To Save a City

MILITARY HISTORY SERIES · TEXAS A&M UNIVERSITY

68

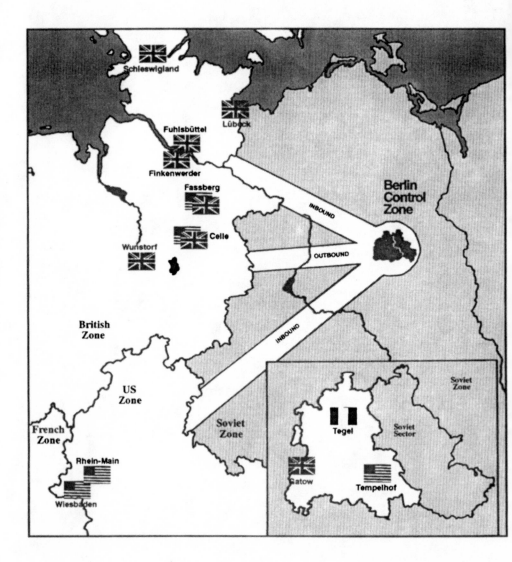

To Save a City

The Berlin Airlift, 1948–1949

Roger G. Miller

Texas A&M University Press, College Station

Library of Congress Cataloging-in-Publication Data

Miller, Roger G. (Roger Gene)
    To save a city : the Berlin airlift, 1948–1949 / Roger G. Miller
      p. cm.
    Includes bibliographical references and index.
    ISBN 0-89096-967-1 (cloth)
      1. Berlin (Germany)—History—Blockade, 1948–1949.
    2. United States. Air Force—History.   I. Title.
    DD881.M525   2000
    943'.1550874—dc21   00-032617
  ISBN 13: 978-1-60344-090-5 (pbk.)
  ISBN 10: 1-60344-090-9 (pbk.)

To Chrissie
and our children,
Travis and Sophia

Contents

Illustrations

Figures

Cartoons by John H. "Jake" Schuffert

Maps and Diagrams

Foreword

In a new century, and although it has hardly begun a forgetful century, one suspects a wondrous time when the United States has not merely survived but flourished economically and now seems dominant over all nations militarily: in such a new time the cares and concerns of the Cold War appear as well into the distant past and therefore almost hardly worth keeping in mind. But surely the course of the American troubles with the Soviet Union that began with the end of World War II and continued until the U.S.S.R.'s collapse are worth looking back to, in hope that they may hold lessons for the present and future.

The author of the pages that follow is not merely a longtime student of American military policy but also an expert on the Berlin airlift, and he has brought novelties to light in regard to the supply of the city of Berlin by air in 1948–49. And his principal novelty concerns the technical side of the airlift. Without the planning and detailed execution of the supply of Berlin, a large city besieged by the Russian forces that surrounded it, a city that lay deep within the Soviet zone of Germany, the airlift would not have been possible. It was one thing for Gen. Lucius D. Clay to telephone, as he did, his Air Force deputy, Lt. Gen. Curtis E. LeMay, and ask if LeMay's planes could supply the city. When Clay then instituted the airlift it was relatively easy, apart from the responsibility involved for President Harry S. Truman to back up Clay and LeMay. It was something else to organize a veritable bridge of planes across the corridors already allotted for American flights to Berlin, to time the resultant flights so as to avoid dangerous overlapping or stacking up. Then at both ends of supply was the need to load and unload. Within Berlin the facilities at the airport were poor and needed organizing. It was necessary, as all students of the airlift understand, to construct another airport in Berlin to handle the traffic.

Curiously there has been little attention to the techniques of organization that brought the extraordinary triumph of the airlift. The work of Maj. Gen. William H. Tunner, the technical expert brought in by the U.S. Air Force, is well-known because Tunner produced a well-written memoir that documented his accomplishment. Beyond that book the authorities on the airlift have seldom gone, even though the airlift has produced perhaps a dozen books of analysis, not to mention the memoirs of participants.

Roger G. Miller has analyzed the technical problems, which were many, and done so in not merely an organized way, based on thorough scholarship, but also in an interestingly written way—his account is no dry-as-dust listing of this arrangement, that enterprise. Perhaps enough books have appeared detailing the diplomacy of the airlift. It is time for discussion of what really happened after the remarkable Truman administration, with all its capacity for careful discussion and equally careful decisions, did what it needed to do. The present book so well sets out what happened behind the diplomatic decisions and the facade of flights, one after the other, that caught the attention of Americans during that event-ridden time. And because of the high importance of the technical accomplishment, the Miller book not merely fills a niche, to use the usual description, but rounds out the story in an utterly necessary way.

Robert H. Ferrell
Indiana University

Preface

This study began as a monograph written in my capacity as a U.S. Air Force historian to commemorate the fiftieth anniversary of the Berlin Airlift in 1998. When I began research, it quickly became apparent that histories of the Berlin Crisis of 1948–49 fell into two general categories. Those in the first explored the diplomatic, political, and economic aspects of post–World War II European history, the treatment of defeated Germany, the presence of the Soviet Union in Eastern Europe, and the origins of the Cold War. These histories usually treated the airlift in outline, although the operation played a significant role in these affairs. The second category of histories concentrated on the airlift itself, based primarily upon a limited number of published works, memoirs, interviews with veterans, and Maj. Gen. William H. Tunner's autobiography, *Over the Hump*. Tunner commanded the Combined Airlift Task Force, and *Over the Hump*, a classic in air power and U.S. Air Force history, has been the main source of material on the Berlin Airlift since its publication in 1964. It was readily apparent that room existed for a study that dealt with the practical details—the "nuts and bolts" as it were—of the Berlin Airlift based on original research in primary documents.

I set out with several goals in mind. First, the National Archives, the Library of Congress, and the U.S. Air Force Historical Research Agency at Maxwell Air Force Base, Alabama, held thousands of declassified documents unavailable to or unused by earlier writers. Mining these should yield new facts and interpretations and provide original insights challenging standard interpretations of the airlift. Second, as a former U.S. Air Force officer, I had an interest in and practical experience with "logistics," the difficulties and challenges posed by the problems of transportation, maintenance, and supply. At its essence, the Berlin Airlift was an exercise in military logistics. I had written previously on various aspects of the history of that esoteric and often ignored military science and believed that this background would provide unique insights into the airlift. Third, with the collapse of the Soviet Empire, historians have had access to many of the archives of the former Soviet Union and its satellites, sources formerly denied to Western scholars. While I could not hope to do research in these areas myself, a great deal of new material had begun to appear that shed light on the situation in postwar Germany and on the Berlin Crisis of 1948 from "the other side." Finally, as much as possible, I wanted to use the words of the veterans of the Berlin Airlift themselves; they did the job and deserve to be heard.

Every historian must acknowledge a great debt to a long list of individuals and institutions for assistance with his or her project. I have been extraordinarily fortunate in this regard.

First, and most important, my personal gratitude goes to friend and scholar Daniel F. Harrington of the United States Air Forces in Europe (USAFE) History Office at Ramstein Air Base, Germany. Dan and I met as doctoral students in the history program at Indiana University in the late 1970s and have remained colleagues, comrades, and co-conspirators. Dan wrote an excellent study of the Berlin Airlift for USAFE at the same time that I prepared my USAF monograph. We exchanged almost two hundred e-mail messages posing questions, arguing interpretations, clarifying issues, and identifying obscure sources. Dan provided rare documents from the USAFE History Office files and made available other materials he had collected during more than thirty years of studying post–World War II U.S. diplomacy. Finally, he compiled the charts that compose the appendixes of this book. In the acknowledgments to his monograph, Dan wrote that he had learned more from me than I from him—it is the only misstatement in an excellent study.

In the Air Force History Support Office at Bolling Air Force Base, Washington, D.C., senior historians Jacob Neufeld and Herman S. Wolk read the manuscript thoroughly as did my associates Priscilla D. Jones and Walton Moody. They provided cogent criticism and sage advice—mixed with a large ration of encouragement—and saved me from many errors. Historians Larry Benson, Rebecca Cameron, Richard Davis, Sheldon Goldberg, William Heimdahl, Perry Jamieson, Eduard Mark, Diane Putney, Wayne Thompson, George Watson, Richard Wolfe, and William T. Y'Blood shared their extensive knowledge of aviation history and unique perspectives on air power generously. David Chenowith's expertise as photographer and editor deserves special recognition. Yvonne Kinkaid and Vicki Crone, Air Force History Support Office research librarians, ferreted out rare sources, answered innumerable questions, and provided suggestions for additional exploration.

The vast majority of the documents that tell the real story of the Berlin Airlift may be found in the stacks at the National Archives and Records Administration's Archives II in College Park, Maryland. Archivist Will Mahoney performed yeoman service in his capacity as a knowledgeable and professional guide through a maze of record groups. In the Manuscript Division of the Library of Congress, the papers of USAF leaders like Hoyt Vandenberg, Curtis LeMay, and Muir Fairchild provided invaluable information. The Air Mobility Command (AMC) History Office at Scott Air Force Base, Illinois, maintains another major Berlin Airlift collection. Command Historian Tom Cossaboom critiqued the manuscript using his extensive knowledge of German history and many years of service as command historian for USAFE. His deputy, John Leland, and historian Betty Kennedy supplied a large number of important documents and answered questions quickly and professionally. Mickey Russell at the Air Force Historical Research Agency, Maxwell Air Force Base, Alabama; Duane Reed of the Manuscript Division at the Air Force Academy Library, Colorado Springs, Colorado; and Terry Aitkin and Dave Menard, curators at the U.S. Air Force Museum at Wright-Patterson Air Force Base, Ohio, made important contributions. Thanks also go to Robert J. Limbrick of the U.S. Air Force Art Program in the Pentagon and Ann DeAtley of the U.S. Air Force Photographic Pre-Accessioning Center at Bolling Air Force Base, Washington, D.C.

Outside of the Air Force history program, John Greenwood and William Stivers at the U.S. Army's Center for Military History in Washington, D.C., provided information on the airlift from the U.S. Army perspective, aided by the archivists at the U.S. Army Military History Institute, Carlisle Barracks, Pennsylvania. Group Captain Sebastian Cox, chief of the Air Historical Branch, Ministry of Defence, and Général Hugues Silvestre de Sacy, chief of the *Service Historique de l'Armée de l'Air* and their staffs furnished information and photographs.

Associate Director Christian Ostermann and his staff of the Cold War International History Project at the Woodrow Wilson Institute in Washington, D.C., were especially helpful in guiding me to published and unpublished papers addressing various aspects of the 1948 Berlin Crisis from the viewpoint of the former Soviet Union. At the National Air and Space Museum, curator R. E. G. Davies provided a different perspective of Berlin Airlift operations. Ron—a native of Great Britain, veteran of the British Army during World War II, and expert on the history of commercial aviation—ensured that I kept the contributions of the Royal Air Force firmly in mind.

Two organizations loomed large during the preparation of this book. My thanks to Col. Kenneth Herman, president, Bill Gross, secretary, and the men and women of the Berlin Airlift Veterans Association (BAVA) for their support and inspiration. Through the BAVA, I had the opportunity of meeting and associating with over two hundred veterans who accomplished the airlift. To list all of them individually would be impossible, but they have my deepest appreciation. Hopefully, this book tells their story adequately. Special thanks are also due to Tim Chopp, president, and Eddie Ide, vice president, of the Berlin Airlift Historical Foundation and to the crew of their Douglas C-54 Skymaster, "The Spirit of Freedom." I visited them at many air shows, and a memorable flight from Baltimore, Maryland, to Washington, D.C., aboard the "Spirit" enabled my son, Travis, and I to "stand where they stood, and see what they saw."

Roger G. Miller
Fairfax, Virginia

To Save a City

chapter I

Crisis in Germany

The Berlin Crisis of 1948 had its origins in the dark mind of Joseph Stalin. Plans to interfere with Western access to Berlin were already hatched and harassment had begun by March 19, 1948, when the dictator met with German leaders of the Soviet-backed Party of Socialist German Unity (SED). During the subsequent discussion, German communist leader Wilhelm Pieck warned that the elections scheduled for Berlin in October threatened to be a disaster for the SED. But, he argued, humiliation could be prevented if, somehow, the Western powers could be removed from the city.

"Let's make a joint effort," Stalin replied, "perhaps we can kick them out."[1]

Germany in Defeat

The war Adolf Hitler had begun in 1939 ended in May, 1945, with the almost total destruction of Germany and its occupation by the victorious Allied powers—the United States, Great Britain, and the Union of Soviet Socialist Republics. The members of the "Grand Alliance" had laid the foundations of the peace during a series of wartime conferences between Pres. Franklin D. Roosevelt, Prime Minister Winston Churchill, and General Secretary of the Communist Party Joseph Stalin. Roosevelt and Churchill first addressed the question of Germany with the acceptance of Roosevelt's controversial demand for unconditional surrender. At Teheran in December, 1943, the "Big Three" leaders discussed partitioning Germany into several smaller states, an idea ultimately abandoned because it threatened to sow the seeds for a rebirth of German nationalism.[2]

The most important meetings were held at Yalta in February, 1945, and at Potsdam the following July. The Allies agreed that their occupation forces would reshape Germany. The German Army would be disbanded; the country's arms industry eliminated; the Nazi Party and all aspects of Nazi influence on government, law, culture, and daily life destroyed; and war criminals punished. Economically, the emphasis would be on developing agriculture and peace-related industries. Germany would be administered as a single economic unit and controls would be introduced to ensure an appropriate distribution of resources throughout the zones. Reparations would be exacted for the horrors inflicted by the Nazi war machine, but enough would be left to sustain the German people without outside financial assistance. The occupation would continue until all reforms had been completed, a satisfactory constitution written, and supervised elections held.[3]

During the war, the Allies had agreed to divide Germany into three occupation zones. The Soviet zone encompassed the eastern third of the nation, while the British and Americans divided the western portion of the nation, with the British zone in the north and the American zone in the south; a fourth zone for France was eventually carved out of the American and British zones. At Potsdam, the Allied powers agreed that the occupation zones would be temporary.[4] The Soviet zone, under normal conditions, produced much of Germany's food, the British zone was heavily industrialized and had to import food in the best of times, and the American zone also produced insufficient food for its population. In retrospect, it hardly seemed a fair division. A contemporary saying opined that "the Russians received the agriculture, the British the heavy industry, and the Americans the scenery."[5] The Allies also agreed to administer the occupation from Germany's capital, Berlin, which lay more than one hundred miles inside the Soviet zone of occupation. In the same way that they treated larger Germany, the Allies divided Berlin into "sectors" garrisoned and administered by the military forces of the four powers. The decision to establish sectors for the Western nations in Berlin deep inside the Soviet occupation zone provided the setting for the Berlin Crisis of 1948.

Another development exacerbated the economic situation for the Allies. As the Red Army advanced across Eastern Europe, Stalin unilaterally moved the Russian-Polish border westward and then compensated Poland by moving its border with Germany fifty miles to the west, giving the Poles about a quarter of Germany's most fertile land and displacing several million Germans, most of whom ended up in the Western zones.[6] To Western leaders, this step seemed to be done with sinister purpose. In Churchill's words, "the Russians, pushing the Poles in front of them, wended on, driving the Germans before them and depopulating large areas of Germany, whose food supplies they seized, while chasing a multitude of mouths into the overcrowded British and American zones."[7] At Potsdam, Churchill argued that Poland and Russia were getting the food and fuel—in the form of Silesian coal—from a prostrate Germany, while the British and Americans were getting the mouths that had to be fed. Stalin refused to concede the point, however, and there was little the Western leaders could do but acquiesce. The Soviet demand for reparations proved systematic and rapacious. By the end of 1945, the United States and Great Britain had poured tons of food into their occupation zones while the Soviets had taken tons of food out of their zone. The result was, in the eyes of Western leaders, an indirect payment of deliveries to the USSR from the two Western nations.[8]

The four military commanders in chief—General of the Army Dwight D. Eisenhower, Field Marshal Sir Bernard L. Montgomery, Marshal Georgi Zhukov, and Gen. Jean de Lattre de Tassigny—met in Berlin on June 5, 1945, to sign the formal "Declaration Regarding the Defeat of Germany and the Assumption of Supreme Authority" and to proclaim the protocols that instituted the zonal boundaries and the Allied Control Council. The movement of Allied military forces into their occupation zones and of the garrison troops into Berlin was completed on July 4, 1945, and the Allied Control Council held its first meeting on July 30. Composed of the military governors of Germany and located in the American sector of Berlin, the Allied Control Council was the four-power agency that would govern occupied Germany.[9] It does not get too far ahead of our story to note that Gen. Lucius D. Clay, Gen. Sir Brian Robertson, Marshal Vassily D. Sokolovsky, and Gen. Pierre Joseph Koenig were the military governors for Germany during the Berlin Crisis in 1948.

Berlin

Like the rest of Germany, Berlin had suffered enormous damage during the war. In May, 1945, roughly 2.8 million people remained in the city, down from a prewar population of 4.6 million. Of the prewar work force, only 28.5 percent remained. The medical profession had been especially hard hit, with only 2,400 of the 6,500 prewar doctors remaining. Housing space had been seriously reduced. Some 70 percent of dwellings had been damaged but could still provide shelter while an additional 10 percent was reparable, but 20 percent had been demolished. Bomb damage had been concentrated within the city center, where 70 percent of the area had been completely devastated. Only 43 percent of the work places in Berlin survived. Hospital beds had been reduced from 33,000 to 8,500. None of Berlin's eighty-seven sewer systems functioned, so diseases like typhus and dysentery spread quickly, a situation exacerbated by the shortage of physicians. Allied bombing had rendered Berlin's drinking water system unusable. The food situation was also critical, as Berlin could produce only 2 percent of its own needs; only the importation of food from the Soviet zone prevented starvation. The USSR refused to allow Western troops into Berlin for two months following the city's surrender on May 7, 1945. During those eight weeks, Berlin and Berliners were subjected to brutal treatment at the hands of the Soviet army.[10] "It was like a city of the dead," General Clay observed soon after the war. "I must confess that my exultation in victory was diminished as I witnessed this degradation of man."[11]

In the confusion of ending the war, negotiating the shape of postwar Europe, and establishing the occupation, Allied planners overlooked a significant detail: no formal agreement guaranteed Western access to Berlin by surface transportation. Opportunities to negotiate access had presented themselves between 1944 and 1946, but other subjects had taken priority. It was variously assumed that the presence of the Western garrisons certified access, that the West would always get along with the Soviets and thus no need existed for written guarantees, or that the occupation would end within a reasonable time thereby making the subject irrelevant. Additionally, the Soviets had recognized tacitly the right of Western access to Berlin from the beginning of the occupation, and Western officials appear to have avoided the issue in their efforts to get along with the USSR. In the final analysis, Britain and the United States placed their trust in Soviet good will, and this trust proved misplaced. In 1948, Soviet harassment would set off a scramble in Washington to locate a copy of any signed document guaranteeing Allied access to Berlin, but none existed. The lack of a formal agreement enabled the Soviets to claim that the Allies were in Berlin only with the special permission of the Soviet Union, not because of their rights as victors, and that this permission could be withdrawn.[12]

Where political leaders had failed, military leaders had to act since access to Berlin was a practical necessity. On June 29, 1945, Marshal Zhukov met with General Clay, Eisenhower's deputy, and Sir Ronald Weeks, deputy to Montgomery, over a request for the use of four rail links: two with the American zone and two with the British; two roads, one to Frankfurt in the American zone and the other to Brunswick in the British zone; and two air lanes with Frankfurt and Bremen (British). Zhukov would only allow them access to one railway, one road, and one air route. Clay and Weeks, conscious of the need to get their troops to Berlin on July 1, accepted Zhukov's proposal, believing that it was temporary and could be adjusted later by the Allied Control Council. Temporary verbal agreements with the Soviets, however, had a tendency to become permanent inconveniences, and the land routes to Berlin quickly fell into this category. The Soviets refused to allow access to additional roads or railways. Further, they limited use of the single rail link: on September 10, 1945, they agreed to allow ten trains daily to cross the Soviet zone, and on October 13, 1947, they increased this allowance to sixteen.[13]

Air routes proved to be another matter. In 1945, concerns about air safety led to a written guarantee signed by all participating nations. The number of flights in and out of Berlin had increased dramatically after the war. With airplanes from several nations involved and much flying done at night or under conditions of reduced visibility, the need for some kind of standard rules and flight patterns was readily apparent. In late 1945, the Aviation Committee of the Allied Control Council proposed the establishment of six twenty-mile-wide corridors between Berlin and the cities of Hamburg, Hanover (Bückeburg), Frankfurt, Warsaw, Prague, and Copenhagen. During subsequent negotiations, the Soviet Union argued that only three, those with Hamburg, Bückeburg, and Frankfurt, were actually necessary. The Allies approved an agreement defining these corridors on November 30, 1945.[14] This agreement failed to provide complete freedom for Western aircraft however. Limitations still applied to altitudes, and Soviet aircraft engaged in military activities often flew through the corridors regardless of the traffic between the Western occupation zones and Berlin. The agreement ultimately would not prevent the Soviets from attempting to control Western aircraft operating in the corridors under the guise of "safety considerations." However, the presence of the three corridors, guaranteed in writing, was unarguable and would make the Berlin Airlift possible.

Breakdown

The wartime illusion that the United States could work with a friendly Soviet Union died a relatively quick and probably inevitable death in the postwar period. Roosevelt had introduced Stalin to the American people as "Uncle Joe," putting a kindly face on the brutal dictator for public consumption during the war. Sometime after 1945, however, Stalin ceased to be the amiable, stouthearted, pipe-smoking friend of World War II propaganda and emerged instead as the dictator he was. Further, the motives that drove each nation in the postwar era were mutually exclusive, and the victorious allies were destined to clash.

American leaders expected to maintain a short-term military and political presence in Europe after the war, a presence that would ensure the reconstruction of a stable Europe. Initially, much hope was placed in being able to reach consensus with the USSR. However, even before Potsdam, the administration of Pres. Harry Truman had recognized the communist nation as a potential threat and had begun operating on the premise that a stable, confident Europe would serve as a "third force" between the United States and the Soviet Union. As Britain, France, and the other nations recovered, they would jointly "redress the balance of power" and constrain the communists. It is important to remember that it is impossible to separate the apprehensions of American leaders about Russian actions in eastern Europe from their apprehension about stability and democracy in western Europe. The chief fear between 1946 and 1948 was not a Soviet invasion of Europe, but the strength of communist parties in France and Italy and their ability to take advantage of economic hardship.[15]

Additionally, it gradually became apparent that Germany had to play a major role in a stable Europe. During World War II, Secretary of the Treasury Henry Morgenthau had proposed eliminating German industry and "pastoralizing" the country's economy. Approved in September, 1944, the U.S. Joint Chiefs of Staff paper governing American occupation policies, JCS 1067, embodied the essence of the Morgenthau Plan and envisioned restricting the German economy to the bare minimum required to satisfy

Figure 1. Gen. Lucius D. Clay (left), *commander of the Office of Military Government, United States, and military governor of Germany, meets with Brig. Gen. Frank L. Howley, the American commandant in Berlin.* Courtesy Brig. Gen. Frank L. Howley Collection, U.S. Army Military History Institute, Carlisle Barracks, Pennsylvania

the population's immediate needs. This directive proved impractical primarily because it prohibited some actions necessary for the occupation government to function. For one, the directive banned personal relations between Americans and Germans, even to the extent of requiring separate toilets in occupation government office buildings. For another, reviving utilities, transportation systems, and factories required hundreds of thousands of experienced Germans, many of whom were ineligible under the stringent rules that governed even nominal members of the Nazi Party. In still another restriction, the traces of the Morgenthau Plan in JCS 1067 worked admirably in preventing a German military revival but also frustrated economic recovery. Gradually, American policy shifted to a belief that a stable, democratic Germany would make a good partner and ally in central Europe. JCS 1779 replaced JCS 1067 in July, 1947. It allowed for the introduction of more liberal occupation practices in the American zone and enabled Clay to take measures necessary to strengthen the German economy.[16]

As the American military governor in Germany, General Clay was a primary instrument in this policy change. A courtly southerner from a distinguished family, Clay was a brilliant military administrator noted for his refined manners, incisive mind, and formidable will. Grandson of a United States senator and son of another, Lucius DuBignon Clay graduated from the U.S. Military Academy at West Point in 1918 and entered the Corps of Engineers. In the peacetime army, he was a nonconformist who had demonstrated energy, intelligence, and the willingness to accept responsibility. Assigned to the headquarters of the Corps of Engineers in Washington, D.C., in the mid-1930s, Clay developed considerable political skills and earned a reputation for ability and efficiency. These qualities served him well during World War II, in which Clay served first as director of Matériel and then as a deputy at the Office of War Mobilization and Reconversion. Clay had been in Germany since the end of the war and became the first U.S. commander in chief, Europe, (CINCEUR) on March 15, 1947, receiving his fourth star in the process. In Germany, Clay's well-honed political savvy proved invaluable. "Clay had political knowhow," Robert D. Murphy, his political advisor in Germany recalled, "the ability to interpret ambiguous regulations, to avoid paper roadblocks, to persuade obstinate officials—these universally useful political talents were bred in Clay's bones." Two operational commands reported to CINCEUR headquarters: the Office of Military Government, United States (OMGUS), commanded by Clay's deputy, Maj. Gen. Frank Keating, and European Command (EUCOM) under Lt. Gen. Clarence C. Heubner.[17] Clay would be instrumental in establishing the position of the United States in postwar Europe, determining the shape of western German democracy, and drawing the line on Soviet expansionism, a line that would begin in Berlin.

Soviet policy in Germany and eastern Europe was largely shaped by that nation's experiences in World War II. Primarily, Stalin wanted to establish a protective belt of pro-Soviet nations on the western border of the Soviet Union and to prevent the rise of a strong, unified Germany outside his control (a policy that he shared with France, which had also suffered terribly from German aggression). Stalin's goals were evident as early as October, 1944, when he and Winston Churchill had tried their hand at dividing up postwar Europe. Stalin demanded that Poland, Czechoslovakia, and Hungary form a belt of "independent, anti-Nazi, pro-Russian states." He wanted Germany broken up and the great industrial areas of the Ruhr and Saar placed under international control.[18] Subsequent developments recognized the impracticality of many of these proposals, but Stalin's plans for a buffer zone of states and a weakened Germany under Soviet control remained. It should be noted that a portion of this policy could be expected: The USSR would establish Soviet-style states because its leaders recognized no other type of government as legitimate and sincerely believed in its efficacy. "This war is not as in the past; whoever occupies a territory also imposes on it his own social system," Stalin told a delegation of Yugoslavian communist leaders in April, 1944. "Everyone imposes his own system as far as his army can reach."[19]

Following the end of the war, Stalin moved rapidly to consolidate the Soviet position, and events on three successive days in 1945 lay the foundation for communist control in Germany. On June 9, Moscow created the Soviet Military Administration in eastern Germany. The following day the Soviet Military Administration authorized the formation of an anti-fascist party and various trade unions in the Soviet areas of occupation. On June 11, German communists, with Soviet backing, established the German Communist Party (KPD). Subsequently, the Soviets followed a standard pattern that would be repeated in other countries. Through the active involvement of the Soviet Military Administration, they pushed for the creation of an anti-fascist front uniting all political parties. Forced fusion of the German Socialist Party with the KPD created the communist-dominated Party of Socialist German Unity in April, 1946, giving the communists a solid political base in the eastern zone and a potent foothold in the western zones. Communist leaders, who dominated the SED, then called for the "establishment of an anti-fascist, democratic regime, a parliamentary democratic republic" while the Soviet Military Administration suppressed all other political activities.[20]

A more immediate Soviet goal was to make Germany pay for the horrors its army had inflicted on the Soviet Union. Stalin demanded ten billion dollars in direct reparations and sought access to the coalfields in the Ruhr. He wanted to acquire German scientific and technological knowledge and deny this to the West; to seize military and industrial assets; and to eliminate the prosperity, power, and position of the German ruling classes which had supported the war. The agreement at Potsdam authorized each nation to seize reparations from its own zone, and the British and Americans allowed Stalin one-sixth of surplus production in their zones. The Soviets also systematically stripped those portions of Germany under their control, leading to the loss of 3,500 plants and factories,

1,115,000 pieces of equipment, and two million industrial jobs. More demands came later. In late 1946, thousands of German technicians, managers, and skilled personnel were forcibly transferred to the USSR. In addition, women in astounding numbers were raped by the conquerors over a prolonged period of time, and those who resisted were often beaten or murdered. This rape and pillage was not limited to the immediate aftermath of the Soviet invasion. Had it been, these actions might have been understandable (though not excusable) given the terrible destruction visited upon the Soviet Union by the Nazi armies. Hitler's plans for the Russian people had been horrific—the majority were to have been starved to death and the remainder reduced to slave labor—and his armies and the murderous Nazi organizations that followed them had made impressive progress toward this end in an extremely short time. The result was warfare characterized by incredible brutality and terrible retribution when the victorious Soviet armies reached Germany. Systematic rape and pillage continued in Soviet-controlled areas for many months and threatened Stalin's long-range program for Germany.[21]

Other Soviet activities in Germany were also of grave concern to American leaders and heightened postwar tensions. The newly formed Central Intelligence Agency's Berlin Operations Base, known by the delightful acronym "BOB," conducted intelligence gathering in Berlin. Early, BOB began tracking Soviet efforts to use German resources to build an atomic bomb. The Russians formed a corporation called "Wismut" to mine and process uranium in eastern Germany and resorted to using forced labor to support the effort by taking German scientists to the Soviet Union to work on the project. A branch of the prewar German industrial giant I. G. Farben at Bitterfield in the Soviet zone produced distilled calcium while the Tewa plant in Neustadt produced wire mesh, both critical for the manufacture of uranium 235. The Soviet Union also began surreptitious efforts to obtain materials and manufactured goods that were unavailable in eastern Germany from the western zones.[22]

Beyond the USSR's more immediate objectives, Stalin's long-range goal was a pro-Soviet, communist-dominated government. As early as June 4, 1945, during a meeting on postwar policies with German communist leaders, Stalin told them that there would be more than one Germany for a time. He expected to establish Soviet dominance in the eastern occupation zone and then undermine the British position in its zone. When after a year or two the United States withdrew, nothing would stand in the way of a united Germany under communist control within the Soviet orbit. The results of the Potsdam Conference were extremely promising, Stalin pointed out, since they called for operating Germany as a single economic unit, a decision that would facilitate Soviet penetration of the other zones. Further, the policies of demilitarization, de-Nazification, and democratization would assist by strengthening those elements that would tend to favor the USSR. This belief apparently continued as part of Soviet policy in the early postwar years. Stalin and other leaders told visiting Bulgarian and Yugoslavian delegations in early 1946 that Germany must be Soviet and communist.[23]

Given the way he treated his own people, the Soviet dictator may have failed to realize that to attain this goal he would ultimately need the German people—and their support would be withheld. The Red Army raped as many as one million German women, and Soviet reparations removed as much as one-third of eastern Germany's industrial capability. The millions of forced refugees, the arrest of German leaders who opposed Soviet policies, and the brutal persecution of eastern European intellectuals did further irreparable damage to Stalin's long-range goal. All of this made little difference as long as Russian policy remained one of retribution. When Stalin shifted from this to reconciliation in mid-1946, the actions of the Red Army and the harsh Soviet occupation proved catastrophic. They left the Soviet Military Government a legacy of hatred and distrust that nothing could redeem. Ultimately, little the Soviet occupation leadership could do would convince the Germans that they had a stake in either Soviet success or a Soviet-sponsored future.[24]

Stalin's policy had another unintended but important effect. The tremendous destruction during the war, combined with Soviet pillage, left eastern Germany in economic ruin. Further, the USSR at best showed little interest in rebuilding its zone, and conditions there by 1948, along with conditions throughout eastern Europe, had shown little improvement since the end of the war. In turn, the economic conditions in eastern Europe and Germany, because they were interdependent, delayed the economic recovery and thus the political stability of western Europe, major postwar goals of the United States.[25] Historian Chuck Pennacchio has argued that "Moscow's decision to rebuild Russia at the expense of Soviet-occupied Germany froze East Germany in a condition of wartime destruction, a situation which weakened the social fabric and alienated the population from the German Communists, associated as they were with the Soviets. The resulting migration of workers to the west and electoral setbacks for the Communist Party of Germany (KPD) heightened the threat of Western economic absorption and unified German recovery."[26] Ultimately, this situation would force the United States and Great Britain to act. The Berlin Crisis of 1948 can best be understood within the context of a recovery in Western Europe that failed to get off the ground after World War II.

One additional point must be made. It is clear that Stalin feared and respected the power that the United States and the Western allies had amassed. The advent of the U.S. nuclear monopoly dashed his belief that the Soviet Union would emerge from World War II equal to or stronger than the Western powers. Further, it ended whatever idea he might have had about dealing with future problems through a partnership with the West. The goal of constructing a secure periphery around the Soviet Union remained. There were limits, however: Stalin refused to face another war and thus was prepared to halt Soviet expansionism in the face of Western resolve. At no point was the Soviet dictator prepared to challenge the Americans or the British when they made their interests clear.[27]

The Marshall Plan and German Unification

Following World War II, Soviet pressure on Turkey over control of the Black Sea straits and support for the Greek communists through Yugoslavia, Bulgaria, and Albania concerned American officials. Initially, Britain aided the Greek government against the communist insurrection; but in March, 1947, British leaders announced that they no longer had the resources to continue their support. The Truman administration proved willing to fill the void, but limiting its involvement to Greece smacked too much of rescuing British imperialism. Consequently, in his address to Congress on March 12, 1947, President Truman announced "the Truman Doctrine," which held that the United States would aid democracies resisting enslavement by a minority.[28]

The winter of 1945–46 was unusually harsh in western Europe, exacerbating economic conditions and raising the specter of political and social instability that could be exploited, many leaders feared, by the Soviet Union. The situation was especially acute in Germany, where the people were ill equipped to meet the added hardship and there was little to suggest that things would improve anytime soon. The German people primarily blamed the Soviets for their suffering, and nowhere was this better reflected than in the local elections held in the fall of 1946, which resulted in a massive anti-communist protest vote, especially in the Soviet sector of Berlin.[29]

Clay moved to address the situation in mid-1946. During the Paris meeting of the Council of Foreign Ministers in July, he suggested a merger of the British and American zones of occupation to Secretary of State James F. Byrnes. The British accepted the proposal and final arrangements for the establishment of "Bizonia" were concluded at the council meeting in December. In Clay's view, his proposal was an effort to address the serious economic problems in Germany and not an attempt to permanently divide the nation. The creation of Bizonia created a detour around French and Soviet intransigence and offered an avenue to a united Germany. As he told his biographer, Jean Edward Smith: "There was simply not enough in the way of resources or industry in the American zone to give it anything but a pastoral economy. And on the other hand, we were supplying the money and the food to keep both our zone and the British zone alive. It was quite evident to me that, with the coal and industry of the Ruhr added to our zone, we would have a self-supporting economic area. . . . It was equally clear that maintaining four small occupation zones made no political sense. If we were going to restore a democratic Germany, we had to create units that at least would be reasonably acceptable to the Germans. So this again made it important to enlarge the sphere we were operating in."[30]

It proved somewhat more difficult to make Bizonia work than originally expected. For one thing Clay and other American leaders feared that the British Labour government would nationalize German industry, institute centralized economic controls, and promote socialism. On the whole, however, Bizonia appeared to make some progress in restoring the German economy and, in Clay's view, would prove an important step toward German unity.[31]

Prompted by concerns over European recovery, the United States also began looking at Germany from a new perspective by early 1947. On the one hand, professional members of the State Department had long distrusted the Soviet Union, as did President Truman. Secretary of State Byrnes, on the other hand, preferred a more accommodating foreign policy. Byrnes, however, grated on Harry Truman, who distrusted him and his motives. Truman forced Byrnes to resign in January, 1947, and replaced him with former Chief of Staff Gen. George Catlett Marshall. Marshall not only had Truman's confidence, but he also shared the president's hard-line view of the Soviets. American policy in Germany underwent an almost immediate change. Under Marshall's direction, "economic unity was felt to be necessary not only to make Germany self-sustaining, but to help contribute to the recovery of Europe." Foreign affairs specialist George Kennan put the situation into clear perspective: "To talk about the recovery of Europe and to oppose the recovery of Germany is nonsense. People can have both or they can have neither." With that link established and the Truman Doctrine announced, Marshall met with his colleagues on the Council of Foreign Ministers—Ernest Bevin of Great Britain, Vyacheslav Molotov of the Soviet Union, and Georges Bidault of France—in Moscow from March 10 through April 24, 1947.[32]

Six weeks of negotiations proved fruitless. Molotov pressed the others for the renewal of reparations. Marshall refused to agree with Molotov's demands unless the Soviets agreed to an economically self-sufficient Germany and provided a detailed accounting of the industrial plants, goods, and infrastructure already removed by the Russians. Molotov refused these demands and the meeting finally adjourned. The participants came away from Moscow with increased suspicions of the others' motives. Profoundly discouraging was Marshall's personal meeting with Stalin, during which the dictator expressed little interest in an immediate solution to German economic problems. The Americans had concluded by then that for Europe's sake a solution could not wait. With the continental economy sinking into turmoil, cooperation with the Soviet Union in Germany took a back seat to economic cooperation in Europe.[33]

The desperate plight of western Europe persuaded Marshall to announce a comprehensive program of American assistance—the European Recovery Act, or "Marshall Plan"—on June 5, 1947. This program in concert with the Truman Doctrine marked a fundamental change in American policy toward Europe, driven by deepening concerns over the consolidation of communist power in eastern Europe, the failure to reach a settlement on Germany's future, and the worsening economic situation in western Europe threatening political stability, especially in France and Italy. The Marshall Plan was open to all nations that wanted to participate, including the Soviet Union and the countries of eastern Europe. As American leaders anticipated, Stalin scorned the offer and refused to allow Soviet satellite states to participate because he feared American political and cultural influence as well as economic penetration. Marshall's announcement appeared, to the Soviets, to be an attempt to use economic assistance to consolidate a Western European coalition and to threaten recent Soviet gains in eastern Europe.[34]

By early autumn, 1947, the Soviets had concluded that the Western powers had settled on a definite goal in Germany. A memorandum on October 3 to Foreign Minister Molotov reported that "Analysis of the materials at our disposal and of steps which were taken by the United States and Great Britain in Germany gives grounds for the conclusion that we are speaking not about a propaganda manouevre or political blackmail but about a real threat of political and [economic] dismemberment of Germany and inclusion of West Germany with all its resources in the Western bloc knocked together by the United States."[35]

This prospect appalled Soviet leadership, which moved to reverse the process. Directives to the Soviet delegation at the meeting of the Council of Foreign Ministers in London between November 25 and December 15, 1947, stressed the imperative need for a peace treaty with Germany associated with the establishment of a "united democratic Germany."[36] The meeting, however, broke down over sharp differences concerning reparations to the Soviet Union, Russian demands for a say over the Ruhr, and Molotov's abuse toward the other representatives. The conference drove home the significant divisions between the Western allies and the Russians over Germany. As a result, the United States announced the end of reparations to the Soviet Union from the Western zones, and France began to move closer toward a united front with the British and Americans. The Council of Foreign Ministers was the final straw in Soviet intransigence, at least as far as Marshall was concerned. Disgusted by Molotov's demands for reparations, the refusal to place the resources of the Soviet zone in a common pool, and the barrage of abuse, insults, and accusations, Marshall finally proposed adjournment. The council did not meet again until May, 1949.[37]

On February 20, 1948, Secretary Marshall wrote that the Soviets were reshaping eastern Germany into a totalitarian nation similar to the Soviet satellites of Eastern Europe. He believed that it was now necessary for the Western powers to integrate the economy of western Germany with that of Western Europe. Unless this step was taken, Marshall reported, "Western Germany too may be at some time in the future drawn into Eastern orbit with all obvious consequences wich [sic] such an eventuality would entail."[38] The Secretary went on to say that the United States believed that a divided Germany was undesirable and it had not abandoned hope that a solution to the problems in central Europe would include a united country. However, "it has long been decided, in collaboration with the British Govt, that desire for an undivided Germany cannot be made an excuse for inaction in Western Germany, detrimental to recovery of Western Europe as a whole." Above all, he continued, the United States would work effectively to prevent Soviet domination of Germany. "It would regard such an eventuality as the greatest threat to security of all Western Nations, including the US." Accordingly, it was important to integrate western Germany into the Western European economy immediately.[39]

The United States and Great Britain, joined later by France, moved quickly to establish West Germany and include it in the Western state system. Representatives of the three governments and the Benelux nations— Belgium, the Netherlands, and Luxembourg—met in London between February 23 and March 6, 1948. Despite Soviet threats to ignore any decisions taken, the attendees put the final touches on the economic merger of the three western zones of Germany and agreed upon the establishment of a federal system of government for that area.[40]

Threat and Response

The aging Soviet dictator initially responded to the hardening of Western attitudes by tightening control over the nations of Eastern Europe already emerging as communist satellites. Foreign Minister Molotov had already announced the formation of the Cominform in September, 1947, to strengthen international communism, especially in eastern Europe. At the first meeting of the Cominform, its leader, Andrei Zhdanov, announced that the Soviet Union and the Western powers were to be viewed as two irreconcilably hostile camps and that this view would serve as the doctrinal basis for Soviet foreign policy under Stalin. Subsequently, Zhdanov began an anti-Western propaganda campaign vilifying Western leaders and called on French and Italian communists to disrupt the economies in their countries and seek the ouster of noncommunists from their governments.[41]

No single event shocked the Western powers more than the Soviet coup d'etat in Czechoslovakia in February, 1948, and the suicide or murder of the Czech patriot and foreign minister, Jan Masaryk. The first forcible communist conquest of a free government, according to historian Walter Millis, placed a new complexion upon the "power, ferocity, and scope of Communist aggression."[42] The brutal overthrow of a neutral government came as a shock to the American people. For many, it called back memories of the Nazi betrayal and seizure of Czechoslovakia in 1939 and confirmed views of Stalin's willingness to attain his ends by any means necessary. "When Czechoslovakia, which had done everything possible to conciliate the Soviet Union, was seized by the communists," Brookings Institution analysts concluded, "little doubt remained in Western minds that the communist ambitions could be checked only through the evidence of superior power."[43] The coup not only set off a short-term war scare, it also swept away the last vestiges of opposition in Congress to the Marshall Plan and accelerated Western plans to consolidate the occupation zones and form a west German state.[44] Unification of the western zones of occupation meant introducing a single currency that would be outside of Soviet control. In response, Stalin "ordered a progressively tightening blockade around the city."[45]

On March 9, Stalin summoned Marshal Sokolovsky and General V. Semionov, political advisor to the Soviet Military Administration in Germany, for urgent consultations. Such an action usually heralded a significant decision or promulgation of a major change in policy. What took place during the meeting remains unclear, but it seems probable that Stalin communicated his decision to step up the harassment of the Western allies, including a blockade of Berlin. On March 12, a secret memorandum to Molotov from an assistant outlined a plan to achieve an Allied policy on Germany favorable to Moscow by "regulating" access to Berlin. (Stalin's comment to the German communist leaders—"perhaps we can kick them out"—was made exactly one week later.) At the Allied Control Council on March 20, Sokolovsky, normally a genial individual, icily demanded to be informed about the activities at the recently concluded London Conference. While this was a reasonable request, General Clay and his British counterpart, Gen. Sir Brian Robertson, hedged, unable to reply, they told Sokolovsky, because they had not yet heard from their governments.[46] Sokolovsky then read a statement condemning the West and walked out, proclaiming, "I see no sense in continuing this meeting and declare it adjourned." The council never met again.[47]

Soviet interference with traffic between the western zones and Berlin started in January, 1948, when Soviet troops began stopping British and American military trains and demanding the right to check the identity of all passengers. Apparently, this was in response to the announcement of the upcoming February meeting of Western nations in London, and it established a pattern of Soviet reaction to Western initiatives in Germany. As British and American leaders pressed ahead, more serious interference was not far off.[48]

The April Crisis and the "Little Lift"

On March 25, five days after Sokolovsky walked out of the Allied Control Council, he issued orders restricting Western military and passenger traffic between the American, British, and French zones of occupation and their sectors in Berlin. Soviet leaders had taken note of some French reluctance to move ahead with establishing a German government in these zones, and Soviet leaders may have believed that a major shock might deter Western actions. The new measures began on April 1 with the announcement that no cargo could leave Berlin by rail without permission of the Soviet commander, an action that would place the Russians in control of all trade with Berlin; this was later extended to passenger trains as well. American commanders had provided manifests in the past and the Soviets had accepted these in good faith. Now Soviet soldiers would inspect each train and truck before allowing it to cross the Soviet occupation zone. In response, Clay requested authority to prevent Russian troops from boarding the trains and to permit his personnel to shoot if necessary. In Washington, Secretary of Defense James Forrestal, Secretary of the Army Kenneth Royall, Secretary of the Air Force Stuart Symington, and the Joint Chiefs of Staff determined that Clay's proposal was too extreme for the situation but did authorize him to test the restrictions. Clay dispatched a train bound for Berlin whose commander refused to allow it to be inspected. The Russians merely shunted it to a siding where it remained for several days before a frustrated Clay, without viable options, ordered the train to return west.[49]

Clay's other response to Soviet interference was more successful. On April 2, he directed the United States Air Forces in Europe (USAFE) and its commander, Lt. Gen. Curtis E. LeMay, to deliver supplies to the military garrisons in Berlin by airplane. In doing so, Clay called upon two legends. "Old Iron Ass" to his men, the forty-one-year-old LeMay was distinguished for his exploits as a pre–World War II pilot and navigator. In 1938, he had guided U.S. Army Air Corps B-17 bombers to intercept the Italian ocean liner *Rex* far at sea in defiance of the U.S. Navy, which considered the defense of American shores from invasion to be its business. In Europe during World War II, LeMay earned a formidable reputation as a resourceful and innovative group commander: he had ordered his men to fly straight and level as they approached their targets in the face of German anti-aircraft measures, and he had invented the "combat box" defensive formation flown by Eighth Air Force. Later, he took command of the Twenty-first Bomber Command in the Pacific, where he ordered his high-altitude, precision-bombing B-29 Superfortresses to fly in mass formations at low altitudes and to attack Japanese cities with incendiary bombs. Beneath his tough, pugnacious veneer, the cigar-chewing LeMay was a cool and creative leader.[50]

The other legend had wings: the Douglas C-47 Skytrain. After World War II, General Eisenhower cited this aircraft as one of the four most important weapons in victory (along with the bazooka, the Jeep, and the atomic bomb). Derived from the DC-3 airliner and first flown in 1935, the C-47 was one of the most widely used aircraft in U.S. Air Force history. Powered by two 1,200 h.p. Pratt & Whitney R-1830-92 engines, the C-47 had a maximum speed of 230 m.p.h.—on the airlift it would cruise at 150 m.p.h.—and carried a maximum payload of three tons.[51]

USAFE officers quickly established an emergency airlift system later termed the "Little Lift." Twenty-five C-47s of the 61st Troop Carrier Group at Rhein-Main Air Base began flying cargo to Berlin. Douglas Dakotas, the British version of the C-47, assigned to the British Air Forces of Occupation (BAFO) continued to support the British garrison in Berlin as well. Aircraft flying other missions were reassigned to the Berlin run, and veteran pilots in non-flying jobs were drafted back into the cockpit to supplement those already on duty. The Little Lift began delivering as much as 80 tons of perishable foods—fresh milk, eggs, vegetables, meat, cheese, and the like—to Berlin daily. USAFE delivered about 310 tons of cargo to Berlin in March and over 1,000 tons in April. Rhein-Main served as the traffic control point, establishing priorities for shipment based upon requisitions from Berlin. While flight and maintenance crews did some loading and unloading, German civilians did most of the heavy labor at both ends of the operation. Despite the recall of qualified flying personnel, the shortage of aircrews remained a serious problem, and the overtaxed airmen ate on the run and napped in odd corners when they could find the time. The Little Lift also led to a shifting of USAFE operations away from Tempelhof

Figure 2. Lt. Gen. Curtis E. LeMay, commander in chief, United States Air Forces in Europe during the April Crisis, the Little Lift, and the early months of the Berlin Airlift. Courtesy U.S. Air Force

Air Base in Berlin to the less vulnerable airfields in the U.S. occupation zone (the 53rd Troop Carrier Squadron moved permanently from Tempelhof to Rhein-Main). All but essential maintenance at Tempelhof was also transferred, and most organizational equipment was removed and used to meet critical shortages in other locations.[52]

The April crisis foreshadowed the Berlin Blockade in June and provided the USAFE with some valuable lessons. "The Soviets made a major mistake," airlift veteran Howard M. Fish summarized years later, "They gave us the opportunity to learn."[53] The Little Lift illuminated the need for a single agency in Berlin to screen and assign priorities to all requirements as well as a central agency in the Western zones to clear all cargo before delivery. Procedurally, the army's Transportation Corps found it best to utilize a shuttle system in which cargo-filled trailers were continually brought to the flight line for immediate loading of aircraft as they arrived. Additionally, the Transportation Corps exercised considerable foresight by briefing a large number of officers on Little Lift operations and by keeping two truck companies on alert in case of further Soviet interference with ground communications with Berlin. Perhaps most important, the U.S. European Command (EUCOM) made a special effort to increase the reserve-stock levels in Berlin during the next few months and to evacuate personnel already due to leave. Coal was given special attention as EUCOM increased rail shipments over this period—1,451 tons in March, 10,062 tons in April, 10,443 tons in May, and 4,749 tons in June—before the Soviets closed the borders. Other military supplies shipped to Berlin amounted to 5,929 tons in April, 6,020 tons in May, and 3,151 tons during the first part of June. In addition, these figures do not convey the full story since two-thirds of the total coal delivered to Berlin came by barge. These additional stocks would provide a valuable reserve during the last months of 1948. At the same time, USAFE flew out of Berlin 212 tons of cargo in April, 337 tons in May, and 193 tons in the first part of June. Most of this was furniture and other personal items as EUCOM reduced its number of unnecessary personnel and civilians in the city.[54]

Soviet leaders concluded from the April crisis that their actions had been effective. "Our control and restrictive measures have dealt a strong blow at the prestige of the Americans and British in Germany," a report to Moscow stated optimistically on April 17. "The German population believe that the Anglo-Americans have retreated before the Russians, and that this testifies to the Russians' strength."[55] Additionally, the Little Lift apparently failed to surprise the Soviets, who seem to have had some awareness of American ability to move cargo by air. Prior to the April crisis, for example, the chief of the Soviet Occupation Forces in Germany reported that the Americans were paying special attention to air transportation.[56] The April 17 report took careful note of the Allied airlift effort during the Little Lift and its conclusion must have been reassuring: "Clay's attempts to create 'an airlift' connecting Berlin with the Western zones have proved futile. The Americans have admitted that idea would be too expensive."[57]

Such mistaken analysis calls for some comment on Soviet intelligence during the subsequent Berlin Crisis. According to the authors of a recent history of CIA and KGB activities in Berlin, Soviet intelligence was uniformly excellent. The KGB had high-level sources in both the French and British governments (and through the latter, the U.S. government as well). However, Soviet intelligence was hamstrung by the fact that Stalin's advisors, who without exception had a well-developed sense of self-preservation, told the dictator only what he wanted to hear. Consequently, Stalin received reports that reinforced his prejudices and confirmed his beliefs and suspicions. Soviet intelligence in 1947 and 1948 repeatedly assured him that the Western powers would abandon Berlin under pressure. Such misleading reports, the authors concluded, while soothing to the dictator and enhancing for careers, "endangered everyone" because decisions based on them could exacerbate any situation. Undoubtedly, misleading reports prolonged the Berlin Blockade by encouraging Soviet leadership to underestimate Western resolve. For example, Ernest Bevin's resolute comments to the British cabinet on September 10, 1948, affirming that British forces would remain in Berlin at all costs, were in Soviet hands almost immediately, and this information might possibly have convinced Stalin that pressuring the West would never halt the creation of a West German state had he learned of it. Instead, Soviet intelligence reports highlighted the great differences between the American and British positions—the sort of thing Stalin obviously preferred to receive but which proved misleading.[58]

From such reports, Stalin apparently concluded that pressure on Berlin would force the Western powers to abandon the creation of a separate Germany, detach the German people from Western governments unable to protect them, and enable the Soviet Union to negotiate from a position of strength. If the Western allies refused to bow to the pressure, then the Soviets would force them out of Berlin and make the city part of the eastern zone. On June 11, the Soviet military government in Germany reported that further restrictions would be placed on traffic to give "another jolt" to Western prestige.[59]

Despite such conclusions, however, the April blockade failed to have the impact that Russian leaders hoped. In fact, a decisive step took place in the midst of the crisis. On April 6, 1948, French diplomat Maurice Couve de Murville visited Clay. Following comprehensive discussions regarding the German situation, Clay prepared a memorandum that called for the election of a German assembly by September 1, 1948. The assembly would draft a constitution that would include a federal structure for the government and guarantee individual rights and freedoms. Once the constitution was approved by three of the four occupation powers and ratified by the German states, the *Länder*, a new government would be elected within thirty days; the new government would have day-to-day control of Germany except for foreign policy. Finally, the memorandum established that while France would not join Bizonia, it would align its occupation policies with that entity. A common banking system and, most significantly, a common currency reform would take place immediately in the three Western zones. Couve de Murville and Clay initialed the memorandum, which subsequently became French policy in Germany. General Clay submitted the document to Generals Robertson and Koenig formally when the London Conference reconvened on April 20, and its provisions were embodied in the final communiqué issued on June 6, 1948.[60]

One serious warning was embedded within the April crisis that the Soviets did heed. On April 5 near Gatow Airport, a Soviet Yak 3 fighter buzzed a British Viking airliner carrying ten passengers, hitting the British plane head on during a second pass; there were no survivors. The Soviets attempted to place blame for the crash on the British pilot and seized the opportunity to demand further restrictions on Western air activities in the corridor. The American and British reaction was immediate and unmistakable: Clay and Robertson ordered fighter aircraft to escort unarmed transports flying the corridor. Such a response might have been expected from the volatile southerner, but it was especially pointed coming from the reserved British commander (who was also known for his confident bearing and immaculate dress). Robertson, however, was genuinely angry over the incident and the Soviet response. Subsequently, Marshal Sokolovsky reversed course, apologized, and assured the Western powers that the Soviets did not intend to interfere with the air corridors.[61]

It is clear that the Russian plan for the blockade called for interruption of the air corridors at some point. An April 17 telegram to Molotov from his military deputy stated that "The plan drawn up, according to your instructions, for restrictive measures to be taken regarding communications between Berlin and the Soviet Union zone with the Western occupation zones is applied from 1 April, except for restrictions from communication by air, which we intend to introduce later."[62] Tragic as it was, the Viking crash may have warned the Soviets away from the latter step. The firm, instantaneous Western response showed how dangerous it would be to attempt to close the air corridors. The KGB reported that Clay had said that he feared the next Soviet step would be to close the air corridors, in which case he would bring in fighters and that "If the Russians wanted to prevent flights of American aircraft through the corridors, they would have to fire on the American machines."[63] During the coming months, the Soviets would harass aircraft and threaten air traffic. They might easily have halted the airlift by interfering with its communications and radar, but, as will be discussed later, the Russians carefully avoided any step that might call forth an immediate military response. First, any action in the air had to be proactive. Aircraft, unlike trucks, barges, or trains, could not be halted at the border or shunted aside. Stopping them required active measures—such as firing warning shots or even shooting an airplane down—that risked war. Second, the incident with the Viking had shown vividly how the West would react. Finally, and perhaps most importantly, the Soviets saw no need to interfere; it was unlikely, in their estimate, that an airlift could succeed.[64]

Another point must also be emphasized. The traditional view is that the Soviets relaxed restrictions on April 10 and thus ended the April crisis and the Little Lift soon thereafter. In truth, Clay and LeMay kept the C-47s flying into Berlin during the succeeding weeks. Some twenty C-47s delivered a few tons of cargo daily, building up local stocks against future Soviet action.[65] The Little Lift instituted on April 2 was still operating when the USAFE officially began what would be called "Operation Vittles" on June 26. The significant difference between these two campaigns lay in the target: the Little Lift supported the military garrison, while Operation Vittles supported the entire population of the Western-controlled sectors of Berlin.

Further Provocations

Soviet leaders themselves viewed the events of April, 1948, as part of an escalating campaign of harassment designed to increase pressure on the Western powers. The April crisis was just a step along the way, and a chronology of subsequent events validates their position: On April 9, the Soviets notified Clay that American military personnel maintaining communications equipment in the eastern zone must withdraw. This measure was extremely important because it eliminated the navigation beacons that marked the air corridor routes, thus forcing aircraft flying in and out of Berlin to navigate by the beacons at each end of the corridors. On April 20, they demanded that all barges secure individual clearances before entering the eastern zone. On April 24, the Soviets refused permission for two international coaches on the Nord Express train to leave Berlin. On May 20, all barge traffic halted for a time when the Soviets levied new documentation requirements. Trains were temporarily halted on June 1 and June 10, and five days later the Soviets closed the autobahn bridge across the Elbe River. On June 19, the Russians announced that only one train at a time instead of three could pass through the Berlin gateway at Marienborn, reducing the average number of trains from twelve or so daily to no more than seven. Then, on the same day, they halted all passenger train traffic and autobahn traffic. Controls on freight train and barge traffic were further tightened. On June 21, Soviet authorities halted a U.S. military freight train at Marienborn; the following day they seized the train, attached their own locomotive, and towed it back to Helmstedt despite the protests of the train's conductor. The most important step, however, took place on June 16 when the Soviet delegates walked out of the *Komandatura*, the four-power council that governed Berlin, evidence that they no longer believed that they could achieve their goals by participating in its deliberations and a signal of increased confrontation with the West.[66]

Western concerns over Berlin's vulnerability to Soviet action had risen relatively early. By late 1947, the Soviet-controlled press had begun to question the legitimacy of four-power control in Berlin, and the U.S. embassy had identified and reported on the Communists' "noisy campaign to force us out." More specifically, on December 22, 1947, the CIA reported that "there was a possibility of steps being taken in Berlin by the Soviet authorities to force other occupying powers to remove [their forces] from Berlin."[67]

During the April crisis, a U.S. Army intelligence assessment on April 8 accurately described Soviet actions as a direct attack on the logistical position of the Western powers in Berlin and as "another move in the Kremlin's latest drive to expand further the Soviet Union's sphere of influence."[68] This assessment concluded that the "Tightening of controls along the western boundary" was evidence of "a complete and final separation of that zone from the rest of Germany."[69] While army intelligence concluded, erroneously, that the Soviet goal was to push the Western powers out of Berlin and recognized the possibility that public utilities and the food supply of the Berlin population might be restricted, it did not envision a blockade.

By June, however, American leaders in Germany recognized that the

Soviets might blockade Berlin but provided Washington with mixed signals on the situation. In response to a request for an evaluation of the ability of the United States to remain in Berlin, Clay reported on June 13 that the situation had cleared up at least temporarily and that while he could maintain the Berlin garrison indefinitely, he could not maintain the city's German population. Nevertheless, Clay recommended that American prestige in Europe required the garrison to stay until Berlin's citizens were threatened with starvation. In a letter the following day, General Huebner, the EUCOM commander, painted a similar picture for Gen. Omar Bradley, the U.S. Army's chief of staff. Interference with the coal trains and threatened "repairs" to the Elbe River bridge indicated, he believed, that the Soviets planned to cut off rail and ground traffic to Berlin, leaving the only available supply routes through the air. Huebner continued that he was uncertain if the air force had the capability of supplying a city of two million by air, and he feared that fuel and food shortages might turn the Germans against the Western powers, making their position in Berlin untenable. Huebner followed this letter with a much less alarming report on the same day advising that interference with the coal trains should not be interpreted as the imposition of new restrictions. Two days later, he noted that checks on vehicles were continuing, but he hoped that no more restrictions would be instituted.[70]

Despite over three months of Soviet harassment and the recognition of Berlin's vulnerability, little real thought and almost no planning had been given to the possibility of a complete blockade of Berlin. By mid-June, the army's intelligence division had considered the logistic effect of Soviet restrictions, but no further planning had taken place. As of June 15 the military lacked any concrete plans for action should the Soviet Union impose a blockade.[71]

Realistic options were almost nonexistent. American leaders would have to rely on diplomacy, though without force to support it since the United States had disbanded most of its military after World War II. Actual U.S. military strength as of February, 1948, was 552,000 men in the army, 476,000 in the navy (including 79,000 marines), and 346,000 air force personnel. The army had little strength in reserve, and activating more than one combat division for operations overseas would require a partial mobilization. In Europe, EUCOM was an occupation force chiefly involved in police duties and with little combat readiness, and the U.S. Army in Germany scarcely deserved the name. "Undisciplined, disorganized, engaged in black-market trading, with high AWOL [absent without leave] and VD [venereal disease] rates," Clay's biographer, Jean Edward Smith, later wrote, "the American Army in Europe was seen by many observers as a blemish on the United States." In April, 1947, Clay decided that the army could turn responsibility for maintaining law and order over to the German police and return to combat training. He ordered General Huebner to reestablish the 1st Infantry Division as a viable combat force. Huebner, a former enlisted man and wartime commander of the "Big Red One," moved quickly, reasserting discipline, order, and authority. He dedicated one regiment from the division and another regiment composed of constabulary troops to tactical training, and by fall Clay could show the two units to visiting General Bradley with some pride.[72]

Two regiments, however, were going to provide little resistance against a serious Soviet attack, and despite continued progress, things were not much better by the summer of 1948. In July, the American Army in Germany was understrength: 90,821 troops were available but around 116,000 were required for an adequate defense. The 1st Infantry Division of 12,180 men provided the main operational force, but its overall combat efficiency rating was a meager 62 percent (except for its third regiment, which was rated at 15 percent). The U.S. constabulary of 15,766 men consisted of six highly mobile, lightly armed regiments committed to a security mission. The 350th Infantry Regiment, less a battalion in Austria, was committed to occupation duties and had a combat efficiency rating of 50 percent. Two infantry battalions and two field artillery battalions rounded out the ground forces. The British Army had 103,426 men organized into four divisions, three independent brigades, and four unassigned infantry regiments. The French had another 75,000 personnel organized into one armored division and five regimental combat teams. In Berlin, the Western allies fielded the equivalent of five battalions without heavy weapons and with minimal combat effectiveness. These battalions faced four Soviet divisions located within twenty-five miles of the city.[73]

The air situation was only marginally better. After his arrival on October 18, 1947, LeMay's efforts to build combat capability met with some success. In June, 1948, the USAFE consisted of one tactical fighter group, two troop carrier groups, and a photo-reconnaissance squadron, while reinforcements in the form of one fighter group were expected in a few months. The 86th Fighter Group consisted of seventy-five World War II–vintage Republic P-47 Thunderbolts, but the group was well trained, had experienced officers, and boasted a 90 percent operational efficiency rating. The 36th Fighter Group and its seventy-five Lockheed F-80 Shooting Stars, the air force's first operational jet fighter, were scheduled to reinforce USAFE and would arrive from the Caribbean after the Berlin Blockade began. Beyond fighters, the 45th Reconnaissance Squadron was a composite unit of twenty-one widely assorted aircraft, including Douglas A-26 and FA-26 Invaders, North American F-6s (the reconnaissance version of the P-51 Mustang), and Boeing B-17s. This unit, too, was experienced and well trained with an 85 percent operational efficiency rating. Additionally, as will be detailed later, the air force had begun rotating Strategic Air Command bombers to Germany, and one squadron of Boeing B-29 Superfortresses was in temporary residence at Fürstenfeldbruck in Bavaria. Outside USAFE, the Royal Air Force fielded thirty-six light bombers in four squadrons and ninety-six fighters in six squadrons, although reinforcements from England were close at hand.[74] The French had committed most of their air power to Southeast Asia.

Military leaders in Europe knew that cooperation was their only chance of success in a crisis with the Soviet Union. Beyond preparing his own forces, General Huebner also began coordinating war plans with the British while LeMay began discussions with both the British and French air forces. And beyond discussions, the aggressive USAFE commander covertly established supply installations in the French occupation zone and on airfields in France using the surplus property and the graves registration units in those areas as cover. This effort would give USAFE operations some depth and reduce its dependence upon the vulnerable forward bases in Germany.[75]

The Western nations faced a formidable foe. Soviet forces in Germany consisted of between one-half and one million men. The 3rd Shock and 8th Guards Armies located along the border of the Soviet zone of occupation formed the first operational echelon, while the 1st and 2nd Mechanized Armies farther to the east comprised the second operational echelon. These units were heavily mechanized with hundreds of IS-2 heavy tanks and T-34s, the best tank of World War II, backed by self-propelled artillery. The demobilization of troops at the end of the war had primarily culled out of service older, wounded, sick, and tired veterans, leaving a residue of the best younger men, most with combat experience. Almost all of the officers, especially at higher levels, had extensive experience in war. The Soviet Air Force operated hundreds of fighters, bombers, and attack aircraft from an extensive network of airfields. However, Russian forces did have weaknesses, primarily in discipline and in a shortage of truck transportation.[76]

Currency Reform—The Trigger for Blockade

In the meantime, creation of an economically stable western Germany required reform of the German currency. The occupying powers had introduced a single currency after the war, but the Soviets had debased it by printing as much as they pleased. Further, Russian leaders opposed currency reform unless they controlled its manufacture without interference from or oversight by the Western powers, something the British and Americans refused to allow. By late 1947, Soviet leaders had concluded that the Western powers were well underway toward the introduction of a single currency in the Western zones and began planning for the introduction of new banknotes for the Soviet zone. On May 18, 1948, the Russian government directed its military administration in Germany to put the currency reform into effect in its zone and to limit the circulation of money in the Greater Berlin area to Soviet occupation currency if the Western powers instituted unilateral currency reform in their zones. The London Conference communiqué issued on June 6 instructed the three Western military governors—Clay, Robertson, and Koenig—to proceed with currency reform. On June 18, they notified Marshal Sokolovsky that the new currency, called "west" marks, would be introduced in the Western zones beginning on June 20. West marks would not, however, be legal tender in Berlin.[77]

In response, the Soviets increased pronouncements condemning the Western powers for splitting Germany and stepped up the harassment of communications with Berlin. On June 19, Soviet guards halted all passenger trains and traffic on the autobahn, delayed Western and German freight shipments with inspections, and required that all water transport secure special Soviet permission. On June 21, the Russians halted a U.S. military supply train and refused to let it go to Berlin. Then, late the following day, they placed armed guards on the train, attached a Soviet engine, and ran it back to Western Germany.[78]

Talks between financial experts from the four powers, held on June 22, went nowhere, but the Soviet delegate to the meeting was explicit in his threats: "We are warning both you and the population of Berlin that we shall apply economic and administrative sanctions which will lead to circulation in Berlin exclusively of the currency of the Soviet occupation zone."[79] On the same day, Marshal Sokolovsky notified Clay, Robertson, and Koenig that, in response to the new Western currency, new Eastern currency would be introduced in the Soviet zone, including Berlin. The Western leaders responded by extending the use of west marks to their sectors of Berlin. (West marks issued in the city were overprinted with a "B" that limited their use to Berlin and thus became known as "B-marks.") In concert with all these actions, the Soviets launched a propaganda campaign notable for its viciousness. By radio, newspaper, and loudspeaker, authorities condemned and disparaged the Americans, British, and French and played on the fears of the Berliners in an effort to turn them against the Western allies. Rumors of Mongolian troops spread, and Russian units began conducting well-advertised maneuvers just outside the city. German communists in the eastern sector of Berlin demonstrated, rioted, and attacked pro-Western German leaders.[80]

On June 24, the Soviets completely severed land and water communications between the Western zones and Berlin, and the next day they added, for good measure, that the Soviet Union would not supply food to the civilian population in the Western sectors of Berlin. As of June 24 the military government halted all rail and barge traffic in and out of Berlin. Motor traffic from Berlin to the Western zones was permitted, but even this required a twenty-three kilometer detour to a ferry crossing, allegedly because of "repairs" to a bridge. Surface traffic from the Western zones to Berlin was blockaded, only the air corridors remained open.[81]

Contrary to popular belief, the purpose of the Berlin crisis was to reverse political decisions already taken by the Western powers, not to force the Western garrisons out of Berlin (although eliminating Western influence and activity in Germany remained a long-term Soviet goal).[82] While the introduction of a new currency in the Western occupation zones triggered the Berlin Blockade, it was clear that the new currency itself was not the problem. What offended Soviet leaders was the new currency as a concrete measure of separation of Western Germany. A July 14, 1948, letter of justification from the Soviet ambassador to the United States, Alexander S. Payushkin, made the Soviet point of view clear: "[T]he Agreement concerning the four power administration of Berlin is an inseparable component part of the agreement for the four power administration of Germany as a whole. After the U.S.A., Great Britain, and France by their separate action in the western zones of Germany destroyed the system of four power administration of Germany and had begun to set up a capital for a Government for Western Germany in Frankfurt-am-Main, they thereby undermined as well the legal basis which assured their right to participation in the administration of Berlin."[83]

It is also clear that Stalin did not want war with the United States. He was committed to attaining his goals using every method available short of an action that would provoke the Western powers. Scholar Michael Narinskii has recently concluded that: "All the Soviet actions were aimed at exerting military and political pressure on the West so as to obtain political concessions, relying on the West's prudence and unwillingness to provoke war. The fundamental mistake made by the Soviet leadership was that they underestimated the resolution of the Western powers to resist Soviet pressure and to press on with realization of the decisions on the German question taken by the London conference of representatives of six countries."[84]

Resolution was one thing; the physical ability of the Western garrisons to remain in Berlin and the capacity of the West to maintain over two million German civilians was quite another. Where Soviet leaders significantly erred was in their assessment of the American and British *capability* to remain in Berlin. Lacking experience with strategic air transport of their own and familiar with the German failure to air supply its forces at Stalingrad during World War II, Soviet leaders drastically underestimated the capability of the American and British air forces to sustain the population of Berlin. "Resolution" would not deliver a loaf of bread or a lump of coal to Berlin. Airplanes of the United States Air Forces in Europe and the British Air Forces of Occupation would deliver both.

Berlin under Siege

Five significant points must be emphasized about this crisis in Germany. First, the Western commitment to remain in Berlin was not inevitable. Only Britain's fiery foreign minister Ernest Bevin and an icily determined Lucius Clay argued the case for Berlin from the beginning. Bevin, who had ascended to power with the British Labour Party, hated Stalin's dictatorship of the Left as much as he hated dictatorships of the Right and proposed to fight communism in Europe as he had in the trade unions. Other leaders, including Marshall and Forrestal in Washington and Sir

Brian Robertson in Germany, had reservations about Western ability to maintain its position in Berlin. Second, the airlift was never a solution to the blockade of Berlin. Flying the necessities of life did nothing to resolve the issues involved. Rather it was a stopgap measure, an expedient that enabled Western leaders to buy the time needed to seek a diplomatic solution to the crisis posed by the Soviet blockade. It enabled them to negotiate without the need either to give in at some point to Soviet pressure or to escalate the situation beyond control. Third, no one, including Bevin and Clay, planned for the airlift or foresaw that it could become the critical element in a crisis. It was a logical device implemented by military leaders in Germany as an immediate response to the situation. Clay had used it on a limited scale during the April crisis, and he resorted to it again in June almost as a reflex action; Clay neither requested nor received permission from Washington for the airlift. Officially, there were 8,973 Americans, 7,606 British, and 6,100 French occupation personnel in Berlin. Their requirements could be met by air. As for the 2,008,943 Berliners, few believed their needs could be met by air transportation alone for any length of time. However, the airlift garnered support over time. Some American military and civilian leaders saw its possibilities early, while others came to accept the airlift only after it proved its ability to supply Berlin. Fourth, the leadership of Ernst Reuter and the tremendous determination of the German people to remain free of Soviet control were critical to the success of the airlift. Finally, and most important of all, the airlift fitted into the prevailing written and unwritten ground rules already established through previous interaction with the Soviets in Germany. Tacit agreement to act within those ground rules was crucial: it prevented the situation from escalating into something neither side wanted—a war in Europe.[85]

In one way, the Berlin crisis took place at a reasonably favorable time. The winter of 1946–47 had been especially harsh and had been followed by a drought during the summer. In contrast, the weather in 1948 was exceptionally pleasant, leading to a magnificent harvest, though not enough to end a critical food shortage. In July, 1948, occupation authorities raised the German ration to a minimum of 1,990 calories each day, the first increase since the ration had been set by nutritionists in 1945. The West had built up the German fishing fleet and imports had also increased. For the first time since the war, Europe had begun to produce surplus food. Beyond these factors, the European Recovery Plan held out great promise across the continent.[86]

Members of the Soviet Military Administration in Germany celebrated when the blockade began. They believed that the Western powers had little option other than to acquiesce to Russian demands or to abandon Berlin to the Soviet Union. None had doubts that the blockade would succeed, and they took for granted that, cut off from food and fuel from the Western zones of occupation, the garrisons in Berlin had no other practical recourse.[87] None of them, of course, anticipated the Berlin Airlift.

chapter 2

The Airlift Begins

Of all the roles played by military air power, that of air transport was perhaps the least anticipated and certainly the least explored prior to World
War II.[1] Consequently, military air transport evolved pragmatically as
needs arose, and its organization in the United States was fragmented from
the beginning as each military service developed the capabilities required
to meet its own commitments during the war.

The U.S. Army Air Forces (USAAF) itself created two distinct transportation organizations. The first was Air Transport Command (ATC), a global
air delivery system that reported directly to USAAF headquarters and whose
units, equipment, and personnel were outside the control of theater commanders. ATC operated much like a civilian airline, following standard
routes, maintaining regular schedules, and making planned stops at designated airports and airfields. While ATC included standardized flying
squadrons, the size and strength of maintenance, supply, and other support units, as well as that of the group and higher headquarters, could be
varied according to need, thus providing the flexibility required by a global organization. The adaptable structure of ATC and the rhythmic operational patterns it followed facilitated a conveyer-system approach to air
operations that proved key to the delivery of large amounts of cargo.

The advent of ATC—and its smaller rival, the Naval Air Transport
Service (NATS)—created a revolution in military transport during World

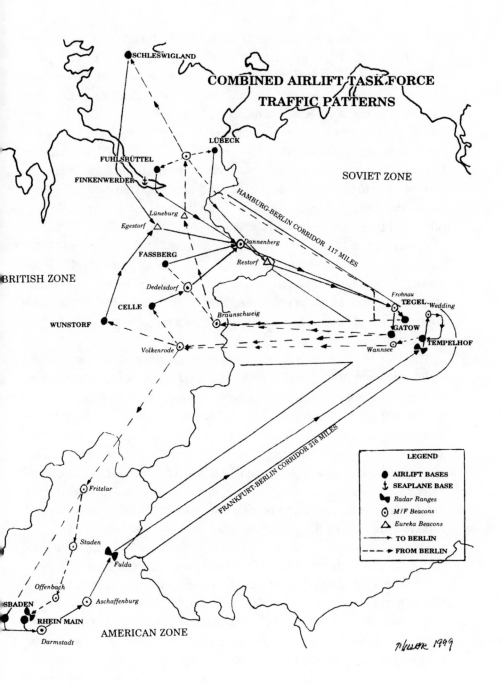

COMBINED AIRLIFT TASK FORCE
TRAFFIC PATTERNS

SCHLESWIGLAND

LÜBECK

SOVIET ZONE

FUHLSBÜTTEL

FINKENWERDER

HAMBURG-BERLIN CORRIDOR 117 MILES

Lüneburg

Egestorf

Dannenberg

FASSBERG

Restorf

BRITISH ZONE

Dedelsdorf

Frohnau

TEGEL

Wedding

CELLE

Braunschweig

GATOW

WUNSTORF

TEMPELHOF

Volkenrode

Wannsee

FRANKFURT-BERLIN CORRIDOR 216 MILES

Fritzlar

Staden

Fulda

Offenbach

SBADEN

Aschaffenburg

RHEIN MAIN

AMERICAN ZONE

Darmstadt

Miller 1999

LEGEND

● AIRLIFT BASES

⚓ SEAPLANE BASE

🦴 Radar Ranges

⊙ M/F Beacons

△ Eureka Beacons

→ TO BERLIN

--→ FROM BERLIN

War II. Military planners envisioned neither the dimension nor the shape that global air transport would take afterward. Based on prewar experience, planners anticipated meeting the needs of the USAAF itself; instead, air transport became a universal requirement. ATC "quickly developed into an agency of the War Department, serving the whole war effort." Historians Wesley Craven and James Cate later wrote: "Its planes carried out from the United States almost everything—from bulldozers to blood plasma, from college professors to Hollywood entertainers, from high-explosive ammunition to the most delicate signal equipment, from eminent scientists to the most obscure technicians, from heads of state to the ordinary G.I.—and they brought back hog bristles and tungsten from China, cobalt and tin from Africa, rubber and quinine from Latin America, and from all over the globe the wounded G.I. who could not expect to find in New Guinea, Luzon, Burma, North Africa, or even western Europe the medical attention he could have in the United States. And when the war ended in Europe, ATC had the capacity to bring home as many as 50,000 veterans per month."[2]

The second USAAF organization was Troop Carrier Command (TCC), which grew out of the need to support the U.S. Army's parachute forces created at the beginning of World War II. Troop carrier squadrons, in contrast to ATC squadrons, were combat units organized and equipped to deliver airborne forces directly into battle and then to support those forces during the subsequent fighting. Each unit had a standard organization and sufficient manpower to enable it to meet the surges of combat operations. In contrast to ATC, troop carrier units operated under the orders of the theater commanders and between missions provided airlift capability to meet local needs within their assigned theater.

During World War II, proposals to unify military air transport had begun to circulate through the War Department. Especially, ATC leaders favored consolidation of all air transport primarily because they believed that a single organization would be more economic and efficient. Despite such advocacy, consolidation gained little real support. Turf wars were rampant: Inter-service rivalry prevented the unification of ATC and NATS. Within the army, experience attained during the war seemed to justify separate tactical and strategic organizations. Further, the troop carrier community jealously guarded its autonomy, arguing that its mission was too specialized for inclusion in a larger organization. Perhaps most important, consolidation contributed little to the main goal of USAAF leaders:

securing independence from the U.S. Army. In fact, to gain backing for independence, air leaders promised army leaders that the U.S. Air Force would continue to provide air support for army airborne units. Consolidating troop carrier units under ATC might have been interpreted as abandoning that promise.

The National Security Act of 1947—which created an independent U.S. Air Force on September 18, 1947—eliminated one major obstacle to consolidating air transport by empowering the Secretary of Defense to mediate between the services and giving him a charter to eliminate unnecessary duplication. In December, 1947, the new secretary, James V. Forrestal, ordered the army and navy to prepare a plan to unite ATC and NATS. Planning proceeded smoothly and on June 1, 1948—just three weeks before the Berlin Airlift began—the Department of Defense activated the Military Air Transport Service (MATS) under the command of U.S. Air Force Maj. Gen. Laurence S. Kuter, with Rear Adm. John P. Whitney as his deputy. Subsequently, MATS assumed a significant war readiness mission of its own, becoming responsible for deployment of Strategic Air Command units to overseas bases and their subsequent support.

Troop carrier units and their combat mission remained, too. A May 3, 1948, memorandum by Secretary Forrestal reaffirmed the essential elements of the military air transport system by declaring that the mission of MATS "does not include responsibility for the tactical air transportation of airborne troops and their equipment, the initial supply and resupply of units in forward combat areas, or that required by the Department of the Navy for internal administration."[3] Air transport thus remained divided into two organizations, one strategic and the other tactical. The Berlin Airlift would begin relying on the tactical airlift capability supplied by troop carrier units assigned to USAFE, but a call for the global airlift capability of MATS would come quickly.

Officially, the Berlin Airlift began on June 26, 1948. Preliminary actions, however, began days earlier. On June 18, EUCOM's Transportation Division established a traffic control point at Rhein-Main based upon the plans developed following the April crisis. On the following day, the 67th Truck Company delivered two hundred tons of supplies from the quartermaster supply depot at Giessen to the control point. On June 19–20, USAFE C-47s delivered fresh milk to Berlin. On June 21, the transportation officer in Berlin expanded the traffic control point at Tempelhof and established a liaison with Rhein-Main.[4] The most significant move took place on

Figure 3. *Secretary of Defense James V. Forrestal signs MATS into existence, observed by* (left to right): *Rear Adm. John P. Whitney, vice commander, MATS; John Nicholas Brown, assistant secretary of the navy for air; unidentified; Charles V. Whitney, assistant secretary of the air force for matèriel; and Maj. Gen. Laurence S. Kuter, commander in chief, MATS.* Courtesy Laurence S. Kuter Papers, Special Collections, Air Force Academy Library.

June 22, when General Huebner directed General LeMay to "utilize the maximum number of airplanes to transport supplies to Tempelhof Air Drome, Berlin."[5] LeMay reported to the air staff in Washington: "I am today providing all available air lift to supply Berlin in the crisis created by Soviet action following the recent currency conversion. This commitment will undoubtedly continue until the Soviets again permit our rail and freight shipments to pass to Berlin without inspection."[6]

LeMay had two experienced but somewhat weary transport units available, the 60th and 61st Troop Carrier Groups. Originally, U.S. Air Force leaders had planned to reduce USAFE's air transport capability to one group of four squadrons performing "airline flights in Europe" and special missions as required. The remaining aircraft would conduct operations with the army, a troop carrier group's standard mission. This arrangement had proved impossible, however, because Clay's demands for support of his military government normally absorbed almost all of the available aircraft. In the spring of 1948, LeMay received authorization to keep two transport groups in Germany instead of one, thus LeMay had the 61st Troop Carrier Group of three squadrons—the 14th, 15th, and 53rd—in position at Rhein-Main and Wiesbaden. The 60th Troop Carrier Group, consisting of the 10th, 11th, and 12th Troop Carrier Squadrons, was farther southeast at Kaufbeuren Air Base in Bavaria. Nominally, these units totaled ninety-six C-47s. LeMay had proposed to use one group to meet theater requirements while the second handled tactical troop carrier duties, but the extensive demands for use of the small number of aircraft prevented this plan from being implemented. In practice, the 61st Group devoted one squadron to operating a regular theater airlines called European Air Transport Service, a second to supporting military government requirements, and the third—supposedly reserved for the tactical support of combat units—to emergency airlift requirements. The emergency demands for airlift to Berlin in April had drained the unit's resources, however; more than twenty aircraft per day had been committed to Berlin since then. The 60th Group was supposed to have a purely tactical mission, however, it actually supported distant American commitments in Tripoli, Palestine, Cyprus, and Berlin—support for Tripoli alone had been a two-month commitment. Other missions were addressed piecemeal but added up to a significant use of available resources. In June alone, the 60th furnished thirty-one aircraft and an even larger number of aircrews to assorted missions, almost two complete squadrons.[7]

From the beginning of the Little Lift in April through the arrival of the first C-54s three months later, C-47s provided military air transport in Europe. The Skytrain, affectionately known as the "Gooney Bird," was a much beloved airplane in air force lore. "No more reliable or forgiving aircraft has ever been built," veteran pilot J. B. McLaughlin later wrote. "We got away with youthful stupidities that would have killed us in any other airplane."[8] They were less popular during the Berlin Airlift, however. USAFE Skytrains were all more than five years old and had thousands of flying hours, most under wartime conditions, on their airframes. Some still wore the faded black and white markings of D-Day invasion stripes or the reddish vestiges of desert camouflage from North Africa. Their limited cargo

Figure 4. USAFE's air transport in June, 1948, consisted of two troop carrier wings of veteran Douglas C-47 Skytrains. These are being unloaded in all too typical weather on the flight line at Tempelhof. Courtesy U.S. Air Force

capacity frustrated those concerned with the build up of supplies, and their age and worn condition hindered the maintenance and supply personnel who had to keep them in the air. In one example, intergranular corrosion and cracks in the fittings of the landing-gear bracing strut attachment grounded many C-47s at a cost of some 850 hours in inspection and maintenance. A shortage of parts threatened routine maintenance and technical order compliance despite every attempt to requisition them. About the only individuals who really liked the Skytrain were the cargo-handling personnel, since C-47 doors were low and caused less fatigue for the loading crews and less damage during cargo transfer. Following the April crisis in Berlin, LeMay had requested larger, more modern transport aircraft, but these would not be available until 1949.[9]

USAFE's response to General Huebner's order was immediate despite its limited means. Overnight deliveries went from just under 6 tons on June 21 to 156.42 tons on the next day, and for the next week the C-47s sustained 80 tons daily.[10] From then on the airlift just grew, LeMay later wrote, "in time-honored Topsey [*sic*] fashion."[11]

Again, however, the early USAFE effort was still directed to support of the military garrison in Berlin. On June 23, General Clay and his political advisor, Robert Murphy, flew to Heidelberg, where they met with General Huebner and his staff. Clay wanted to break any blockade by sending a regimental combat team supported by artillery and armor along the autobahn connecting the American zone with Berlin. By June 24, when the Soviet blockade went into effect, EUCOM plans called for an experienced engineer, Brig. Gen. Arthur Trudeau, to command the task force, which would include an engineer battalion with bridging equipment and the capability to repair the bridge over the Elbe that the Soviets had "closed for repair." Backing this force, Curtis LeMay and USAFE planned to attack Russian airfields in Germany. Clay believed from intelligence reports that the Soviets were bluffing and concluded that forcing the blockade immediately was the correct response. But an armed convoy was also a calculated risk, and Clay knew that gaining Washington's approval for such action would be difficult. Moreover, support from his allies, he quickly discovered, was nonexistent.[12]

Prime Minister Ernest Bevin had ordered the British military commander in Germany, Gen. Sir Brian Robertson, to explore every possible means of remaining in Berlin, including aerial supply. Air Commodore Reginald N. Waite, director of the Air Branch of the British Control Commission in Berlin, calculated that enough resources were available to supply the population of the city by air for a short time and presented a rough plan for an airlift to Robertson on June 24. During Robertson's visit to Clay later that day, the British general was appalled to find the American planning a direct military confrontation with the Soviets. "If you do that, it'll be war—it's as simple as that," he told Clay. "In such an event I'm afraid my government could offer you no support—and I am sure Koenig will feel the same." Drawing on Waite's plan as an alternative to Clay's armed convoy, Robertson proposed supplying the Berlin population by air temporarily until diplomatic negotiations could end the blockade. Clay was dubious. Delivering cargo to the Western garrisons by air was comparatively easy; supplying an entire population, even in the short term envisioned, posed potentially insurmountable difficulties. Clay remained committed to a direct military solution, and on June 25 he forcefully advocated the use of an armed convoy during a long-distance teletype conference with his superiors, Secretary of the Army Kenneth Royall and Chief of Staff Gen. Omar Bradley, in the Pentagon. To the general's dismay, Royall and Bradley ordered him not to send the convoy and stressed that any action risking war must be avoided.[13]

This decision ruled out any plan of ending the blockade by force for the time being and left Clay with no real options. Later that day he met with the Lord Mayor–elect of Berlin, Ernst Reuter. "I may be the craziest man in the world," he told the German leader, "but I am going to try the experiment of feeding this city by air." Reuter was skeptical about the resolve of the Americans as well as their technological ability to supply Berlin's citizens. But he was also determined that his city would not fall under Soviet control and promised Clay that, come what may, Berliners would make the sacrifices necessary to survive.[14] Reuter's support was essential to any relief effort. Until the Berlin Crisis, Clay had developed little communication with Reuter, but under the pressure of events the two cultivated a mutual respect and soon became friends. "[Reuter] was a strong man and a forceful speaker," Clay told his biographer years later. "It was unfortunate that he died when he did [September 29, 1953], because I think he would have become one of the truly great men of Europe."[15]

Clay, like Reuter, remained skeptical about the long-term success of the airlift and was extremely thankful that the USAFE effort probably would have to last only a short time, a few weeks at most. Once he decided on air supply, however, the general moved quickly. Berlin's immediate need was food. On the afternoon of June 25, Clay asked Col. Frank Howley, the tough ex-cavalryman and irrepressible commander of the American garrison in Berlin, what he needed first. Howley specified flour, since it was easy to handle and of high nutritional value. At 4:15 P.M. Clay called LeMay's chief of staff, Maj. Gen. August W. Kissner, and requested estimates on the maximum amount of cargo that USAFE could deliver to Berlin. Kissner reported that USAFE could furnish 225 tons daily. USAFE headquarters mobilized its limited resources, and 200 tons of flour reached Berlin the next day.[16] Howley watched the first Skytrains land. To him, they were a harbinger of the future: "They wobbled into Tempelhof, coming down clumsily through the bomb-shattered buildings around the field, a sight that would have made a spick-and-span air parade officer die of apoplexy, but they were the most beautiful things I had ever seen. As the planes touched down, and bags of flour began to spill out of their bellies, I realized that this was the beginning of something wonderful—a way to crack the blockade. I

Figure 5. Lord Mayor Ernst Reuter, here with General Clay, refused to allow Berlin to fall under Soviet control. Courtesy U.S. Air Force

went back to my office almost breathless with elation, like a man who has made a great discovery and cannot hide his joy."[17]

Superfortresses to Great Britain

As the airlift began, the deployment of B-29 heavy bombers to Europe came under consideration as well. Thousands of U.S. bombers had been based in Great Britain during World War II, but all of these were gone by the end of 1946. Soviet actions in Germany now brought American warplanes back to the island nation. At the end of the war, though, runways on existing RAF airfields had the length to handle B-17s and B-24s but not the huge B-29s. In 1946, Air Chief Marshal Sir Arthur Tedder, chief of the air staff, and Gen. Carl Spaatz, commanding general, U.S. Army Air Forces, both concerned over the growing Soviet threat in Europe, reached a "gentlemen's agreement" whereby the British lengthened and widened the runways at several bases during the next couple of years; by the time of the crisis over Berlin, airfields in England were ready for the larger planes.[18]

In 1948, the initiative came from the British. On June 26, Bevin told American ambassador Lewis W. Douglas that the airlift would provide time for negotiations and recommended that the United States also send heavy bombers so that the Soviets would understand that the West meant business. In Germany, Sir Brian Robertson learned of his government's position and tipped off Clay. After discussions with LeMay on June 27, Clay requested a group of B-29s. During the meeting in the Pentagon that same day, Secretary Forrestal discussed moving two B-29 groups to England and sending two squadrons of Superfortresses to join the one already in position at Fürstenfeldbruck in Germany. Gen. Hoyt Vandenberg especially supported this move, since he had wanted to base additional Strategic Air Command units in Europe for some time. The Berlin Crisis now offered him the opportunity. President Truman approved the movement on June 28. The Strategic Air Command immediately ordered two squadrons of the 301st Bombardment Group to Goose Bay, Labrador, the normal staging base for air units bound for Europe. These joined the third squadron of the 301st at Fürstenfeldbruck on July 2. The deployment of B-29s to England, however, had to wait until the British cabinet granted approval, which came on July 13. Once Strategic Air Command received the green light it reacted quickly. On July 17–18, 1948, the first of sixty B-29s of the 28th Bombardment Group from Rapid City Air Force Base, South Dakota, and the 307th Bombardment Group from MacDill Air Force Base, Florida, landed at airfields in Great Britain for what was billed as thirty-day temporary duty (TDY).[19] This deployment subsequently became sixty days, then ninety days. On November 13, the Air Ministry advised Washington that long-term use of RAF stations by U.S. aircraft "was assumed."[20]

The deployment of the two heavy bomber groups was a serious demonstration of American commitment to the defense of Europe and of its partnership with Great Britain. However, it is uncertain in terms of mili-

Figure 6. Boeing B-29 Superfortresses of the 28th Bombardment Group from Rapid City, South Dakota, over Dover, England. Courtesy U.S. Air Force

tary might how much deterrence the two groups of B-29s actually provided. Despite conventional belief, these aircraft were incapable of carrying atomic bombs. B-29s configured to deliver nuclear weapons, designated SILVERPLATE, were just coming into service; only the 509th Bombardment Group at Roswell Air Force Base, New Mexico, had them, and none of the 509th's bombers were sent to Europe until July, 1949. The two groups of Superfortresses in England were a powerful conventional bombing force in their own right and a forceful symbol of American resolve, but the lack of ability to deliver atomic bombs made them a much weaker deterrent than has commonly been believed.[21]

Soviet intelligence reported the arrival of the 28th and the 307th Bombardment Groups, but it remains unclear if the Soviet leadership knew that the B-29s lacked nuclear capability. In any case, the U.S. nuclear monopoly had already provided an effective deterrent to any idea on Stalin's part of settling the Berlin situation through military means. Despite a scare in September, 1948, when two Soviet divisions moved closer to the border with Western Germany, there is no indication that the Soviets considered military force. The combat training and level of military activities of Russian forces in Germany did not change significantly. Small-unit tactical training continued, but large-scale operational exercises of the type that usually preceded offensive action were absent, and Soviet units maintained normal levels of combat readiness throughout. Further, the only discussion of a military nature in the Politburo during the Berlin Crisis took place on June 30, 1948, and concerned the question of antiaircraft defense of the Soviet Union. This discussion certainly reflected Russian concerns over the U.S. Air Force and the nuclear monopoly. It is less clear that it reflected the deployment of B-29s to Europe.[22]

Armed Convoy Option Continued

Lucius Clay remained committed to forcing the blockade despite the reaction of his British and French allies and his superiors in Washington. He and his political advisor, Robert Murphy, wanted to challenge what they saw as a Soviet bluff, and they may have been correct given the lack of Soviet military planning for such a contingency. Further, since most high-level leaders viewed the airlift with considerable skepticism, an armed convoy remained an option for several months. The National Security Council on July 16, for example, concluded that after October and the onset of winter the United States would have to consider using an armed military force to break the blockade.[23]

In contrast to Clay's optimism, however, an analysis by the Pentagon on July 13 presented a bleaker assessment. The autobahn route to Berlin was 125 miles long and averaged three bridges per mile. A force large enough for the operation would be difficult to assemble and support, and every bridge represented a choke point where even a weak defensive force could delay or halt the advance. Even if this route could be seized and defended, it then would take a prodigious logistical effort to supply Berlin by truck estimated by Pentagon planners as "a system of transportation and traffic control equal to that in effect on the Red Ball Highway of OVER-LORD OPERATION. . . during World War II."[24] The Soviet military administration controlled the railroads and canals, however, and to gain access to these would require the seizure and defense of all locks, marshaling yards, switches, and bridges between the American zone of occupation and Berlin. The U.S. Army had neither the combat capability nor the means of transportation for such a mission. And above all, any such action ran the risk of war. Clay continued to express confidence in EUCOM's ability to run an armed convoy to Berlin without serious trouble. However, in Clay's estimate the plan had to be implemented soon or the chance of success would be severely reduced.[25]

On July 22, the Joint Chiefs directed Clay to prepare contingency plans for an armed convoy. By September 8, EUCOM had completed a plan for "Task Force TRUCULENT" calling for the 2nd Constabulary Regiment, 1st Engineer Battalion, and five to six truck companies with unspecified contingents of British and French troops to deliver one thousand tons of supplies to Berlin per day by truck. The convoy would be organized and equipped for combat and to remove any obstructions from the route. Depending on the Soviet reaction, EUCOM would then follow TRUCULENT with regular convoys on the same route sufficient to deliver one thousand tons of cargo to Berlin daily.[26]

Although planning continued, it is clear, that little interest existed at the highest levels for forcing convoys into Berlin. The Joint Chiefs of Staff generally believed that the idea was impractical and that the combined strength of both the U.S. and British forces was insufficient to fight convoys through any kind of interference. Further, neither the British nor the French were willing to back the use of armed force until all diplomatic measures had been exhausted. Afterward, the British probably would support the option, but the French probably would not favor it. Additionally, one thousand tons per day was far below the minimum cargo tonnage required, and by mid-July the airlift had already exceeded that amount by a substantial margin.[27]

Fortunately, the need for an armed convoy faded. The airlift's growing success eliminated the need for more direct action and this was probably for the best. General S. Ivanov, chief of staff of Soviet forces in Germany, later confirmed that his command had considered the possibility of the United States attempting to run an armed supply convoy to Berlin. However, since Soviet intelligence reported that the Americans were not preparing to supply the city by land, further contingency planning was unnecessary. Armed convoys would have been extremely dangerous, according to former officers of the Russian forces in Germany, and would have been viewed as an invasion of Soviet-controlled territory. They most likely would have been fired upon with unpredictable consequences.[28]

Operation Vittles: An Expedient in Action

Facilities to support the airlift in Germany were limited. In the American zone of occupation, Rhein-Main Air Base outside Frankfurt was the major airport in the country. USAFE had built most of its facilities, and these were already operating at full capacity when the airlift began. It had one 6,000-foot concrete runway and dispersed hardstands for tactical fighters. Despite the concrete infrastructure, however, conditions were such that the field would quickly become known by the apt nickname "Rhein-Mud." The second base in the American zone, Wiesbaden (just northwest of Rhein-Main), was a former *Luftwaffe* fighter base with minimum facilities and utilities beyond a 5,500-foot concrete runway and attendant taxiways and hardstands. Tempelhof in Berlin was the city's municipal airport prior to the war. When the Americans took over, they built a 6,150-foot pierced-steel-planking runway, a concrete apron and taxiway, and dispersed hardstands for tactical aircraft.[29]

The British, conversely, were reasonably well supplied with airfields. Most were former *Luftwaffe* fields improved and expanded by the RAF's airfield construction wings and the Royal Engineers. The RAF had built a hard-surfaced runway at Wunstorf near Hanover after the war, and by 1948 it had the capability of handling ninety-four transport aircraft. Fassberg had been one of the *Luftwaffe*'s largest airfields, and the British would complete a 6,000-foot concrete runway at that location during the airlift. Nearby Celle was a small field with a pierced-steel-planking runway on the major rail line to Hanover. Schleswigland had a concrete runway used by Messerschmitt Me-262 jet fighters during the war, and its 160,000-gallon underground fuel storage system would make it attractive for handling the liquid fuels needed in Berlin. Lübeck was another former *Luftwaffe* field located only two miles from the Soviet zone of occupation. Fuhlsbüttel was a civilian airfield at Hamburg. Finkenwerder was a stretch of the Elbe River west of Hamburg that served as a seaplane base. The British opened these bases to airlift operations one at a time as needed, and all were in operation by the end of 1948. In Berlin the situation was less satisfactory. The British airlift had to operate out of Gatow until, as will be described later, the construction of another field at Tegel. Gatow was originally a training center for the *Luftwaffe* and lacked a hard-surface runway until the RAF constructed a 4,500- foot pierced-steel-planking runway.[30]

Figure 7. Completely surrounded by buildings, Tempelhof was the primary American-operated airfield in Berlin. Courtesy U.S. Air Force

Thanks to the stockpiles built up in Berlin after the April crisis, the city could manage without outside shipments of goods for a time. Stocks as of June 30 included a twenty-five-day supply of flour, eighty-one days of sugar, nineteen days of meat, fifty-six days of fat, eighteen days of potatoes, fifty-four days of cereal, nineteen days of milk, and eighteen days of coffee. These stocks meant that Berlin did not have to rely on air support immediately, provided a margin of safety in case of failure or error, and furnished time to expand the existing airlift capacity.[31]

In Berlin, OMGUS planners became deeply involved in determining what types of goods should compose the cargo to be airlifted. Most often this featured intricate calculations that balanced short-term burdens against long-term needs. For example, was it better to fly in flour and coal and manufacture bread in Berlin, or, since a loaf of bread was 30 percent water, to pay the price in weight and fly in loaves? The answer in this case was to deliver flour and coal. On the other hand, it was smarter in terms of cargo space to airlift real coffee rather than provide the fuel required to manufacture ersatz coffee in Berlin. Dehydrated potatoes, known as "Pom," were one-fifth the weight of fresh ones. Other decisions involved altering the infrastructure of the city. Construction of a bridge between Gatow and the city reduced the amount of gasoline needed to haul airlift cargo, and altering electrical plants to use diesel fuel meant that they would consume less coal. These and literally thousands of similar calculations enabled the planners to reduce essential airlift cargo to a practical minimum.[32]

The American military government set the city's basic daily food ration at 646 tons of flour and wheat, 125 tons of cereal, 64 tons of fat, 109 tons of meat and fish, 180 tons of dehydrated potatoes, 180 tons of sugar, 11 tons of coffee, 19 tons of powdered milk, 5 tons of whole milk for children, 3 tons of fresh yeast for baking, 144 tons of dehydrated vegetables, 38 tons of salt, and 10 tons of cheese. Beyond food, the primary need in Berlin was the raw materials of power: coal and liquid fuel. The major difference between the World War II airlift over the Himalaya Mountains from India to China—known as "flying the Hump"—and the Berlin Airlift was that gasoline was the major cargo in the former, while coal became the most important cargo in the later. In addition, quantities of raw materials would be required to keep Berlin industries operating, together with a wide assortment of smaller necessities ranging from medical supplies to newsprint. Initially, Howley and his experts figured that they could get by with the delivery of 3,475 tons of cargo per day in August, September, and October.[33]

Additionally, it is now clear that the Berlin Airlift was aided by the fact that the Soviet blockade was loosely applied, especially during the first few months. According to historian William Stivers, "the Soviet blockade neither attempted nor achieved the isolation of West Berlin."[34] The Western sectors of Berlin simply could not be walled off from the rest of the city: The railroad system wound in and out of the Western and Eastern sectors and occasional Soviet attempts to reroute trains proved fruitless. Canal traffic from the Elbe and Oder Rivers also passed through the British sector of Berlin. In addition, thousands of Germans who lived in one sector and worked in another traveled between the sectors daily. Such access offered endless temptation and little hazard to German traders, who often had to do little more than falsify their manifests to show a delivery destination in the Soviet zone and then deliver their cargo to the Western sectors. American military intelligence reported the arrival in August of large amounts of foodstuffs—including fish products, vegetables, cereals, soups, and fruits—fodder, firewood, coal, and building materials in this manner. Such deliveries were documented well into October and apparently continued throughout the blockade.[35]

The enterprise of individual Berliners with access to the Soviet occupation zone contributed as well. Before the blockade, citizens had foraged for food in the countryside in the Eastern zone to supplement bare shelves, and that practice continued even after the borders closed. During the crisis, Germans developed a "widespread and efficient smuggling organization" that brought truckloads of food into the Western sectors of the city. Berliners flocked to the *Potsdamerplatz* in the center of Berlin, where black market items were available in substantial amounts to those who could afford them.[36] Frank Howley counted on the porousness of the Soviet blockade: "Tight lines were drawn between the Soviet sector and the three Western sectors, but they didn't prevent intermingling during the blockade .... About eighty thousand Germans, living in our sector and working in another, or doing business outside their own sector, went back and forth daily.... Theoretically, the Germans were not permitted to bring anything into our sectors, but the Russians, so keen on searching people on the slightest pretext, shrank at the formidable task of searching eighty thousand every day."[37]

Additionally, the Soviets kept the doors to Berlin half open because they needed the West as much as, if not more than, the West needed them. Close economic ties existed between Western Berlin and the Soviet occupation zone. Industries in Berlin were able to negotiate deals with suppliers in the Eastern zone in exchange for finished goods that the Russians were interested in obtaining. The Soviet Military Administration and German Economic Commission continued to procure the more stable and valuable currency circulating in Western Germany by selling luxury goods, textiles, and silk hose in those zones. When Marshal Sokolovsky and Col. Sergei Tiulpanov met with members of the East German Industrial Committee on June 28, they appear to have been shocked when their hosts explained that industry in the Soviet zone would soon cease to function without access to raw materials and parts from the Western zones. Seemingly, Soviet leaders lacked any understanding of the extent to which their region of Germany depended on Western materials and industries. Ultimately, various sources estimate that as much as five hundred thousand tons of supplies reached the Western sectors of Berlin through either authorized or unauthorized means during the months of the blockade.[38]

The interdependence of the sectors was demonstrated by an incident that bordered on the farcical. The U.S. commander in Berlin, Frank Howley, took special glee in bedeviling the Soviets. At one point during the blockade, the irrepressible Howley learned that Marshal Sokolovsky's home was serviced by a gas main that went through the Western sector. He turned off the heat, forcing the marshal to move. When Soviet soldiers loaded Sokolovsky's furniture on a van and tried to cross the American sector, Howley's alert men confiscated it all.[39]

The dependence of the Soviet occupation zone on the Western zones was the Achilles' heel of the Soviet blockade, and Lucius Clay began playing his own economic card early with devastating impact. On June 24, the Soviets halted milk delivery to the Western sectors but quickly resumed it when U.S. authorities halted meat deliveries to the Eastern zone. When the Soviets cancelled the Berlin Food Agreement on June 25 and ordered that food supplied by their zone be distributed only in the Eastern sector of Berlin, American authorities immediately had the city magistrate transfer American-supplied flour from the main food warehouses to storage areas in the Western sectors. When the Soviets announced that all food received in the Soviet sector would be distributed in that area only, the Western allies cut out all shipments of food and medicine to Eastern Berlin.[40] The United States officially began a counterblockade in September, 1948. Self-denial had limited impact on the Western areas of occupation, where "rations of bread, sugar, and potatoes suffered little as a result of the stoppage of meager deliveries previously received from the Soviet zone."[41] On the other hand, the Allied counterblockade severely impacted the economy of the Soviet zone of occupation and caused a major headache for the Soviet Military Administration in Germany.

The British could initially deliver 75 tons of cargo per day but could increase this to 400 tons with aircraft from England. Once they completed some runway repairs at Gatow on July 3; however, the potential British capacity almost doubled to 750 tons per day. BAFO could maintain this level for one month at the expense of all other air traffic (except with Berlin and with Warsaw), though with repercussions on British civil air transport. The American capacity was terribly limited as well. Based on a figure of seventy trips per day, USAFE planners calculated that the command could provide about 225 tons of supplies. LeMay believed that with an all-out effort he could fly one hundred roundtrips per day providing, at most, about 300 tons of cargo daily. Theoretically, then, the airlift could deliver about 1,000 tons per day. To meet these goals, late on the evening of June 27, USAFE ordered the 60th Troop Carrier Group from Kaufbeuren to Wiesbaden. The first of the 60th's C-47s reached Wiesbaden early in the morning and were loaded and ready to fly into Berlin that evening.[42]

LeMay knew that USAFE would be unable to sustain its efforts for long, however, and he had reached the end of his own resources. He had a critical need for modern airlift capability, making reinforcements from the United States mandatory. On June 27, LeMay sent a message to Washington asking for the transfer of a group of Douglas C-54 Skymasters to Germany immediately; he also wanted air force headquarters to consider advancing the schedule for converting the 60th and 61st Troop Carrier Groups from C-47s to C-54s. Clay, at LeMay's urging, made his own request for C-54s on the following day.[43]

In the Skymaster, Clay and LeMay were calling on another successful veteran of World War II. Douglas had begun development of a four-engine transcontinental airliner in the late 1930s, and the U.S. Army Air Forces commandeered the production line after Pearl Harbor. Orders for a military cargo version quickly followed. The C-54 first flew in March, 1942, and the USAFF bought a total of 952 while the U.S. Navy purchased an additional 211 as the R5D. Four 1,290 h.p. Pratt & Whitney R-2000-7 engines gave the airplane a top speed of 265 m.p.h. and enabled it to carry over thirteen tons of cargo. During the airlift, however, the C-54 seldom carried more than ten tons because of the added wear to the tires and the increased strain on the brakes during landings. LeMay needed C-54s even though few spare parts and little maintenance support were available in Europe for the big aircraft. The Skymasters thus needed to be self-sustaining, with their own stocks of equipment, parts, and spares, especially engines.[44]

On Sunday, June 27, Secretary of Defense Forrestal held a meeting that included Secretary of the Army Royall, Under Secretary of State Robert Lovett, Secretary of the Navy John L. Sullivan, and air force Maj. Gen. Lauris Norstad. The conferees estimated that Berlin could survive for thirty days on existing reserves and the cargo delivered by air. The use of dried foods could increase this to sixty days. One decision by this group was implemented immediately: the secretary of defense ordered four C-54 squadrons from Alaska, the United States, Hawaii, and the Caribbean to

Figure 8. The Douglas C-54 Skymaster, the U.S. Air Force's primary strategic air transport during the 1940s, was the workhorse of the Berlin Airlift. These aircraft are awaiting takeoff at Rhein-Main. Courtesy U.S. Air Force

Germany. U.S. Air Force Chief of Staff Hoyt Vandenberg passed the news to LeMay. Three squadrons of thirty-nine C-54 Skymasters from the Alaskan, Caribbean, and Tactical Air Commands would be leaving their bases within twenty-four hours carrying spare air crews and maintenance personnel. A fourth squadron, thirteen C-54s from the Seventh Air Force in Hawaii, was also ordered to Germany with additional crews and maintenance personnel.[45]

On Monday, June 28, Forrestal, Royall, and Lovett presented the options to President Truman. The president interrupted their briefing by affirming that abandoning the city was beyond discussion. The United States was in Berlin by agreement, Truman affirmed, and the Soviets had no right to push its forces out. He then approved the decisions sending additional B-29s to Germany, upgrading the B-29 squadron in Germany to a group, and deploying two groups of B-29s to England. For the time being, no B-29s would go to France, however, and the transfer to England was delayed until the British government gave its approval. At the same time, the Strategic Air Command directed the 301st Bombardment Group at Goose Bay, Labrador, to send two squadrons to Fürstenfeldbruck, Germany, immediately.[46]

That same day USAFE submitted an estimate to the director of EUCOM's logistics division that showed a planned increase in tonnage from 450 tons per day by June 30 to 1,500 tons as of July 10. The increased tonnage requirements demanded a more efficient organization, and LeMay himself got a firsthand look at the problems when he flew a C-47 into Tempelhof on June 29. Cleared and ready to depart Rhein-Main at 10:45 A.M., he was forced to wait until noon because of difficulty in getting runway clearance at Tempelhof. Once in Berlin, however, things went smoothly; it took only twenty minutes to unload the aircraft. LeMay also conferred with Clay while in Berlin about the complex and difficult task of delivering coal. Ultimately, they agreed that the only way to move coal in sufficient amounts was to use B-29s. Tempelhof, however, lacked the ability to handle the Superfortresses, and LeMay determined to try dropping the coal at low altitude. He directed Col. Henry Dorr, the commanding officer at Tempelhof, to find a suitable location away from the active runway to test the concept. As a result of his visit, LeMay also directed the air traffic control center to revise landing procedures at Tempelhof by eliminating standard instrument approaches where possible in favor of a straight-in approach during inclement weather. At Tempelhof, he saw pilots going to the operations office to fill out forms as they would under normal conditions. LeMay ordered operations officers to go to the aircraft with the proper forms instead and also had coffee and refreshments brought to the airplane. After returning to Rhein-Main, LeMay directed the 60th Troop Carrier Group to reduce the fuel load in the C-47s by two hundred gallons, thus increasing payloads in each plane by about 1,500 pounds.[47]

Perhaps most important, after his return, LeMay appointed Brig. Gen. Joseph Smith, the headquarters commandant for USAFE, to be temporary commander of the airlift operation with orders to integrate the airlift activities at Wiesbaden, Rhein-Main, and Tempelhof to achieve the maximum number of missions to Berlin. Smith had begun his military service in the cavalry and then transferred to the Army Air Corps in 1928. He flew the airmail in 1934 when the air corps had that responsibility temporarily and later found his niche in bombardment. During World War II, he served in a variety of important posts, including senior air member of the Joint War Plans Committee for the Joint Chiefs of Staff. Smith ended the war as chief of staff of Twentieth Bomber Command flying B-29 Superfortresses out of India and China. After the war, the general served as chief of staff for Air University and commander of the Air Tactical School before going to Europe. Smith had little experience with airlift operations, however, and was reluctant to take on what appeared to be an ill-defined, open-ended task. LeMay assured him that it was only a two-week job. Smith accepted and established his headquarters at Camp Lindsey, Wiesbaden, with two main sections, "Operations" under Col. Carl R. Feldman and "Supply and Maintenance" under Lt. Col. William H. Clark; "Public Information" and "Statistical Control" rounded out the small, ad hoc organization. As the airlift expanded over the next few weeks, this headquarters grew dramatically. Smith's "two-week" tenure lasted from June 29 through July 28, during which he and his staff made several fundamental decisions that shaped the Berlin Airlift.[48]

Most histories credit Smith with giving the American portion of the airlift its codename. The traditional story has it that when several USAFE officers proposed fancy names to glamorize the operation, Smith responded bluntly: "Hell's fire, we're hauling grub. Call it Operation Vittles."[49] It is possible that the source of the codename may be more prosaic, however. When General LeMay requested C-54s in Germany, he caused a flurry of activity at U.S. Air Force headquarters in the Pentagon. On Sunday, June 27, the Operations Division alerted the four C-54 squadrons by telephone to prepare for an immediate move. In the meantime, operations personnel prepared a written directive to be issued as soon as the movement received approval from the Secretary of Defense. The directive required a codename so that agencies like supply, personnel, transportation, finance, and others could identify their activities with the operation and its priority. A codename was normally selected from the official codebook, but on that Sunday the book was unavailable. Brig. Gen. Oliver S. Picher, the director of operations, asked Col. William R. Large, Jr., of the Operations Division for suggestions. Large responded that since the airlift would deliver clothes and food, why not call it Operation Vittles? Large further recommended that the word be spelled "vittles," instead of "victuals," because the term would be unfamiliar to the Russians.[50]

The first C-54 from the United States arrived at Rhein-Main on the morning of July 1 and was cleared for Tempelhof just over ten hours later.

Figure 9. Brig. Gen. Joseph Smith was a distinguished pilot and veteran commander who established many of the basic procedures followed by the Berlin Airlift. Courtesy U.S. Air Force

By July 2, seventeen Skymasters had reached Rhein-Main. Of these, three had already flown missions into Berlin, two were in poor condition, and twelve were undergoing routine maintenance and would be ready the next day. Nine more planes were en route while one was on the ground at Bordeaux, France. Smith and his staff quickly established a plan for the subsequent waves of C-54s arriving from the United States. The first twenty-five went directly to Rhein-Main, where they were fed into the C-54 squadrons at that base; an additional thirty were absorbed into the 60th Troop Carrier Group at Wiesbaden, replacing its C-47s. As more C-54s arrived, the C-47s were returned to their home bases but their crews stayed behind. For support, C-54 engine "buildup" remained at Rhein-Main, and

C-54 parts and supplies were centralized at the same location. Three days later, on July 12, Smith and his staff followed this plan to its logical end and made Rhein-Main an exclusive base for C-54s. The remaining squadron of C-47s was transferred to another mission on Cyprus, and the last ten Skytrains were moved to Wiesbaden shortly thereafter. Smith also decided to centralize all C-54 support at Rhein-Main.[51]

Smith and his staff established a "block system" to control the two types of aircraft—which had significantly different cruising speeds and flight characteristics—operating from two different bases. For the first three weeks of the airlift, flights into Tempelhof were organized into three eight-hour shifts, or "blocks," each day. Each block was further divided into a C-54 section and a C-47 section. Under this arrangement, as many C-54s as could be prepared were loaded and at alert stations by take-off time. The first took off precisely at the block start time followed by other C-54s at four-minute intervals. Four minutes after the last C-54 took off, the first plane in the C-47 section became airborne followed, in turn, by the other available C-47s. During the last week of July, Smith's headquarters quickened the pace of the airlift by shortening the blocks to six hours each at shifts of four per day. Further, the C-54s received priority over the C-47s to take advantage of their larger cargo capacity. The C-54 blocks from Rhein-Main took off first followed by the C-47s from Rhein-Main. The C-47s at Wiesbaden acted as fillers, taking off after the C-54s had cleared Rhein-Main and ceasing operation when the C-47s at Rhein-Main were scheduled to fly. Once in the air, the controllers assigned the aircraft to altitudes from 5,000 to 10,000 feet at 1,000-foot intervals. To ensure further separation, each C-54 climbed at a fixed 155 m.p.h., then increased to a cruising speed of 175 m.p.h. when it reached its proper altitude. The C-47s climbed at 130 m.p.h. and cruised at 150 m.p.h. in the corridors. General Smith and his staff also established the radio codes for airlift aircraft as follows: "Easy" for eastbound C-47s, "Willy" for westbound C-47s, and "Big Easy" and "Big Willy" for the C-54s. These designations were followed by numbers, beginning with "1," assigned in order of takeoff followed by the last three digits of the aircraft's serial number.[52] "Big Easy," the code for eastbound C-54s heavily laden with cargo for Berlin, became perhaps the most recognized words on the radio during the Berlin Airlift.

Beyond these measures, Smith instituted the minimum "in commission" rate for airplanes at 65 percent of unit strength and directed that each aircraft in commission would make three round trips each day. On

July 21, General Smith requested that improvements be made to the navigation beacon at Tempelhof, and he coaxed American Forces Network to broadcast all night, providing a positive fix for radio compass. Efficiency measures also extended to cargo management. On July 26, Smith and his staff had made final arrangements for all military and industrial supplies to be shipped through Wiesbaden and for Rhein-Main to handle cargo destined for the civilian population.[53]

The arrival of the huge Skymasters quickly caused problems. Simply, no field in Germany was designed for an aircraft of its size operating in large numbers. No sooner had the C-54s begun to land in Berlin than Tempelhof reported that its runway had begun to break down. Engineers estimated that it would not last more than sixty days under the continued pounding. Smith requested authorization to begin construction of a second runway at Tempelhof on July 9, and ten days later his headquarters had completed plans for transporting construction materials to that facility. Planners allotted 50 tons daily on the airlift for construction materials, and by July 31 the airlift had delivered 274.6 tons of materials for runway construction.[54]

Other problems, including the limited runway and ramp space at the two bases in the American zone and the longer distance of the southern than the northern corridor, suggested another measure. On July 23, in a farsighted move that will be discussed in detail later, Smith approached Royal Air Force Group Captain K. B. B. Cross about the possibility of basing C-54s at one of the RAF airfields in the British occupation zone. Cross recommended either Fassberg, Wunstorf, or Gutersloh.[55]

By the latter half of July, the airlift showed considerable improvement in organization and efficiency. The headquarters at Camp Lindsey had expanded and now commanded four main units. The 60th Troop Carrier Group at Wiesbaden and the 61st Troop Carrier Group at Rhein-Main were in the process of replacing their C-47s with C-54s. At Rhein-Main, the Provisional Troop Carrier Group of C-54s consisted of four squadrons organized by their geographic origin: the 48th Troop Carrier Squadron was the "Texas Squadron," the 54th the "Alaska Squadron," the 20th the "Caribbean Squadron," and the 19th the "Hawaiian Squadron." In addition, an element of officers and enlisted men at Tempelhof handled operations at that end of the airlift.[56]

With the arrival of the Skymasters, the average daily delivery rate began to climb, tripling the just over 500 tons per day achieved by the end of

June. On July 31, Operation Vittles delivered 1,719.5 tons of cargo; additionally, the British airlift delivered 1,437 tons on the same day for a combined total of 3,156.5 tons, a huge amount but still well under the 4,500 tons per day required by Berlin. The figures for July 31 also demonstrate the relative efficiency of the C-54 over the C-47: 122 C-54 sorties had delivered 1,072 tons, while 200 C-47 sorties had delivered just 647.1 tons. Despite the fact that the daily tonnage requirement for Berlin had yet to be met, great effort had yielded significant results. From June 26 through July 31, the combined cumulative total for the airlift was 69,005.7 tons of cargo: 39,971 tons delivered by U.S. aircraft and 29,034.7 by British airplanes.[57]

Operation Plainfare

While the American effort developed, the British buildup proceeded at an accelerating pace as well, first under Air Marshal Sir Arthur P. M. Sanders, then after November, 1948, under Air Marshal T. M. Williams. Like the U.S. Air Force, the Royal Air Force of 1948 was a shadow of the service that had defended the British Isles and brought terrible destruction to Germany during World War II. The decommissioning of aircraft and demobilizing of personnel after the war had proceeded with reasonable smoothness. The drastic reductions and prolonged vacillation in London over the postwar shape of the force, however, had a depressing effect on morale and cost the service hundreds of experienced airmen who otherwise might have remained on active duty. Further, while the RAF had begun the transition to jet fighter aircraft, its other elements continued to depend upon older planes. In particular, Transport Command, the RAF's equivalent of MATS, had been reduced to three air groups—Nos. 38, 46, and 47—equipped with rapidly aging cargo aircraft. RAF participation in the Berlin Airlift was further complicated by overseas commitments in the Middle East, India, and especially Malaya, where Transport Command had four squadrons supporting "Operation Firedog," the suppression of a communist insurrection that began in 1948.[58]

The British airlift, codenamed "Operation Plainfare," enjoyed several significant advantages. First, the weather tended to be milder in the British zone with less fog than the Americans would face in the Frankfurt area. Second, the route between the British zone and Berlin was relatively flat while the Americans had to fly over the Taunus Mountains; aircraft

Figure 10. Air Marshal T. M. Williams, air officer commanding, British Air Forces of Occupation, in November, 1948. Courtesy Crown copyright, 1998/Ministry of Defence

flying the northern corridor could thus operate at much lower altitudes. Third, and perhaps most significant, aircraft operating from British bases had a shorter distance to fly. The southern corridor was 50 percent longer than the northern corridor, and aircraft flying in the latter thus could make more round trips to Berlin each day. As will be discussed later, airlift leaders would soon take advantage of these conditions by basing larger, more efficient C-54s at two bases in the British zone, and long-range plans—should the airlift have to continue indefinitely—called for removing all British aircraft from the airlift and basing Skymasters at the British airfields.

Against these advantages, the British faced two major problems that would eventually determine the shape of Operation Plainfare and dictate the contribution it would make to the airlift. The first problem was that the British flew from several widely dispersed bases, complicating aircraft routing and air traffic control. Second, in contrast to the U.S. Air Force, the Royal Air Force flew several types of less efficient aircraft and was unable to standardize operations around one airplane like the C-54 Skymaster. The RAF's shortage of transport aircraft also forced it to draw heavily on small civilian firms flying a hodgepodge of mostly surplus military aircraft. Coordinating and controlling a variety of different aircraft, each with its own unique performance characteristics, posed a serious challenge to British air operations and ultimately meant that the northern part of the airlift would never be as productive in landing large numbers of aircraft daily as the southern operation. On the other hand, the variety of aircraft made available several distinct—in some cases unique—cargo carrying capabilities. Airlift leaders gradually took advantage of these capabilities by shifting much of the responsibility for cargos requiring special handling (like liquid fuel and salt) to the British operation, while the Americans concentrated more on bulk cargos, especially coal. Operation Plainfare, while it did deliver substantial tonnage to Berlin, thus landed a much smaller amount of cargo than Operation Vittles. However, by assuming primary responsibility for several vital cargos, Operation Plainfare made an absolutely essential contribution to the people of Berlin.

The British were about as prepared for the crisis in Berlin as were the Americans. In May, 1948, following the mini-blockade of the previous month, Headquarters No. 46 Group directed a squadron of Douglas C-47 Dakotas based in England to stand by to support the garrison in Berlin in case of another emergency. By June 19, working with the British Army of the Rhine, No. 46 Group had expanded the number of "on call" squadrons to two and had prepared a plan under the title "Operation Knicker" that called for twenty-four Dakotas to deliver roughly sixty-five tons of cargo daily to the British garrison in Berlin for up to one month. The British C-47s formed the backbone of British air transport in the late 1940s, and like their U.S. Air Force counterparts, these planes had seen extensive operational service in every theater of World War II. Worn veterans though they were, the Dakotas were reliable and tough, and by removing excess equipment the British would increase their average cargo load to over three tons.[59]

When the Berlin crisis erupted, Foreign Minister Ernest Bevin abandoned his vacation and rushed back to London for a June 25 meeting with the cabinet. Gen. Sir Neville Brownjohn, Robertson's deputy, provided a briefing that stressed the inadvisability of using troops to force the blockade and also indicated that, while an airlift would be a useful interim measure, it would be impossible to supply all of Berlin by air for any length of time. Bevin disagreed. He demanded that all available cargo aircraft be placed at the disposal of the forces in Germany, called for immediate consultation with the French and Americans, and proposed assignment of a small number of ministers to review and manage the situation as it developed.[60]

The first RAF reinforcements reached Germany before the foreign minister spoke. On the evening of June 24, 1948, in accordance with Operation Knicker, eight C-47s under the command of Wing Commander G. H. Ganteral departed the RAF airfield at Waterbeach in England for the RAF station at Wunstorf. Each transport carried its own ground crew, and all of the crews took enough personal equipment for ten days' temporary duty. This squadron was followed by a second squadron of Dakotas on June 28, the same day that the British cabinet gave formal approval to the operation, which officially began that same day. The British Army, in the meantime, assembled some two hundred tons of supplies, mostly flour and meat, at Wunstorf. During the first twenty-four hours of the British operation, thirteen Dakotas delivered forty-four tons of cargo to Berlin; between June 28 and 30, the British delivered seventy-five tons of cargo. It was clear, however, that something more than two squadrons would be required. Air Commodore John W. F. Merer, air officer commanding, No. 46 Group, ordered additional squadrons from No. 38 and No. 47 Groups to Germany under the code name "Carter Paterson," the same name as a noted British moving firm. Transportation Command issued operational orders for an expanded airlift on June 30, and an additional thirty-eight airplanes reached Wunstorf on the same day. Somewhat confusingly, in the midst of this activity the Dakotas of No. 30 Squadron, which had been based temporarily at Schleswigland on the Baltic coast in May, 1948, returned to England on June 25 only to have to fly back to Germany. By the beginning of July, Wunstorf, a small field to begin with, had been saturated by the Dakotas of Nos. 30, 46, 53, 77, and 238 Squadrons, plus a portion of No. 240 Operational Conversion Unit. Despite best efforts, though, poor weather, shortages of ground equipment, and maintenance problems prevented Wunstorf from reaching the planned 160 sorties per day expected during the first phase of the operation from June 30 to July 3. In the meantime, RAF leaders took note of a biting Soviet remark that the moving firm of Carter Paterson specialized in "removals." On July 19, the RAF replaced "Carter Paterson" with an intentional and utterly appropriate pun: the British airlift became "Operation Plainfare."[61]

Command problems probably contributed to the early difficulties as well. On June 29, Transport Command's No. 46 Group sent Group Captain Noel Hyde to Wunstorf to take charge of the operation. At the same time, the

British Air Forces of Occupation dispatched Group Captain Wally Biggar to the same base with the same instructions. It took a few days to sort out the situation, and on July 3 new instructions recognized that BAFO Advanced Headquarters had been formed at Wunstorf and would command all air transport resources allocated to BAFO. This decision solved the immediate command situation, though it caused some bad feelings among senior officers. BAFO, like USAFE, was a tactical command with limited experience in the complexities of air transport operations. Group Captain (later Air Chief Marshal Sir) Kenneth Cross recalled that "we were decent, Tactical Air Force chaps with fighter-bombers and we did not go into these transport operations with any enthusiasm." Logically, Transport Command's No. 46 Group had the necessary experience, and although it would ultimately take command of Operation Plainfare, it would have been better had that assignment been made at the beginning of the airlift. The arrival of Headquarters No. 46 Group at Bückeburg under Air Commodore John W. F. Merer on September 22 placed transport experts in charge. No. 46 Group was responsible to the BAFO for operational control of transport activities during Plainfare and to the commanders of Transport and Coastal Command for operational control over all aircraft and personnel furnished by their commands.[62]

Again, in a pattern that mirrored that of the American airlift effort, it was immediately apparent to the British command that Dakotas would be unable to carry the responsibility imposed by the expanded airlift. On July 12, the first twelve four-engine Avro 685 Yorks reached Wunstorf. The York was the transport version of the RAF's superb Lancaster bomber. Powered by the even more superb Rolls Royce Merlin engine, the York had a maximum speed of 310 m.p.h. and an airlift speed of 185 m.p.h. The shoulder-wing configuration of the York made it relatively easy to load and unload, and during the airlift the RAF altered the aircraft, enabling it to carry an average load of a little over eight tons. Eight squadrons of Yorks ultimately served in the Berlin Airlift. The orders that committed most of Transport Command's aircraft forced the RAF into three significant decisions. First, the Berlin Airlift received priority over all other operations. Second, the RAF halted all crew training, something that never occurred before even in wartime. Third, Transport Command ceased all scheduled air operations worldwide.[63]

By mid-July, the large number of Dakotas and Yorks had overtaxed Wunstorf's facilities, and the RAF transferred all Dakotas to Fassberg, a

Figure 11. Avro Yorks in front of the unloading hangars at Gatow in Berlin, September, 1948. Courtesy U.S. Air Force

former RAF fighter base in caretaker status at the beginning of the airlift. Subsequently, the decision to base U.S. Air Force C-54s at Fassberg forced the Dakota squadrons to move once again, and they transferred to the base at Lübeck beginning on August 20. The final major addition to the airlift was the arrival at Schleswigland in early November of No. 46 Squadron equipped with Handley-Page Hastings. A four-engine aircraft expected to replace the York in RAF service, the Hastings featured an eight-ton payload and a cruising speed of over 300 m.p.h. Ultimately, two squadrons of Hastings joined the airlift from England while two other squadrons, one of Dakotas and one of Yorks, converted to Hastings by the end of the operation.[64]

Despite a relatively good maintenance record, the C-47 Dakotas were smaller and gave way to other aircraft if block time was lost or the airlift flow was interrupted. The much larger Avro Yorks and Handley-Page Hastings suffered from maintenance problems. The former lacked the robustness necessary to withstand the extreme stress caused by frequent takeoffs and landings under full loads, while the latter had "teething problems" following its introduction in November, 1948.[65]

Another RAF aircraft deserves honorable mention for its role in the airlift. The availability of Lake Havel next to Gatow in Berlin suggested the use of seaplanes, and that large body of calm unobstructed water thus served as the delivery base for Short Sunderland flying boats operated by RAF Coastal Command. Each plane could carry five tons of cargo, and on July 5, Sunderlands from Nos. 201 and 230 Squadrons began delivering food to Berlin from their temporary base at Finkenwerder on the Elbe River outside Hamburg. While Lake Havel was ideal, operations at Finkenwerder were a severe trial. The Elbe was choppy and full of wrecks, and the base lacked the necessary fueling system for flying boats. In the words of one of the crewmen, "the moorings themselves were in a basin attached to the factory and would have been excellent had there not been so much rubble from the Hamburg firestorm in the water; scrap metal, sunken submarines and the like littering the area."[66] Until a system could be improvised, fueling had to be done by hand from forty-gallon drums. The ponderous flying boats were also slow and difficult to schedule through the corridors. The Sunderlands operated under increasingly difficult conditions until December, when Lake Havel froze and the planes were withdrawn from Plainfare.[67]

The greatest problem for the RAF came in a shortage of both flight and ground personnel, which severely effected utilization rates. The British called up reservists, delayed demobilizing those men already in service, and terminated training programs, thus making additional personnel available. Operation Plainfare, however, still fought a continual battle with Transport Command in England for experienced aircrews, mechanics, and technicians. By September, when it was obvious that the airlift would have to last well into the future, the RAF reinstated the training programs cancelled earlier and returned twenty Dakotas and ten Yorks to the United Kingdom for that purpose. RAF leaders also called on the Dominions for assistance; ten Australian Dakota crews reached Lübeck in September, ten South African crews arrived in October, and three crews from New Zealand reached Germany in November. Skilled maintenance personnel were also overworked and in short supply, and their morale was difficult to keep up. Reopening the training programs helped, and finally in the spring of 1949, Transport Command established standard overseas tours for all maintenance staff.[68]

Maintenance also proved to be a serious problem for the RAF. Its aircraft underwent major inspections every one hundred hours conducted at bases in Great Britain, which necessitated constant ferry flights to and from Germany. Many of the problems discovered during these inspections were the same as those faced by the Americans. The tremendous number of take-offs and landings strained engines and airframes; tires, brakes, and undercarriages also took a terrible beating.[69]

Elements of the Royal Army Service Corps handled the receipt, storage, and loading of all cargo handling at the dispatching bases. Designated the Rear Airfield Supply Organization, these units employed large numbers of German laborers. Similarly, the Forward Airfield Supply Organization accomplished all cargo handling in Berlin.[70]

There was no railroad between Gatow and Berlin, so transporting supplies from the airport to the city posed another challenge for the British. However, Lake Havel offered a satisfactory solution to getting heavy cargo to Berlin since about forty big barges capable of carrying some fifteen thousand tons of freight had been trapped on the lake by the blockade. This was a much more economical way to move cargo than over roads: Three thousand tons of cargo moved by vehicle would cost some fifteen tons of gasoline or five tons of diesel oil, but a single tug could tow the same load on barges and burn only one ton of coal. Liquid fuel was also moved by barge, delivered from Gatow to Lake Havel though sections of oil pipe. These were taken from PLUTO, the oil pipeline that had been laid across the English Channel to supply oil to the Allied armies in France after D-Day.[71]

One area in which the British airlift effort differed significantly from the Americans was the use of civilian aircraft under contract. Following World War II, the British government lifted its wartime ban on private aviation, and companies established and manned by veterans and equipped with surplus military aircraft of marginal commercial utility proliferated. A postwar boom had subsided by 1948, however, and many of these operations were on the verge of bankruptcy. When the Royal Air Force turned to civilian firms to carry a portion of the airlift load many companies responded; indeed, several had already made proposals to participate in the airlift shortly after it began. Members of the Air Ministry, Ministry of Civil Aviation, RAF, and BAFO initially opposed using civilian aircraft. However, the need to expand cargo delivery beyond Transport Command's capacity led to a reversal in attitude. The subject was discussed during a meeting in the Air Ministry on July 19, and the superintendent of British European

Airways Corporation (BEA) was asked to obtain proposals from charter companies. During a subsequent meeting on July 28, the participants agreed that BEA would act as the British agent for the civilian operation and its commercial manager in Germany, Edwin P. Whitfield, would be in general charge.[72]

Several of the private firms, it should be noted, had specialized aircraft that could meet some of the unique requirements of the airlift. Flight Refueling, Ltd., a company established before World War II with extensive experience delivering aviation fuel, offered its services shortly after the airlift began. The company owned several Avro Lancastrian tankers, a transport version of an interim commercial airliner modified to carry liquid fuel. A Lancastrian made its first flight into Berlin on July 27, flying all the way from Tarrant Rushton in Dorset. Subsequently, on August 4, the first contract aircraft arrived in Germany. These included nine Dakotas, two Hythe flying boats (converted Short Sunderlands), one cargo version of the Consolidated B-24 Liberator, and a Handley-Page Halton.[73]

The Halton was a passenger-carrying conversion of the Halifax bomber developed for use by British Overseas Airways Corporation. British charter operators used several to carry freight, including liquid fuel with which its six- to eight-ton payload was invaluable. Further, a detachable pannier slung under the fuselage allowed the Halton to carry salt without incurring internal damage to the aircraft. Other aircraft flown by civilian firms included the four-engine Avro Tudor, which had been unsuccessful as an airliner but proved a workhorse on the airlift despite ground-handling problems. The Bristol 170 Freighter, a transport with a four-ton payload designed to be loaded through the nose, proved useful for awkward and bulky cargo. Avro Lancasters, Avro Lincolns, and Consolidated Liberators also operated as tankers.[74]

Use of civilian contract aircraft posed serious problems. The companies and their aircraft varied greatly in resources, procedures, efficiency, and operating standards. Created largely for charter work over long distances, the civilian firms were poorly prepared and ill equipped for high-intensity, sustained operations. The company managers tended to do things their own way, and the fact that they operated almost exclusively during daylight played havoc with RAF crew and maintenance schedules. Problems with supplies, parts, maintenance, and integration into the RAF operations provided continued challenges. Operating on a shoestring, the civilian companies arrived without servicing capability of any sort and

Figure 12. A civilian Avro Lancastrian, owned by Flight Refueling, Ltd., discharges liquid fuel at Gatow in Berlin. Courtesy Crown copyright, 1998/Ministry of Defence

had to borrow even the most basic equipment from the RAF. They had few parts or spares for their rickety, run-down aircraft and lacked the capital to buy these materials. None of the companies had enough mechanics, and since each was in competition with the other, the idea of pooling tools, parts, and personnel was beyond consideration. Other problems revolved around pilots and pay. The pilots ranged the gamut from veterans respected by the RAF aircrews to those who did the minimum of work and were regarded as overpaid mercenaries. Worse, the contracts, which paid by the flying hour, rewarded sharp practice: if they carried short loads, civilian pilots reduced operating costs and cut their time on the ground at each end of the route, giving them more time in the air. Despite such problems, the RAF successfully folded the civilian operations into the airlift, and they made a significant contribution to its success. Nevertheless, the problems faced by the British provide evidence that justifies the U.S. Air Force's refusal to hire civilian operators for Operation Vittles.[75]

Perhaps the most important contribution by the civilian operators was the delivery of liquid fuels, especially gasoline. By the end of 1948, the liquid-fuel stocks in Berlin had been drawn down and the city became dependent upon fuel delivered by the airlift. Plans called for a fleet of thirty-one tankers to deliver 220 tons per day by January 1, 1949, but on that date the British had only eleven tankers delivering about 148 tons per day. By the end of the month, however, some twenty-seven tankers—thirteen Haltons, nine Lancastrians, and five Tudors—were in operation. Two Liberator tankers joined the airlift in mid-February. These, however, overtaxed the facilities at Wunstorf and Schleswigland. While Schleswigland and Gatow in Berlin had fixed underground systems, Wunstorf lacked such facilities until late in the airlift. As a result, fuel was pumped from "cistern wagons" positioned on the rail spur servicing Wunstorf into fuel trucks, or "bowsers," in the proper amount for each type of aircraft. This was an adequate process, but was complicated by numerous equipment breakdowns. The Shell Oil Company controlled the offloading of fuel at Gatow, while the Standard Oil Company did the same at Tegel.[76]

All told, forty-one Haltons/Halifaxs, eighteen Dakotas, seventeen Lancastrians, nine Tudors, four Bristol Freighters, three Hythes, three Liberators, three Yorks, two Vickers Vikings, two Bristol Wayfarers, and one Lincoln comprised the civilian fleet that flew cargo to Berlin, a total of 103 aircraft operated by twenty-five different civilian companies. Ultimately, the civilian fleet flew 21,921 sorties to Berlin and delivered 146,980 tons of cargo. The Berlin Airlift was both the greatest opportunity and the greatest success for these companies. Created and mostly run on a shoestring by veteran World War II fliers, most had gone bankrupt by 1950.[77]

By the end of 1948, Plainfare had settled into a pattern of operations. RAF Hastings carrying coal and civilian Haltons and Liberators delivering liquid fuel operated from Schleswigland. Lübeck-based Dakotas handled food and some coal. Civilian Haltons and Bristol Freighters from Fuhlsbüttel delivered food, salt, and a variety of bulky freight. From Wunstorf, RAF and civilian Yorks carried food, coal, and supplies for the British occupation forces and civilian Lancastrian and Tudor tankers ferried liquid fuel. Finally, American Skymasters based at Fassberg carried coal while those at Celle carried both coal and food.[78]

The difference in air speed and flight characteristics between the types of aircraft prevented the development of the steady, sustained stream of aircraft that ultimately characterized the airlift in the southern corridor. And as already mentioned, the numerous, widely dispersed bases seriously challenged the air traffic control system. When Operation Plainfare began with only Dakotas flying from one base in the British zone to one airport in Berlin, the timing was simple and the C-47s were merely spaced a minimum of six minutes apart. The advent of the bigger, faster Yorks posed a potential conflict. The solution was a block system by aircraft type with sufficient intervals between blocks so that the first York in a block would not overtake the last Dakota in the previous block. This system, however, placed an uneven burden on the ground crews. Planners later developed a more complex system that fed the two types of aircraft into the corridor on a timed schedule, enabling them to land at four-minute intervals at Gatow. Additionally, when bad weather intervened, the bigger Yorks received priority over the Dakotas, to the chagrin of the latter's aircrews. As the Skymasters and Hastings joined the airlift, the block system continued to provide the primary means for organizing the various aircraft. The result was blocks of from twelve to twenty aircraft with similar performance flying at separate, fixed altitudes for additional safety. Within the blocks the intervals varied from seven-and-a-half miles for the slowest aircraft to nine miles for the fastest, and the blocks and intervals were timed to ensure three-minute to five-minute separation for arrivals at Gatow and Tegel. Blocks flying at different altitudes did not maintain fixed intervals, and a faster block at one altitude could overtake and pass a slower block flying at another.[79]

The pattern of operations flown to Berlin from the British zone of occupation also differed somewhat from the pattern in the American zone. All aircraft in the latter flew into Berlin through the southern corridor and out through the central corridor. All aircraft in the former flew into Berlin through the northern corridor, but while most aircraft returned through the central corridor, others, especially those based in the north at Schleswigland and Lübeck, returned through the northern corridor. Aircraft on their way to Berlin flew down one side of the twenty-mile wide corridor, while those flying out utilized the other side of the corridor.[80]

Navigation through the northern and central corridors depended on a system of medium-frequency radio beacons and "Eureka" radar beams. Medium-frequency beacons provided a continuous signal received by the radio compass in each aircraft. Eureka beacons, in contrast, responded to impulses from the "Rebecca set" aboard each aircraft and displayed the bearing and distance from the beacon on the aircraft's radar screen. RAF aircraft thus carried navigators and often radio personnel, or "signalers," while American pilots operating in the southern corridor relied on radio aids. The key beacon for regulating operations was the medium-frequency Frohnau beacon located outside of Berlin at the end of the northern corridor. Each base feeding aircraft into the corridor received block times, and it was the base's responsibility to ensure that its aircraft were over the Frohnau beacon at the scheduled time and that all had passed Frohnau when the block time was over. When a base received its Frohnau beacon times, its controllers calculated when the first and last aircraft had to take off to maintain the schedule. These were the base's block times, which were based on factors including the runway used, standard rates of climb and cruising speeds, and standard headings. Within the blocks, pilots announced their arrival times over the Frohnau beacon, enabling the other aircraft to adjust their intervals.[81] The Frohnau beacon was, thus, all important. An American air controller, Bill Morrissey, recalled the greetings of a Royal Air Force group captain when American Skymasters began operating from the base at Celle: "Righto, Yanks! Welcome to our zone. We know we can count on you to enhance our efforts. One thing though—our British pilots compute their own times and they are quite punctual, so keep your interval—and make sure you make good your Frohnau beacon times—for if you don't you'll get one of our kites up your rear! Good luck, chaps."[82]

British pilots relied on Beam Approach Beacon Systems (BABS) for final approaches to their bases. Under this system, a single transmitter sent two beams, a stream of short pulses and one of long pulses, to the navigator's screen in the aircraft. The navigator had an accurate position when the airplane was oriented so that both pulses were the same size. BABS equipment was already based at Gatow and Wunstorf when Plainfare began, and the RAF installed additional units as other air bases were activated, including a mobile BABS system at Tegel. The Royal Air Force and the U.S. Air Force both relied on Ground Controlled Approach (GCA) radar for landing. Through GCA, operators on the ground guided each aircraft to the runway, enabling them to perform blind landings. The fact that they shared this technology facilitated the establishment of American aircraft in the British zone and their integration into the northern corridors.[83]

Additional Airlift: French and Commercial

The French also flew cargo during the Berlin Airlift. Following World War II, the *Armée de l'Air* committed most of its limited air transport capability to operations in Indochina, but it did play a small role in the airlift using a modest number of mismatched aircraft, including three Douglas C-47 Dakotas of *Groupe de Transport 1/61 "Touraine,"* one Avro York of the *Aéronavale* (French Navy), a Douglas C-54 Skymaster from *Groupe de Liaisons Aériennes Ministérielles,* and a Handley-Page Halifax from the *21e Escadre de Bombardement* that flew the route for evaluation purposes. Most surprising was the contribution of three German-designed, French-built Junkers Ju-52s from *Groupe de Transport 1/61 "Maine."* Known as "Toucans" in the French service, the Ju-52 was a three-engine, low-wing, corrugated-skin commercial aircraft from the 1930s that had served as a bomber during the Spanish Civil War and subsequently became the standard German military air transport during World War II. Second only to the C-47, the "Iron Annie" was probably the most common transport aircraft of the period. A French company, *Ateliers Aéronautiques de Colombes,* built four hundred Ju-52s under contract during the war, and Toucans remained in French service well into the 1950s. Ju-52s were a startling sight to pilots, especially Americans, who chanced upon them flying low and slow in the air corridors.[84]

The *Armée de l'Air*'s effort was a valiant, though modest, contribution. French airmen flew 424 missions, delivering 881 tons of supplies to the French garrison in Berlin and carrying 10,367 passengers, mostly French military personnel and civilians evacuated from Berlin. Early operations used airfields at Wunstorf, Bückeburg, and Baden-Baden in the occupation zones and Tempelhof and Gatow in Berlin; later operations took place primarily between Wunstorf and Tegel. Ultimately, however, the French could contribute little. French historians Charles Christienne and Pierre Lissarrague later wrote, "It must be admitted that the French participation proved rather troublesome for the [airlift] organizers." Especially, the Ju-52s simply did not fit the airlift system. First, their cargo capacity of one-and-a-half tons was too small to be efficient. Second, the Ju-52's cruising speed made it next to impossible to fit smoothly into the flow of aircraft in the southern corridor. Third, the French lacked adequate communications equipment; combined with the language difficulty caused by the use of English as the standard language on the airlift, this posed a serious safety hazard. Ultimately, it proved easier and more efficient to deliver supplies for the French garrison in American aircraft. The Toucans were removed from the air corridors by the end of September, 1948.[85]

At the beginning of the airlift, USAFE turned to American civilian air-

Figure 13. A three-engine, French-built Junkers Ju-52 Toucan of the type flown by the French Air Force during the Berlin Airlift. Courtesy COLLECTION S.H.A.A.

lines to supplement its meager resources, although these never attained the status that British commercial carriers earned. American Overseas Airlines (AOA), the international division of American Airlines, was the most active participant. AOA began operations between the United States and northern Europe following World War II and by 1948 flew scheduled air routes serving Great Britain, Scandinavia, and Germany. On March 2, 1948, AOA began service between Frankfurt and Berlin flying the civilian version of the C-54, the DC-4. On the first day of the airlift, AOA began flying cargo to Berlin using its DC-4s and a single London-based DC-3 (the civilian equivalent of the C-47).[86]

The majority of commercial aircraft, however, flew nonscheduled routes between the United States and Europe carrying engines, equipment, parts, and other items required to keep the airlift operating. The most prominent of the nonscheduled carriers was Seaboard & Western Airlines, which had begun operations to Europe in May, 1947. Other active carriers included Transocean Air Lines (whose slogan was "we fly anything, anywhere"), Transcontinental & Western Air (later Trans World Airlines), Pan American Airways, and Alaska Airlines (which included in its "cargo" eleven loads of war brides flown to the United States). Pan American achieved distinction when one pilot took the spirit of help a step further than either military or civilian authorities approved: he flew a load of cargo into Berlin despite the fact that Pan American lacked official permission to enter the corridors.[87]

One of the main cargos delivered by private air carriers were Cooperative for American Remittances to Europe (CARE) packages. Begun as an organization that enabled Americans to help relatives and friends in wartorn Europe, CARE had grown into a major general relief organization by 1948. CARE had developed a standard food package that weighed just over twenty-two pounds and included canned meats, bacon, lard, preserves, dried eggs, powdered milk, coffee, rice, flour, and chocolate—furnishing 42,649 calories—and soap. Other packages provided clothes, baby food, blankets, and other necessities.[88]

One More Worry: The "Vienna Airlift"

At the same time that they struggled with the situation in Berlin, Western leaders kept a wary eye on Austria, where Vienna posed problems similar to Berlin and even fewer options should the Soviets choose to blockade the city. The treatment of Austria after World War II differed from that of Germany in significant ways. Importantly, Allied leaders classified Austria as a liberated country. This allowed the nation to retain its unity and establish a democratic government early. Austria was subject to less intense political infighting than in Germany, and the four powers continued to cooperate long after relations had turned confrontational elsewhere. The victorious Allies did divide Austria into four occupation zones, as in Germany, and the capital, Vienna, which like Berlin lay deep in the Soviet zone of occupation, was divided into sectors. The July, 1945, agreement on the occupation zones guaranteed access to Vienna by surface routes. In June, 1946, the four powers established two air corridors, one from Hörshing in the American zone one hundred miles from Vienna and the other from Klagenfurt in the British zone.[89]

The February, 1948, coup in neighboring Czechoslovakia, as already noted, came as a severe shock to European and American leaders. Subsequently, Soviet authorities in Austria became less accommodating, tightening controls over land and air transportation between the city and the West and ordering the removal of a radio station located on Soviet-controlled territory near the American airfield at Tulin-Langenlebam. To Western leaders, the pattern of Soviet activities in Austria as of late summer, 1948, appeared suspiciously similar to those that had preceded the blockade of Berlin in June. The Soviets had the capability of closing all land access with Vienna and completely isolating the Western garrisons in the cities.

Most significantly, the air option available in Germany was absent in Austria. Attempts by the Western allies to define Vienna according to the post-1938 boundaries established by the Nazis failed in the face of Soviet insistence on the much smaller pre-1938 boundaries. Had the larger boundaries held, four airfields would have been located within the city. The smaller boundaries, however, meant that only two airfields were available to Great Britain and the United States, Tulin-Langenlebam and Schwechat, which were located several kilometers outside the city and could be reached only through Soviet-controlled territory. The Western allies did build two small fields in their sectors, but these were only suitable for light aircraft. Further, a survey in July, 1948, concluded that the densely packed areas of the city prevented the creation of drop zones for parachute deliveries and landing strips for gliders while Soviet control of the Danube River eliminated the use of seaplanes. The only real option lay in stockpiling huge amounts of supplies and constructing an airfield in the city.

As early as June 24, U.S. Army authorities in Vienna had been warned that the Soviets might attempt to blockade the city, and by July 2 plans were in the works for airlift support to the garrison. Planners feared that a blockade would isolate the big airfields at Schwechat and Tulin, leaving only two small fields and one larger field in the British sector of Vienna available. Construction of two 5,000-foot pierced-steel-planking runways at the latter would allow C-54s to deliver some 4,560 tons daily.[90]

Construction of a 3,600-foot emergency runway out of a stretch of road near Dornbach in the American sector of Vienna was already part of the "Protective Security Plan" developed earlier by the commander of the U.S. forces in Austria, Lt. Gen. Geoffrey Keyes. Planners estimated that this strip could be built in less than a month using local resources and would handle twin-engine C-47s. The surrounding terrain, however, made instrument landings hazardous, thus severely limiting the site's value; even under the best conditions, the field could only meet the needs of the military garrison. EUCOM planners found a more suitable site located on flat farmland near Kaiser-Ebersdorf in the British sector where an airfield had once stood. The Kaiser-Ebersdorf location appeared capable of supporting a modern airfield with two 5,000-foot runways that could handle C-54s. Planners concluded that 110 Skymasters utilizing the two air corridors could deliver sufficient cargo daily to supply the city. General Keyes approved plans for construction at Kaiser-Ebersdorf and forwarded them to the Joint Chiefs of Staff in late July, 1948. At the same time, he requested 1.9 million square feet of pierced planking for runway construction. Other plans called for establishing an eighty-four-day stockpile of food and a six-month supply of coal in the city.

While the chief of staff, General Bradley, approved the delivery of enough planking for one runway on August 11, serious concerns about the proposal arose quickly. For one thing, the limited number of bases in Austria would mean that an airlift would have to depend on one base at each end of the corridor. For another, the supply line, which ran from Trieste to Austria, would have to be shifted to Bremerhaven, where it would conflict with the operations in Germany. EUCOM planners also had some doubts about conducting two airlifts at the same time, even given the USAF's global air transport capability. Other critics questioned the location selected for an airport in Vienna. A team of air experts surveyed the proposed site in mid-August and concluded that it was unsuitable for C-54s and that even C-47s would find approaches and takeoffs difficult. General Keyes disagreed, and ultimately he and General LeMay agreed that the site was satisfactory for a field in an emergency. Plans called for the American and British to pool their resources and construct one 5,000-foot runway. The British would then build a shorter runway for their Dakotas, which would operate from two fields, Zeltweg and Klagenfurt-Annabichl, in the British zone of occupation. General Keyes had stockpiled 1.5 million square feet of planking for the first runway by October 21, and the necessary navigation and communication equipment was on hand as well.

Stockpiling supplies in Vienna was a necessity. First, since it would take three months to build the airfield, the population of Vienna would have to live off the supplies available until the runway was complete. Further, American planners estimated that the daily requirement for all of Vienna was 4,230 tons. The maximum deliverable tonnage was only 3,600 tons, however, leaving a daily deficit of 630 tons. The situation was somewhat better if an airlift only supplied the population of the three western sectors. While these would require only 3,235 tons each day, the estimated daily average still provided too narrow a margin in the face of the European winter and other hazards. Under "Operation Squirrel Cage," the U.S. forces in Vienna salted away supplies in some twenty-eight warehouses spread across the Western sectors of the city. The U.S. Army rapidly built up a four-month supply of food and some stocks of coal in Vienna, collected enough pierced steel planking to construct one landing strip, established a two-month supply of petroleum oil lubricants at Trieste, and cached other supplies at depots in Austria.[91]

Even with these stockpiles, serious doubts remained. In April, 1949, the U.S. Army chief of staff directed the Joint Logistics Plans Committee to examine the possible courses of action in case of a blockade of Vienna. The committee concluded that airlift provided the only possible course of action, but that it could only deliver food. Other minimum requirements could not be met. The U.S. Air Force chief of staff, General Vandenberg, however, demurred. He stated that the committee had underestimated the difficulties an airlift to Vienna would face and overestimated airlift capabilities to meet those challenges. Further, as he had continually emphasized during discussions over the Berlin Airlift, Vandenberg stressed that the committee's report omitted "any mention of the crippling affect such an operation would have upon an Air Force in performing its primary missions, either in peacetime or in the event of emergency."[92]

Ultimately, of course, Soviet forces never blockaded Vienna and all of the preparations for an airlift proved unnecessary. Concern over possible Soviet action in Austria nagged at Western leaders during the early weeks of the Berlin Blockade, however. Austria was one more potential problem area that might have to be dealt with despite the limited means at hand.

To Stay or Go

On July 16, Cornelius V. Whitney, assistant secretary of the air force for matériel, presented a pessimistic view of the airlift's prospects to the National Security Council (NSC). The maximum cargo capacity of 180 C-54s and 105 C-47s, he calculated, was only about 3,000 tons per day. Combined with the British limit of about 1,000 tons, this totaled well below the 4,500-ton requirement set in Germany and the 5,300 tons that Whitney used for calculations. Worse, the ability to sustain even these levels was questionable. The runway at Tempelhof was breaking up, Whitney stated, and the aircraft were deteriorating because of lack of proper maintenance and facilities. He also voiced a major fear that concerned U.S. Air Force leaders in the Pentagon: supporting Berlin would require the air force's entire transport reserve, which could be easily destroyed in the event of war. Whitney concluded that "the Air Staff was firmly convinced that the air operation is doomed to failure." Others echoed his comments. Robert Lovett agreed that the airlift was an "unsatisfactory expedient," while Secretary Royall, expressing a prevailing opinion, maintained that it could not last through the winter. Secretary Royall wanted to continue the airlift, however, because it enabled the government to delay a decision on breaking the blockade with an armed convoy. The members of the NSC generally agreed that the airlift could not be continued after October and deferred a decision on sending additional aircraft.[93]

At the highest level, the commitment to remain in Berlin for the immediate future was firm. On July 19, President Truman met with Secretaries Forrestal and Marshall. Marshall pointed out that Soviet aspirations had been thwarted in Italy, Greece, and France; had been reversed in Finland; and had been severely shaken by Josef Broz "Tito" of Yugoslavia. Failure in Berlin, Marshall expounded, would jeopardize the current trend in halting communism. Truman agreed and reaffirmed his commitment to remaining in Berlin.[94] Yet again, there was little faith in the airlift as a means of sustaining the city for more than a few months. "The airlift by that time had begun to demonstrate its power," Forrestal wrote, "immediately the situation was a trifle easier; but the long-term possibilities were formidable."[95]

The National Security Council's collective backbone required stiffening, and a visitor from Germany provided the necessary remedy. On July 22, 1948, General Clay met the NSC with President Truman in attendance. Clay was adamant and in fine form. He urged that everything be done to ensure that the United States stay in Berlin. He lauded the commitment of Great Britain and France and extolled the steadfastness of the German people and Berlin's city magistrate. But, he told those assembled, USAFE needed additional air support or the airlift might let them down. The estimates Clay brought with him were somewhat more optimistic than those presented by Whitney a week earlier. USAFE was operating, he reported, fifty-two C-54s and eighty C-47s, which were averaging about 250 landings per day. An additional seventy-five C-54s would provide the capability to deliver 3,500 tons per day, which, with the British delivering 1,000 tons, would increase the capacity to 4,500 tons. Clay emphasized that the Soviets would not risk war. Intelligence verified the lack of troop movements and preparations for combat, and their threats to interfere with the corridors had proven to be propaganda. The Soviets might harass Clay's airplanes, the general reported, but he foresaw little probability of serious interference.[96] He concluded with a ringing description of the airlift's impact: "The air lift has increased our prestige immeasurably. It has been impressive and efficient and has thrown the Russian timetable off. Two months ago the Russians were cocky and arrogant. Lately they have been polite and have gone out of their way to avoid incidents."[97]

In response, Hoyt Vandenberg expressed deep reservations about what the airlift would do to the air force's worldwide responsibilities. He again pointed out that a complete commitment would disrupt MATS operations, threaten its supporting infrastructure, tie up aircraft intended for emergency use, and expose them to destruction if hostilities erupted. Vandenberg further stressed that a depot would have to be established in England with a subdepot in Germany manned with MATS maintenance personnel, and a full air force effort would require the construction of at least one more airfield in Berlin. Clay responded that a location in Berlin for the additional airfield had already been surveyed, and German manpower was available to carry out the construction using materials available locally. Delivery of paving equipment would take the equivalent of one day's cargo away from the airlift.[98]

The destruction of the U.S. Air Force's vital strategic airlift capability was of serious concern to Vandenberg. MATS aircraft were an integral part of the Strategic Air Command's mobility, and the loss of a significant number of C-54's threatened the U.S. Air Force's primary mission, nuclear deterrence. Further, if MATS aircraft went to Germany, aircrews, maintenance personnel, parts, and spares would have to be diverted to Europe and their potential loss in the event of war also posed a serious threat to the mission. Vandenberg's concerns were well taken. The chief of staff had to maintain a global view of the dangers the nation faced, to evaluate the hazards of committing his limited resources to a single operation, and to keep the air force's principal mission in mind at all times; during meetings with his colleagues, he voiced his positions effectively. Notwithstanding his well-founded concerns, however, Vandenberg also expressed faith in the air force's airlift capability—if it were committed completely and resolutely. "If we decide that this operation is going on for some time, the Air Force would prefer that we go in wholeheartedly," he told the NSC. "If we do, Berlin can be supplied."[99]

As a result of this discussion, the NSC agreed that construction of the new field in Berlin should begin immediately and approved Clay's recommendation for seventy-five additional C-54s, with a decision to be made on additional aircraft in the near future. Finally, the NSC "reiterated the determination to remain in Berlin in any event." It was this document that would be cited over the next few months as justification for increasing the number of aircraft assigned to the Berlin Airlift.[100]

However, doubts persisted. Only a few days later, on July 26, the Joint Chiefs of Staff reported that the full commitment of air transport would enable the United States to meet the minimum requirements of Berlin. But, they emphasized, the airlift would probably fail if it had to continue. They further warned that a full commitment would seriously impact the essential support that the Military Air Transport Service provided to the air force's emergency war plans. The airlift also threatened existing stocks of gasoline and its costs were certain to increase dramatically as the airlift expanded.[101] The chiefs recommended that negotiations continue and that another alternative be sought: "It is assumed that diplomatic effort together with all practicable counter-pressure will continue to be used to arrive at a peaceful solution of the Berlin problems. In this connection, it may not be altogether out of the question to consider, during the time that is to be gained by concentration of major effort on air transport supply, the possibility that some justification might be found for withdrawal of our occupation forces from Berlin without undue loss of prestige."[102]

While the Pentagon vacillated and USAFE set the air bridge to Berlin in motion, efforts to resolve the crisis through diplomatic measures continued. On June 29, Marshal Sokolovsky suggested to General Robertson that the blockade could be lifted if the results of the London Conference were discussed and reconsidered.[103] A few days later, on July 3, the three Western commanders—Clay, Robertson, and Koenig—met with a polite but forbidding Sokolovsky, who interrupted their protests over Soviet actions with the bald assertion that "technical difficulties" would continue until the West abandoned its plans for a West German government. This, according to Clay, was the first Soviet admission of the real reason behind the Berlin Blockade. There was nothing further to discuss, Clay recalled, and "our farewell was as cold as our reception."[104]

When it became evident that discussions at lower levels would not lead to a solution to the crisis, American, British, and French leaders sought to have their ambassadors in Moscow talk with Stalin himself. During a meeting on August 2, Stalin stressed his opposition to the unification of the Western occupation zones into a single entity. He was willing, he said, to lift the blockade upon the receipt of assurances that the London Conference decisions would be postponed until all aspects of the German question were considered by the four powers and when the B-marks were withdrawn from Berlin. American ambassador Walter Bedell Smith was pleased following this meeting with Stalin, and State Department personnel sent to Moscow for the negotiations reported that the Soviet dictator and Molotov had agreed to lift the blockade seemingly on terms the United States could accept. Writing recently, a historian of the period concluded that the meeting with Stalin was a mistake. It confirmed in the dictator's mind that he was master of the situation, that the Western powers were weak, and that the Soviet Union needed only to continue the pressure. While subsequent negotiations with Molotov appeared to go well, the hopes of the Western powers were soon dashed. By August 10, both the United States and Britain had been disillusioned by Soviet language that looked forward to the end of four-power control of Germany and suggested that the Western powers were in Berlin by sufferance rather than right.[105]

The Soviets drafted a proposed joint communiqué on August 15 that essentially announced complete victory for the USSR. The communiqué stated that the B-marks would be withdrawn from Berlin, a meeting of the Council of Foreign Ministers would be convened in the future to consider outstanding questions affecting greater Germany and Berlin, and that the representatives of the three Western powers would announce they would table the idea of creating a government for West Germany.[106] In staking out this position, Stalin and Molotov—gambling that the airlift would fail—ignored the possibility of a compromise with the Western powers.

The Soviet communiqué was never issued. On September 1, a parliamentary council convened to write a constitution for the new West Germany, ending hopes that the Western powers would accept the Soviet position in any form. While subsequent talks between Molotov and representatives of the Western powers on September 18 concerning control of currency in Germany showed that the Western allies were still willing to compromise, Molotov failed to seize this opportunity.[107]

Negotiations between the military governors in Berlin on September 5–6 regarding technical details proved fruitless. Sokolovsky appeared to renege on Stalin's agreement to end the blockade and, at the close of the meeting, he increased the pressure on the airlift by announcing Soviet air exercises in the Berlin area, including the corridors. At the same time, Soviet-sponsored riots in Berlin combined with the threat to the air corridors appeared to form a pattern of persistent Russian pressure designed to force the Western powers into signing an unfavorable agreement forcing them out of Berlin, to place the responsibility of any breakdown in negotiations on Great Britain and the United States, or to provoke the Western powers in an overt act that could justify a Russian attack.[108]

On September 14, the Western diplomatic representatives presented an *aide-mémoire* charging that Marshal Sokolovsky's intransigence had stalled the talks in Berlin. The Soviets replied on September 18, blaming the Western powers for the breakdown and repeating the demand that Russian control be extended to civil aircraft traffic. Clearly, according to Clay, they did not intend to work toward an agreement. On September 24, the Soviet government presented its own *aide-mémoire*, which Clay described as "the usual combination of half-truths, distorted facts, and malicious charges."[109] The Western powers responded by placing the issue of Berlin before the United Nations Security Council. Marshall summarized the Western position to Dr. Philip C. Jessup, the American representative on the Security Council: The United States wanted the blockade lifted, but would not negotiate under duress. The United States was prepared to allow the Soviet mark to be the only currency in Berlin, but only under adequate four-power control. Above all, Marshall told Jessup, "we will not, repeat not, be forced out of Berlin."[110]

It cannot be overemphasized that the Berlin Airlift played a crucial role in diplomatic dealings with the Soviet Union. "The air lift into Berlin alone has given us time for these negotiations and time to present the case before the United Nations," Secretary Royall wrote to Secretary Symington on September 26. "Without the air lift we would long ago have been faced with the alternative of either using force to maintain communications for the supply of Berlin or to have withdrawn from Berlin in virtual defeat."[111]

By the end of September, Stalin's options in Germany appear to have dwindled to continuing the blockade only. Negotiations with the Western powers had failed to influence developments in his favor while Soviet-sponsored riots and an attempt to stack the municipal government of Berlin with pro-USSR appointees in early September had miscarried, causing the Western powers to harden their position. Worse, the airlift was now dividing Germany into the two separate camps the dictator feared. In response,

Stalin avoided the Western ambassadors, postponed a meeting with officials from eastern Germany, and went on a ten-week vacation. For all practical purposes, it seems he decided to rely on the mighty partner that had enabled Russia to destroy Napoleon's army over a century earlier and the Soviet Union to defeat Hitler's forces less than five years before—Russia's great ally, "General Winter."[112]

The Western powers were still willing to negotiate, but in the face of Soviet intransigence they had no other alternative than to allow the diplomatic process to wend its way slowly through the United Nations. The airlift, the operation that enabled Western diplomats to deal with the Soviets without undue duress, would have to continue to serve that function. "We must look forward now to supply Berlin through the winter," Royall continued in his September 26 letter to Symington. "This will mean increasing further the present air lift capacity."[113]

Western leaders, with negotiations stagnant and without other viable options, thus ended up betting all on a roll of the dice in an operation that few really believed would succeed. They wagered Berlin, western Germany, and the American position in postwar Europe on the steady thunder of Pratt & Whitney engines.

chapter 3

Tunner and the MATS Connection

On July 28, 1948, a C-54 touched down at Wiesbaden, and forty-two-year-old Maj. Gen. William H. Tunner stepped out. Tunner was a brilliant, dedicated, meticulous leader whose steel-blue eyes and index-card mind missed nothing. A workaholic, he labored long hours at an intense pace and drove his staff relentlessly.[1] Tunner was one thing more—he was the U.S. Air Force's preeminent authority on air transport. An admiring Curtis LeMay called him "the transportation expert to end transportation experts" and later wrote that his assignment to the airlift "was rather like appointing John Ringling to get the circus on the road."[2]

Tunner's credentials validated his reputation. A talented pilot during the interwar years of the air corps, he had found his way into air transport and had helped create the U.S. Army Air Force's Ferrying Command in the early days of World War II. Sent to the Far East late in 1944, his imagination, determination, and organizational skills had made "flying the Hump" into China legendary. The Hump operation had begun out of necessity when Japanese forces cut off China from all military support from the Allies by closing the Burma Road in early 1942. The only route that remained was by air from India over the Himalaya Mountains. The air operation initially limped along under local control, and when Air Trans-

Figure 14. Brilliant, dedicated, and meticulous, Maj. Gen. William H. Tunner was the U.S. Air Force's preeminent authority on air transport. Courtesy U.S. Air Force

port Command took charge in December, 1942, it was barely delivering 1,000 tons per month. Over the next few months, painfully achieved improvements increased deliveries to 31,935 tons in December, 1944. Then Tunner took command. He refined every aspect of the system, instituted assembly-line maintenance, systematized cargo-handling procedures, and imbued the operation with a driving commitment to increased tonnage. His intense effort paid off: in July, 1945, alone, Air Transport Command delivered 71,042 tons of cargo to China.[3]

After World War II, however, Tunner spent much of his time closing bases and dismantling the powerful air forces that had been instrumental in victory. Military air transport appeared to have little future, and he considered leaving the service. His sense of duty prevailed, however, and when Air Transport Command combined with Naval Transport Command to form MATS in mid-1948, Major General Kuter selected Tunner as his deputy commander for operations. The Berlin Crisis had begun almost immediately afterward, and while USAFE delivered cargo to Berlin, Tunner chafed at his desk. He believed fervently that, despite increases in tonnage delivered, the bomber people operating the airlift needed his knowledge and experience. To a veteran specialist in air transport, elements of the Berlin Airlift most celebrated in the press—air crews flying until they were exhausted, pilots on the USAFE staff rushing to the flight line to fly any aircraft standing on the tarmac, and frantic hustle and bustle—were signs of inefficiency, and he wanted to put things right. Frustrated at having to sit on the bench during the big game and by the fact that USAFE was doing the mission for which MATS had been created, he pressed Kuter to propose that MATS take responsibility for the airlift.[4]

Kuter proved more cautious than Tunner. A brilliant and outspoken military intellectual, Kuter was a long-time advocate of an independent air force and precision strategic bombing who had helped prepare the USAAF's strategic air plan for World War II in 1941. Subsequently, as chief of plans on the air staff, he produced many of the doctrines and policies that provided the foundation of the U.S. Air Force after the war. He earned his airlift spurs at the end of the war by planning and directing the transfer of 23,000 occupation troops to Japan by ATC, and later he commanded ATC's Atlantic Division. Kuter had his share of detractors as well. His views of strategic bombardment before the war had alienated more conservative military leaders while some suspicion that he had been reluctant to fly combat missions as a group commander with Eighth Air Force concerned some peers. His postwar assignments, historian Robert Charles Owen has concluded, suggest that he was viewed as a valued but potentially sensitive asset and that "command of MATS may have been a way to 'rehabilitate' Kuter with an important, but not too important operational command." Probably aware of his position and apparently with less taste for bureaucratic infighting than he had once shown, Kuter declined to press for direct MATS involvement in the airlift.[5]

Frustrated for the time being, Tunner went on an inspection tour of MATS bases. But he left a trusted subordinate, Col. T. Ross Milton, haunting the halls of the Pentagon and reporting the latest information. "He called each night," Milton later wrote, "and he was not happy with my news, for there appeared to be no sentiment for a major effort and no mention of Tunner going over to run it."[6]

Tunner only had to stew for a short time. U.S. Army Lt. Gen. Albert C. Wedemeyer, director of plans and operations of the General Staff, had commanded in China during the latter part of World War II and knew Tunner well. If the Berlin Airlift must succeed, he told Hoyt Vandenberg, then it required the man who had operated the Hump. Undersecretary of the Army William H. Draper, Jr., seconded Wedemeyer, urging that Tunner be sent without delay. Vandenberg apparently had not considered giving Tunner command until after the July 22 meeting of the National Security Council. When it became apparent during that meeting that the airlift would be expanded, Vandenberg realized that he had to send the best man that the U.S. Air Force had for the job. Tunner went to Germany, and with him came some of his old hands to make the airlift work: Lt. Col. Robert D. "Red" Forman as chief of operations, Maj. Edward A. Guilbert as director of traffic for cargo, Col. Orval O. McMahon as chief of supply, Lt. Col. Kenneth S. Swallwell as director of air installations, Lt. Col. Manuel "Pete" Fernandez as chief of communications, Maj. Harold H. "Hal" Sims as chief navigator, and Maj. William P. Dunn as chief of maintenance along with his assistant, Maj. Jules Prevost. Although others, like his chief of staff, Colonel Milton—last seen roaming the Pentagon—had no connection with the Hump, the red, white, and blue insignia of the China-Burma-India Theater quickly became a common sight in Germany.[7]

Tunner arrived in Germany convinced that the Berlin Crisis was "the first conflict between the free and the slave world." This belief led him to one conclusion: "We can't afford to lose it."[8] The Berlin Airlift at the end of July, 1948, contrasted sharply with Tunner's ideal. He later described his vision of an airlift in plain, often quoted words: "The actual operation of a successful airlift is about as glamorous as drops of water on stone. There's no frenzy, no flap, just the inexorable process of getting the job done. In a successful airlift you don't see planes parked all over the place; they're either in the air, on loading or unloading ramps, or being worked on. You don't see personnel milling around; flying crews are either flying, or resting up so that they can fly again tomorrow. Ground crews are either working on their assigned planes, or resting up so they can work on them again tomorrow. Everyone else is also on the job, going about his work quietly and efficiently."[9]

Under Tunner, the monotony of repetition replaced the romance of flying. The more humdrum things were, the better. "The real excitement from running a successful airlift," he summarized, "comes from seeing a dozen lines climbing steadily on a dozen charts—tonnage delivered, utilization of aircraft, and so on—and the lines representing accidents and injuries go sharply down. That's where the glamour lies in air transport."[10] Tunner was determined to establish an airlift that functioned with machine-like efficiency. Only this type of organization could move sufficient food and fuel to defeat the Soviet blockade.

Tunner's approach required the careful coordination of every aspect of the airlift, including detailed procedures and exact duplication and precise execution of each phase of the operation from loading cargo to the return landing. Aircraft maintenance teams, aircrews, supply personnel, and thousands of lesser-known activities were sharply regimented. Everyone performed their duties according to strict directives, and statistical charts and tables tracked the process at every stage. Tunner wanted all activities to take place in a constant unvarying cadence. "This steady rhythm, constant as the jungle drums, became the trade-mark of the Berlin Airlift," he later wrote. "I don't have much of a natural sense of rhythm, incidentally. I'm certainly no threat to Fred Astaire, and a drumstick to me is something that grows on a chicken. But when it comes to airlifts, I want rhythm."[11]

Tunner emphasized the use of all 1,440 minutes of the day. He dreamed of landing one airplane every minute, an almost impossible goal in 1948 but an accurate indicator of the proficiency he sought. Ultimately, he settled for the more practical goal of one landing every three minutes. This rate, he noted, "provided the ideal cadence of operation with the control equipment available at the time." He explained: "At three minute intervals, this meant 480 landings at, say, Tempelhof, in a twenty-four hour period. Ultimately, under ideal circumstances, this schedule could mean 1,440 landings daily at three air fields."[12] At ten tons per aircraft, the airlift could—in theory— deliver 14,400 tons in a single day. Tunner viewed the corridors between western Germany and Berlin as a conveyor belt with aircraft spaced evenly along the route. All the aircraft moved at the same speed, executed their maneuvers at the same spot, and followed the predetermined schedule to the second. Like a conveyor belt, the airlift could be slowed down or sped up as necessary, but it was relentless in its regimentation.[13]

Tunner practiced an intense personal style of leadership. He worked eighteen hours a day, often sacking out on a cot in his office, but not all of that work was accomplished behind a desk. He visited flight lines, hangars, loading and unloading facilities, and the maintenance lines. He observed, talked, and, above all, listened. Aircrews met him as they climbed from their aircraft; maintenance personnel saw him studying repair work at midnight; control tower operators found him looking over their shoulders at three in the morning. In the dark, wearing his worn flight jacket or covered with coal dust, he often appeared to be just another officer, slightly older than most. Airmen laughed at the story of the pilot who ordered Tunner to "shake a leg and get a move on." These visits, discussions, and casual talks often led to immediate changes. For example, when pilots complained about their aircraft being sluggish on take off, he noticed that all of the complaints came when they were hauling coal. He visited the Main River where German workers loaded coal from barges into one-hundred-pound sacks. Noting that the workers only weighed one sack out of every hundred, he ordered fifty bags checked immediately. These weighed, he found, an average of 115 pounds. In their zeal to see that every pound of coal possible reached Berlin, the workers were overfilling the bags. Aircraft were taking off with 15 percent more weight than the crew believed. Tunner immediately ordered that every bag be weighed.[14]

The challenge of motivating personnel uprooted from their homes and families, thrown into uncomfortable quarters, required to fly long hours, and not knowing when the lift would end would tax the ingenuity of any commander, and morale was a priority on the airlift. Major Sims suggested establishing a newsletter. The *Task Force Times*, which kept the airmen "in the loop," was Tunner's pride. And Tunner found a talented cartoonist in the radioman on his own airplane, John H. "Jake" Schuffert, whose uncensored cartoons poked fun at every aspect of the airlift and captured its essence for everyone. Above all, Tunner pushed competition as the antidote to ennui. He set goals for each base and recorded the results on huge "Howgozit" boards for everyone to see. The *Task Force Times* also publicized the efficiency of each unit, and Tunner rewarded those with the best daily records, most notably by sponsoring special cargo delivery efforts such as one on Air Force Day, September 18, 1948, and the fabled "Easter Parade," on Easter Sunday in 1949.[15] He pitted commanders against each other with gusto. During the Easter Parade, Tunner visited Celle, which was delivering 12 percent more cargo than its quota. He then traveled to Fassberg, where he found the commander boasting of delivering 10 percent more cargo than his quota. "That's fine, but of course it's not up to what they're doing over at Celle," Tunner responded. "They're really on the ball over there."[16] By the time Tunner left Fassberg, its commander had charged down to the flight line to urge his people to redouble their efforts.

While Tunner cared for his men and made every effort to improve living and working conditions, he ultimately was a hard-nosed, determined commander deeply committed to the success of his mission. William H. Tunner was called many things in his lifetime: "Tonnage" Tunner has the ring of a public affairs effort, and Rep. L. Mendel Rivers nicknamed him "Mr. Airlift" in later years. Thanks to his ruthless drive for absolute precision with Ferrying Command, on the Hump, and on the Berlin Airlift, however, the nickname that stuck was "Willie the Whip."

Airlift Task Force (Provisional)

With Tunner came more Skymasters. At the time General Clay met with the NSC on July 22, USAFE had 54 C-54s and 105 C-47s assigned to the airlift. Following the decision to augment Operation Vittles, General Vandenberg, on July 23, directed MATS to form a task force consisting of additional squadrons of C-54s. "Task Force Vittles" as established by MATS consisted of a task force headquarters based upon the 518th Air Transport Group from Kelly Air Force Base, Texas, and eight air transport squadrons of 9 C-54s each for a total of 72 aircraft. Contingents of support and maintenance personnel rounded out the deployment. The task force included three aircrews for each aircraft, which imposed a terrible drain on the U.S. Air Force's global air transport operations since this accounted for roughly two-thirds of the C-54 aircrews available worldwide. Obviously, the decision to commit MATS drew deeply on scarce American airlift assets. The United States had a total of 866 C-54s and their variants, both military and civilian. Most were with MATS, which had 214 air force C-54s and 54 navy R5Ds, a total of 268; the USAF troop carrier groups had an additional 168 planes. Beyond these, the air force had another 40 or so aircraft and the navy another 80 in various commands doing miscellaneous duties. Outside of the military, civilian airlines that flew scheduled routes had 267 C-54s—41 leased from the air force—while airlines operating on a non-scheduled basis flew another 44. From these, and subtracting those already in Germany, air force planners calculated that 393 C-54s could be made

"QUIT CLOWNIN', HARLOW AND GET ON NR. 4."

"OH, OH, I FORGOT TO WAKE SGT. HOGAN BEFORE WE TOOK OFF!!"

Figure 15. S.Sgt. John H. "Jake" Schuffert captured the humor of the airlift as cartoonist for the official Combined Airlift Task Force newspaper, Task Force Times. All cartoons are from issues of the Task Force Times

available to the airlift in an extreme emergency. The first of the Task Force Vittles squadrons begin arriving on July 30, and all had reached Germany by mid-August, giving the airlift a total of 126 C-54s.[17]

General Tunner's orders placed him in charge of airlift operations at the three bases already in use, Rhein-Main, Wiesbaden, and Tempelhof. In addition to these, he also took charge of the base at Oberpfaffenhofen in the American zone of occupation and any other depots required for heavy maintenance; the Frankfurt Air Traffic Control Center and any other centers required for control of the airlift; and all airplane operations in the Frankfurt-Berlin air corridors. He was further given direct communications with the Military Air Transport Service and the U.S. Army's European Command. On July 29, Tunner established his headquarters as the 7499th Air Division. Two days later he activated the Airlift Task Force (Provisional).[18]

Tunner began his assignment with a letter that recognized the contributions of General Smith and his USAFE personnel, but which also staked out the MATS claim to participation in the operation: "The world has been increasingly conscious of the outstanding air transport accomplishments of 'Operation Vittles.' Specifically, the American people have been unstinting in their praise of your tremendous achievement with the numbers of people and equipment you have had available. The formation of the Military Air Transport Service 'Task Force Vittles,' under the Commanding general, USAFE, will bring more personnel and equipment to carry on the job you have so magnificently pioneered."[19] Tunner thus made it clear that while he recognized that USAFE operated the Berlin Airlift and that he served under USAFE, Military Air Transport Service had arrived: Operation Vittles would be his program.

The relationship between Tunner's airlift and USAFE would remain a problem throughout 1948. In Tunner's view, the Berlin Airlift should have been a MATS operation from the beginning. However, the operation's origins as a short-term, temporary program directed informally by USAFE using resources already in Germany kept MATS from taking charge. This meant that the airlift commander reported to the USAFE commander and properly had to go through USAFE headquarters to communicate with individuals and organizations critical to the airlift's success, including General Clay, MATS, and Air Matériel Command. Further, certain USAFE facilities vital to the success of the airlift—the supply depot at Erding in the American zone, the maintenance depot at Burtonwood in Great Britain, and the base facilities necessary for his men's comfort, for example—were outside Tunner's direct command. As long as LeMay was USAFE commander, this arrangement posed comparatively few problems. Mutual admirers, LeMay and Tunner worked well together, and LeMay allowed his airlift commander freedom to deal with other headquarters. According to Tunner, when Lt. Gen. John K. Cannon replaced LeMay in October, 1948, the situation changed for the worse at a critical time.[20]

Tunner's first inkling of a problem took place over the agreement that established the Combined Airlift Task Force (CALTF). LeMay had made unified command a major priority and had worked diligently first with Smith and then with Tunner to overcome British opposition to the united organizational structure both men saw as vital (as will be detailed below). USAFE and BAFO signed the agreement on October 14, the day before LeMay left Germany. On the day after LeMay departed, Tunner, as custom re-

Figure 16. Lt. Gen. John K. Cannon succeeded General LeMay as commander in chief, United States Air Forces in Europe, in mid-October, 1948. Courtesy U.S. Air Force

quired, paid a visit to his new boss, who greeted him with a roar of anger over the agreement. Tunner pacified Cannon with the explanation that the negotiations had been lengthy and complex, and that he and LeMay had hoped to conclude them before Cannon's arrival so as not to burden him unnecessarily. This explanation seemed to appease Cannon, but relations between the two men remained poor. Tunner later acknowledged that he caused a good deal of the problem. As a brash young expert on air transport, he viewed Cannon as an aging fighter commander with little knowledge of airlift operations and treated him with less deference than was politic. Cannon, on the other hand, found that he had a rather free-wheeling operation under his command and was determined to bring it under complete control.[21]

Tunner's letter of instruction from Cannon specifically prevented him from dealing directly with Military Air Transport Service, Air Matériel Command, and almost everyone of significance—all contact had to be made through USAFE headquarters. The impact on his operations was critical, Tunner later complained, and he could no longer get immediate action. Before, four days after he requested any special personnel, they were on the runway in Germany. Now, he was lucky to get the request through USAFE in the same amount of time. There was a shortage of housing for airlift personnel and ground transportation was inadequate. Tunner could only send requests to USAFE headquarters, which responded slowly. The British maintenance depot at Burtonwood, near Liverpool, proved a special problem. Tunner counted on seven two-hundred-hour inspections per day at that facility and had transferred maintenance personnel from the airlift to ensure that rate. In November, however, output at Burtonwood fell to only two inspections per day, which figured to be a loss of thirty-five aircraft per week or one hundred fifty per month on the airlift. Burtonwood presented many problems. The location was bleak, the food terrible, the housing poor, and the weather "English." Critical supplies, equipment, and tools failed to arrive from the United States The local commander was capable, so the problems lay at a higher level of command. However, since Tunner could not talk directly to Air Matériel Command, he could do little. Instead of action from USAFE, Tunner later fumed, he received promises and excuses. Finally, he shifted responsibility for the two-hundred-hour inspections back to the squadrons, which were short the men transferred to Burtonwood and thus had to do double duty with a reduced workforce.

All of this took place just as the airlift entered its most critical month. November was the low point of the airlift as bad weather, especially fog, set in. The airlift managed to deliver some cargo daily, but on many days deliveries were well below the airlift goals. On November 30, for example, just ten out of forty-two aircraft that took off actually reached Berlin. Tunner's men delivered the least amount of tonnage during the entire airlift that month, which came close to justifying Soviet intransigence. Conquering November became a major turning point in the success of the airlift, and in Tunner's view, that goal was hampered by the command system and his relationship with Cannon.

The airlift continued to struggle through December and the Christmas season, and entertainer Bob Hope, of all people, became the problem in miniature. Word came that Hope would bring a Christmas show to entertain the airmen delivering freedom to Berlin, and the men eagerly anticipated the event. On December 23, Tunner learned that Hope would give two shows—one downtown in Wiesbaden and another downtown in Berlin. Neither would be at an airlift base where airlift personnel could attend. Tunner exploded. He sent an ultimatum to USAFE: either Hope entertained the airlift, which had attracted him to Germany in the first place, or all mention of the airlift must be removed from advance publicity, something the American press would have noticed and questioned. Within twenty-four hours, USAFE gave priority for the show to all airlift personnel, and three additional performances were scheduled for airlift bases.

Ultimately, it took Secretary of the Air Force Stuart Symington to break the USAFE logjam. He toured Rhein-Main on Christmas Day, poking and prying, talking to the men, and asking pertinent questions. He learned from the men themselves about the poor living conditions and the shortages of suitable tools, equipment, and parts, things Tunner had been complaining about for weeks. Following his tour, Symington demanded facts and figures and thorough descriptions of the problems. The response to Tunner's detailed report on airlift problems, given to the secretary on December 27, was immediate. According to Tunner: "Orders came down to requisition better housing, and construction began on emergency barracks. Burtonwood was shaken up from top to bottom, and the increase in two-hundred-hour inspections began almost immediately. Long-needed supplies began flowing in. Frankly I was amazed at both the amount and the immediacy." In addition, the air force established a rotation policy, ending one of the worst morale destroyers, the extended TDYs. Problems remained though: "It was still somewhat difficult operating under an unsympathetic command, and I am still convinced that we could have performed our mission more successfully had we had greater authority to run our own show, but at least from then on we had sufficient tools to work with."[22]

In addition to settling these problems with USAFE, the resolution of airlift command between the American and British efforts (mentioned above) was another critical step in success. Operational control of the airlift had become a concern as both programs expanded. General LeMay and Air Marshal Sir Arthur P. M. Sanders, air officer commanding, BAFO, both agreed that their goal was to lift the "maximum tonnage in the safest and most expeditious manner possible, with [the] resources at hand and that some form of joint control of air traffic is required."[23] From here, the two positions diverged. The British wanted the USAFE traffic control center at Frankfurt and the British center at Bückeburg to operate independently, coordinating their activities through the Airlift Task Force headquarters in Wiesbaden and BAFO in Bückeburg. In the Berlin air control area, where the streams of aircraft merged as they approached Gatow and Tempelhof, they proposed a form of joint control with a "master controller" who alternated between the Americans and the British.[24]

LeMay and Tunner, on the other hand, wanted to place operational control of all air traffic in and out of the airfields and through the corridors under one headquarters. "I feel that the basic principle involved is the necessity for vesting in one commander operational control . . . of all units as they become involved in the airlift effort," LeMay told Vandenberg. "I do not visualize this one commander assuming personnel, logistics, and administrative, maintenance, or operational control . . . of these operating units, but I do visualize his asserting some control over such matters within these units during the time they are actively engaged in the airlift effort."[25] Cutting minutes, even seconds, off every aspect of the process required, in LeMay's view, a closer relationship than coordination would allow. Further, delivering the maximum amount of cargo to the beleaguered city ultimately meant basing U.S. aircraft in the British occupation zone, making joint control a necessity. Finally, since the bulk of the airlift fell to USAFE, LeMay wanted Tunner in command.[26]

While discussions continued, the growing operations tied the two airlifts together. Planning for basing C-54s at Fassberg had already begun. General Smith, as noted above, had approached the British about using one of the RAF bases in July. Fassberg offered three distinct advantages over the two U.S. bases: it was close to the port at Bremen, its fifty-five-minute flying time to Berlin was less than half that from the Frankfurt area, and it tended to have better weather conditions. Studies projected that twenty-seven C-54s operating from Fassberg would deliver 988 tons in an eight-hour day, while twenty-seven based at Wiesbaden would only deliver 518 tons in the same time. Serious negotiations began on August 4, and at a meeting with the British on August 6, the conferees concluded that Fassberg would not require a runway extension for C-54s; the British would continue to load all aircraft; the RAF would maintain runways, hangars, and facilities; and USAFE would provide fuel pumps and the personnel to man them, the parts and equipment for maintenance, and rations for the 407 officers and 1,950 enlisted men planned for the facility. In an interesting "joint" activity, RAF air traffic controllers supervised the air-control system while USAFE personnel manned the radios so that the C-54 crews might hear an American accent. Personnel from the 7496th Air Wing began to arrive at Fassberg on August 13, the first supplies three days later, and the first refueling units on August 18. The first of the twenty-seven C-54s reached Fassberg on August 21.[27]

In the meantime, one of Tunner's planners, Col. John W. White, began a study on the use of Gatow in Berlin. On August 2, the Berlin Airlift Task Force began developing procedures for directing aircraft to either Tempelhof or Gatow depending on which had less traffic. A liaison detachment from Tempelhof, known as the "Gatow Flight," was established at the British base, and by the end of August, U.S. aircraft were using Gatow, further merging airlift operations.[28]

Several meetings with Air Marshal Sanders in mid-August failed to resolve the command and control issue to LeMay's satisfaction, and he elevated the problem to USAF headquarters, asking Vandenberg to raise the issue with the Air Ministry.[29] In the British reply to the USAF chief of staff on September 28, Air Chief Marshal Sir Charles Medhurst, chief of the British Joint Services Mission in Washington, D.C., reiterated that there was no need for unified command and directions of operations. The Air Ministry believed, he reported, that the two services were operating in separate spheres 140 miles apart using separate fields, corridors, and navigational techniques. The exception was Fassberg, but the ministry anticipated that the RAF C-47s would soon be transferred from that facility. The Control Center in Berlin should provide the necessary integrated control for that city. At the same time, Medhurst informed Maj. Gen. Samuel E. Anderson, director of plans and operations at USAF headquarters, that a new, small Transport Command Task Force would replace the shared control of the RAF airlift element by BAFO and Transport Command. Designated Advanced Headquarters, No. 46 Group, this would be commanded by Air Commodore Merer, air officer commanding, No. 46 Group, and

Figure 17. Royal Air Force and U.S. Air Force radar personnel operate GCA equipment at Gatow in Berlin. Left to right: Cpl. William Black, Aberdeen, Scotland; Flight Lt. Allen Green, Bournemouth, England; M.Sgt. Wilfred Kranz, Harbor Beach, Michigan; Flight Lt. Edward Attwell, Lincolnshire, England; Cpl. Eric Renshall, Liverpool, England; and Aircraftsman Peter Stephenson, Liverpool, England. Courtesy U.S. Air Force

would coordinate all of the RAF, USAF, and British civilian airlift operating from the British zone under the overall direction of BAFO.[30]

In the meantime, during a meeting with Air Vice Marshal C.B.S. Spackman on August 30, LeMay agreed on a temporary arrangement establishing a Joint Traffic Control Center at Tempelhof similar to the British proposal. A committee meeting on September 2 worked out the details, and the resulting "Task Force Approach Control" handled traffic in and out of Tempelhof and Gatow.[31]

As LeMay expected, the C-54 operations at Fassberg ultimately convinced the British of the need for unified command. The C-54s were allotted six block times for takeoff. Within these blocks, schedules called for the aircraft to depart at three-minute intervals under good conditions (five in poor) and to fly at three altitudes: 2,500 feet, 3,000 feet, and 3,500 feet.

Air Traffic Control routed them into Berlin through the northern corridor and they returned, along with C-54s from Rhein-Main and Wiesbaden, through the center corridor. After a C-54 block at Fassberg became airborne, the controller notified BAFO that the corridor was available for the Yorks and Dakotas based at Lübeck. Although the C-54s had little trouble getting block times from the British controllers, it became obvious that the operation of dissimilar aircraft from takeoff through the narrow corridors to landing and return required a single unified agency. The difficulties coordinating the operations of aircraft with widely varying flight characteristics flying in close proximity in the narrow confines of the Berlin corridors demonstrated the need for unified command and control.[32]

In early October, Sir Brian Robertson recommended that airlift operations be placed under Tunner with Air Commodore Merer as deputy. The merger agreement was signed on October 14, and the next day the Combined Airlift Task Force, headquartered at Wiesbaden, set to the task of delivering to Berlin "in a safe and efficient manner, the maximum tonnage possible, consistent with the combined resources of equipment and personnel made available."[33] Merer remained at No. 46 Group headquarters in the British occupation zone while Group Captain Noel Hyde—a veteran airman who had spent much of World War II engineering escapes while a German prisoner of war—represented the Royal Air Force at Wiesbaden. Additional RAF officers served in the Plans and Operations Sections at Wiesbaden while U.S. Air Force officers joined the Operations Section of No. 46 Group. On November 5, the U.S. forces involved in the airlift were reorganized as the 1st Airlift Task Force.[34]

Der Schokoladen-flieger

As the airlift changed, it gained an unanticipated but potent symbol. In many ways, 1st Lt. Gail Halvorsen, a quiet Mormon from Garland, Utah, demonstrated all that was best about the Berlin Airlift. Uprooted from his station at Brookley Air Force Base, Alabama, on short notice, Halvorsen had stuffed his duffel bag with handkerchiefs to deal with his raging cold, parked his car near the flight line, and departed for Germany, reaching Rhein-Main on July 11. The bustling German base was a shock: "As we came within communication range of the tower we were astounded by the non-stop transmissions," he later wrote. "We had never heard so much traffic on the radios."[35]

Figure 18. Among the key Western military leaders in Europe during the Berlin Airlift were (left to right): *Lt. Gen. John K. Cannon, commander in chief, United States Air Forces in Europe; Air Marshal T. M. Williams, air officer commanding, British Air Forces of Occupation; Maj. Gen. William H. Tunner, commander, 1st Airlift Task Force and Combined Airlift Task Force; and Air Commodore John W. F. Merer, commander, No. 46 Group, and deputy commander, Combined Airlift Task Force.* Courtesy U.S. Air Force

On July 17, after several missions, he visited Berlin as a passenger hoping to take movies of the city. While walking near the barbed wire fence off the end of the Tempelhof runway, he noticed children watching the airplanes. These German children acted differently from other children, Halvorsen noted, as they did not ask for candy or gum—expecting nothing, they asked for nothing. He divided among them the only two sticks of gum he had left, and then made a rash promise: if they returned to the fence, Halvorsen told the kids, he would drop gum and candy from his airplane.[36] The children asked him how they would recognize his airplane. "Well, I'll do like I did when I was a kid over Garland, Utah," he told them. "I'd fly up over a farm, wiggle the wings of the airplane at the folks, and let them know that was me."[37]

The delivery system Halvorsen invented was pretty basic. The handkerchiefs destined for head-cold relief became parachutes instead, and the C-54's flare chute became a "bomb bay." Flying into Tempelhof on July 18, Halvorsen spotted the children, wiggled his wings, and dropped three parachutes through the flare chute. He then landed and discharged his official cargo. Happy to have gotten away with the escapade, he taxied his empty aircraft to the runway for takeoff. Small hands waving tiny parachutes through the airfield fence testified that the parachute drop had worked. It was just the beginning, however. In the days that followed the children not only returned, their numbers increased, and they searched each airplane for the one that wiggled its wings. Halvorsen tried to ignore them, but then made a fateful decision to continue his own "chocolate" airlift, making six more drops. These failed to satisfy the children, though, and several days later Halvorsen stumbled across a stack of mail in the Base Operations Office at Tempelhof all addressed to *Onkel Wackelflugel* ("Uncle Wiggley Wings") and *Der Schokoladen-flieger* ("The Chocolate Flier").[38]

Finally, airlift headquarters caught on that something strange was taking place, and Halvorsen was ordered to report to his squadron commander, who demanded to know what he had been doing. The lieutenant temporized, but his commander was abrupt: "Look, I am not *stupid*—it's all over the front pages of the Berlin papers," he told Halvorsen. "You nearly hit a journalist on the head with a candy bar."[39] Then, to Halvorsen's surprise, he was given the go-ahead to continue the candy drop. Tunner not only approved, he was enthusiastic about the lieutenant's initiative, which he later called "One of our most delightful cargos."[40]

Figure 19. Der Schokoladen-flieger, *1st Lt. Gail S. Halvorsen, 17th Air Transport Squadron, of Garland, Utah, rigs some candy bars to miniature parachutes for delivery to German children in Berlin.* Courtesy U.S. Air Force

Dubbed "Operation Little Vittles," Halvorsen's candy drop expanded at a dizzying rate. Pilots and aircrews from his squadron, dependent USAFE wives, and other military personnel helped supply him with parachutes and candy. Publicity in the United States made him a celebrity, and he began receiving sacks of mail each day, much of it containing handkerchiefs. Candy arrived from all over, including over three tons from the American Confectioners Association. Soon, most of the aircraft from his squadron were dropping candy bars and chewing gum. Instead of a few parachutes dropped through the flare chute, boxes were emptied out cargo doors. So many children surrounded the perimeter of Tempelhof that they literally became a hazard. Children in the eastern sector asked for the "Candy Bomber," and Halvorsen made several drops to them before Soviet protests halted his deliveries. Ultimately, Halvorsen was assigned a full-time German-speaking secretary to handle his mail, an unheard of luxury for a lieutenant in the 1940s. *Der Schokoladen-flieger* became the most widely publicized symbol of the Berlin Airlift for hundreds of thousands of Germans and Americans.[41]

The Search for Additional Bases

With the arrival of additional C-54s, crews, and ground personnel in August, congestion and the lack of facilities became a serious problem for the bases in both the Western zones and in Berlin. Rhein-Main and Wiesbaden had become severely crowded, reducing efficiency at both bases. A long-term program of construction and modernization helped ease the situation, however. Two major decisions in August, while taken

Figure 20. 1st Lt. Gail Halvorsen makes an aerial delivery to children outside the fence at Tempelhof. Courtesy U.S. Air Force

primarily for other reasons, also addressed congestion. First, the opening of Fassberg and the stationing of twenty-seven C-54s at that base, which took advantage of the shorter distances available from the British zone, eased the pressure on the American facilities. Second, the replacement of C-47s with C-54s, which removed the less efficient aircraft from the airlift, allowed more productive use of existing facilities. The C-47s were withdrawn from the airlift by the end of September, 1948. In addition, by the end of September, LeMay and Tunner were developing plans to base forty C-54s at Celle in the British occupation zone beginning in December. Ultimately, the American airlift would dispatch aircraft from four bases, Rhein-Main and Wiesbaden in the American zone and Fassberg and Celle in the British.[42]

The critical choke point, however, was at the receiving end, Berlin. None of the runways at either Tempelhof or Gatow were built to handle the tremendous pounding by heavily laden aircraft every few minutes, twenty-four hours a day, day in and day out. Work gangs of German men and women armed with a motley assortment of shovels, picks, crowbars, and other tools maintained the runway around the clock. As soon as an airplane landed, they rushed out to fill holes and generally shore up the surface at a frantic pace. When a piercing whistle signaled the approach of another airplane, they rushed off until it had passed and then repeated the cycle. USAFE personnel also marked off two sod airstrips for use by C-47s, thus reducing damage to the main runway.[43]

Despite such efforts, the runway at Tempelhof quickly deteriorated. At the end of June, LeMay's air engineer surveyed the situation and reported that it was rapidly breaking down under the impact of the heavily loaded C-47s and that the Skymasters threatened greater damage. He recommended construction of a second asphalt-and-pierced-steel-plank strip. This plan received quick approval, and on July 8 U.S. Army engineers and German contractors began work on a 5,500-foot runway parallel to and south of the original runway. Laborers excavated the surface to a depth of two feet then installed a two-foot layer of compacted rubble covered by a two-inch layer of crushed stone. A layer of asphalt and pierced steel planking covered the crushed stone. American enlisted personnel operated the heavy machinery, including graders and bulldozers, while German civilians, both men and women, did the rest by hand. Almost all materials except rubble had to be flown in from the United States occupation zone, adding significantly to the airlift burden. Brick rubble, readily available thanks to the Allied bombing campaign in World War II, replaced the standard limestone base while stone streets and rail sidings provided a plentiful source of crushed stone. The pierced steel planking was later removed and the runway resurfaced with asphalt.[44]

By August, construction on the south runway at Tempelhof was well along, but it was already apparent to Airlift Task Force planners that with more C-54s on the way a third runway would be required. On August 20, LeMay ordered construction to begin on another runway to the north of the main strip. However, even with additional runways, Gatow and Tempelhof were too cramped to meet the projected demands of the airlift. By late July, USAFE survey teams had found a former *Wehrmacht* tank training area in the French sector of Berlin that offered an excellent location for a new airfield. Plans for Tegel received approval on August 5.[45]

On August 26, Tunner set forth his priorities for base construction to facilitate increased tonnage delivered to Berlin. His highest priority was completion of the south runway and the taxiway at Tempelhof; work on the north runway would continue, but it was secondary to this effort.

Figure 21. This photograph of Tempelhof was taken after construction of the second runway. Contrast this with the image in chapter 2 of the airport prior to the Berlin Airlift. Courtesy RG 7185, Helga Th. Mellman Collection, U.S. Army Military History Institute, Carlisle Barracks, Pennsylvania

Tunner's second priority was to assist the British in every way possible with construction of the parking apron and taxiway at Gatow. These two steps would provide maximum immediate aid to the airlift by permitting quick turnaround at Tempelhof in all weather and by expediting loading and unloading at Gatow, which would take advantage of the shorter route from Fassberg. Tunner's third priority was the completion of Tegel, which offered the greatest long-term improvement in airlift capacity.[46]

Through tremendous effort, U.S. Army engineers and German work crews completed the south runway at Tempelhof on September 12. LeMay had expected the third runway to be completed by October 20, but construction took longer and it was not opened until November 23. Work also began on Tempelhof's expanded network of taxiways and hardstands on September 17. These were completed in October.[47]

Tegel required a monumental effort. Construction began on August 5 and included a 5,500-foot runway of brick rubble with an asphalt surface; 6,020 feet of taxiway; 4,400 feet of access road; 2,750 feet of access railroad; and over one million square feet of apron. Administrative, operations, and support buildings, a control tower, and ground controlled approach (GCA) radar sites rounded out the program. General LeMay initially expected completion of Tegel in February, 1949, but this estimate displeased an impatient Clay. "I don't accept the February 1949 estimate for Tegel," he tersely told the USAFE commander on August 20, "It is much too long."[48] Construction followed the pattern at Tempelhof. Over seventeen thousand Berliners, working three shifts and paid slightly over one mark an hour and a hot meal, did the work. Crushed brick provided a solid base for the runway. The city of Berlin razed buildings designated over 60 percent destroyed, and civilians, mostly women, sorted out the whole bricks and loaded them on trucks; the bricks were then crushed at the construction site. American forces furnished essential heavy construction equipment manned by fifteen officers and one hundred fifty men from the army's Corps of Engineers. The airlift delivered critical materials unavailable in Berlin from the Western zones. Ultimately, dedication ceremonies at Tegel took place on October 29, and operations began on November 5, three months after construction began. On March 14, 1949, construction began on a second runway at Tegel. This was a 6,500-foot runway with an additional 1,500-foot base, allowing it to be extended to 8,000 feet if necessary for bigger aircraft. In contrast to the first runway, which was built mostly by hand, the airlift had brought in enough heavy

Figure 22. Construction of a parking ramp at Tegel in the French sector of Berlin continued as C-54s stationed at Fassberg maintained a constant stream of traffic. Courtesy U.S. Air Force

equipment for the work on the second to be done by just over four hundred laborers and technicians. The blockade provided an extra impetus for completing the structure, and work was done on August 4.[49] It is significant to note that from the first, American commanders planned Tegel to be a lasting facility: "Tegel Airport is no wartime strip whipped together for a limited operation with the intent of abandoning it when the need is over. It is a permanent installation complete with an all-weather runway, standard lighting, and permanent buildings to house the administration offices, firefighting equipment, and air traffic control personnel. . . . All access roads will be hard surfaced."[50]

Two aircraft made major contributions to the construction program in Berlin with their ability to deliver bulky outsized cargo. Development of a truly global air transport, the Douglas C-74 Globemaster, began during World War II. The aircraft first flew in September, 1945, and for a time it was the largest land-based transport in the world. In all, Douglas delivered twelve Globemasters to the air force. A single C-74 reached Rhein-Main Air Base on August 14 for service tests and made its first trip to Berlin three days later, landing at Gatow with twenty tons of flour. Prior to its return to the United States on September 21, the C-74 delivered 445.6 tons of cargo in twenty-five trips for an average of 17.82 tons per trip, proving itself as superior to the C-54 as the latter was to the C-47. On Air Force Day, September 18, 1948, the lone Globemaster made six round trips, delivered 125 tons of coal, and set an airlift utilization record by flying twenty hours that day. Additionally, the C-74's great size gave it the capability of delivering bulky industrial and construction equipment. The Globemaster completed one maintenance cycle before returning to the United States for its three-hundred-hour inspection. Despite its success, the C-74 left the airlift permanently. The weight of the giant aircraft over stressed the available runways, and its performance envelope interfered with the tight scheduling demanded by the air corridors. Also, the Soviets allegedly felt threatened, complaining that the C-74 might be used offensively by dropping bombs from its loading elevator located under the fuselage. Subsequently, the U.S. Air Force found that its C-74s were more valuable delivering C-54 engines and other parts from the United States to Germany. On October 4, 1984, the air force initiated "Goliath," special delivery flights from Brookley Air Force Base, Alabama, to Rhein-Main via Westover Air Force Base and the Azores. C-74s flew four Goliath flights each month, which increased to fourteen in January, 1949, and sixteen in February.[51]

The second airplane was the Fairchild C-82 Packet, the first aircraft designed for the U.S. military specifically as a cargo aircraft and produced in quantity. In 1941, Fairchild began design of the twin-engine aircraft featuring direct loading through the rear of the fuselage between twin tail booms. Delivery began in 1945 and Fairchild ultimately produced 220 planes. The C-82's capacity was relatively unimpressive—each carried about five tons—and it was slow and lacked range. However, they performed well on the airlift. Between September 14 and November 30, five Packets made 252 flights delivering 1,054 tons of cargo, about 4.18 tons per trip. The Packet's advantage lay in its wide fuselage and access through the rear, which made it excellent for hauling vehicles. Initially, plans called for the aircraft to evacuate vehicles from Berlin, but they provided tremendous assistance hauling bulk items and heavy construction equipment like bulldozers, asphalt machines, and graders. Tunner had originally planned to use the C-82s for a short time; however, their particular

Figure 23. The Douglas C-74 Globemaster and one of the five Fairchild C-82 Packets that flew on the Berlin Airlift at Rhein-Main Air Base on September 22, 1948. Courtesy U.S. Air Force

value changed his mind and they remained a part of the airlift for several months. As in the case of the C-74 and the later C-124, the C-82 was the forerunner of a more successful airplane—the C-119 Flying Boxcar.[52]

The French occupation force made its most significant contribution to the Berlin airlift by allowing the construction of Tegel in its zone and managing the unloading and distribution of the cargo it received. After Tegel opened, the French garrison made its most spectacular and best-remembered gesture. Two radio towers between 80 and 120 meters high belonging to *Berliner Rundfunk* but controlled by the Soviet military administration provided a serious landing hazard at the new field. On November 20, Gen. Jean Ganeval, the French commander in Berlin, warned the Soviets that if the towers were not moved, he would remove them. The Soviet commander apparently failed to take the warning seriously. On the morning of December 16, French soldiers closed off the roads around the radio installation and peremptorily ordered the station personnel to abandon their offices. Engineers and dynamite did the rest, and a massive explosion brought the towers down.[53]

"Black Friday" and New Patterns of Operations

Under Tunner, the 1st Airlift Task Force staff monitored the flow of traffic through the corridors, issued orders for diversions when necessary, and maintained records on the tonnage delivered. Air traffic control centers located in both occupation zones and Berlin had complete authority over all airlift routes and terminal areas. These centers controlled the rate of flow from takeoff to landing, the traffic patterns in and out of Berlin, and all airlift operational procedures.[54] It was their responsibility to develop the standard procedures required to translate Tunner's vision of an airlift into practical terms. Some of the measures were already in place when Tunner arrived; others were developed over time through trial and error. The basic elements of the airlift were fundamentally simple in theory but extremely complex in practice. While it may seem like indulging in unnecessary military minutia to examine these in detail, the operational patterns were actually the key to expanding the tonnage delivered to Berlin and, thus, played a major role in the success of the airlift.[55]

The complexities of the system for aircraft flying in the northern corridor from the British zone have already been described. Tunner's major impact was on the southern corridor from the American zone. As mentioned earlier, the temporary commander of the airlift, General Smith, had established a system that allotted separate blocks of time within which aircraft from Rhein-Main and Wiesbaden departed for Berlin. Within each block, air traffic controllers at each base determined the altitudes and spacing of the aircraft in accordance with standard Civil Aviation Authority (CAA) and International Civil Aviation Organization (ICAO) regulations, over which the airlift headquarters had no control. In general, the altitudes were set at 1,000-foot intervals from 5,000 feet to 10,000 feet, subsequently reduced to 4,000 feet and 8,000 feet. The air traffic controllers determined the intervals between aircraft based upon the weather conditions at the take off and landing sites. The aircraft usually departed four minutes apart or at greater intervals depending on the weather.

Bad weather, common in Germany, posed significant problems and was, of course, one factor Stalin counted on to halt the flow of coal and food into Berlin. When bad weather reduced conditions to below minimum standards, air traffic control grounded the airlift. If necessary, the control centers diverted aircraft to other airfields in Europe, some as many as six hundred miles away.[56] Further, if an aircraft missed its landing at Tempelhof or Gatow for any reason, air traffic controllers resorted to the time-honored technique of "stacking." As the aircraft circled to land again, those behind it had to enter the holding pattern over the base at a higher altitude. As more aircraft entered, the airplanes circling to land stacked higher in the pattern. Stacking posed several problems. For one thing, landing a stack of aircraft took excessive time—nine aircraft stacked up to 9,000 feet, for example, took over ninety minutes to land—and the process interrupted the smooth flow of the airlift that Tunner sought to establish. More significantly, stacking aircraft was extremely dangerous, especially in poor weather conditions. A pyramid of heavily laden aircraft circling in close proximity high into the sky encountering gale-force winds, heavy rain or snow, and limited visibility presented a terrible risk of disaster that no commander could ignore.[57]

The solution to stacks of aircraft in the narrow confines over Berlin provided a significant key to the success of the Berlin Airlift as well as one of its most dramatic moments. As of Friday, August 13, 1948, the airlift had been in operation for seven weeks. Tunner had been in command for two weeks, and things were beginning to shape up the way he liked. On that date, he flew into Berlin to present an award to Lt. James O. Lykins, the pilot who had made the most flights into Berlin to that point. Tunner's Skymaster took off from Wiesbaden under black clouds and heavy rain. Ahead, he later wrote, stretched a long line of heavily loaded C-54s. Behind him the line extended back to Wiesbaden and Rhein-Main.[58]

As Tunner's airplane neared Berlin, the weather grew worse. Clouds dropped to the tops of buildings, sheets of rain obscured radar, and everything generally "went to hell." One C-54 missed the runway, crashed, and burned; a second landed and blew its main tires when the heavily loaded aircraft avoided hitting the wreck; a third missed the main strip entirely and ground-looped on an auxiliary runway. Aircraft began stacking over Tempelhof. Berlin Control fitted Tunner's aircraft into a slot at 8,000 feet, but those behind had to enter higher. Soon a huge, confusing, milling mass of aircraft circled in a stack from 3,000 to 12,000 feet in danger of collision or of drifting out of the corridors completely.[59] It was one of the worst backups experienced during the airlift, and Tunner later wrote that he had to react quickly.

"This is 5549," I said. "Tunner talking and you better listen. Send every plane in the stack back to its home base."

There was a moment of silence, then an incredulous-sounding voice said, "Please repeat."

I said: "Send everybody in the stack below and above me home. Then tell me when it's O.K. to come down."

He got the message that time. "Roger, sir," he answered.[60]

Once on the ground, Tunner ordered Col. Red Forman, his chief of operations, and Lt. Col. Sterling P. Bettinger, his chief pilot on the airlift, to work out a solution to the problem. With limited authority—again, the air corridors were under CAA and ICAO regulations—Forman and Bettinger could take only two actions immediately. The first was to eliminate second landing attempts. Airlift Task Force headquarters ordered that all aircraft landing at Tempelhof would be allowed one attempt. If for any reason the aircraft failed to land, it would return through the center corridor to its home station, where it landed and was then slotted back into the flow of aircraft to Berlin. The second decision was to eliminate all visual approach patterns. All landings in Berlin would be accomplished following instrument approach patterns even in clear visibility. In essence this meant every airplane followed exactly the same route and turned at exactly the same point in the landing pattern, and two beacons were established near Tempelhof to define the route. Beyond these immediate measures, Colonels Bettinger and Forman spent a great deal of time studying the procedures for lowering inbound aircraft from the 4,000- through 8,000-foot cruising altitudes to the 2,000-foot approach control altitude for landing. They made little additional progress, however, and stacking still occurred, though the number of disruptions and the length of delays decreased significantly.

The situation changed further in mid-October, 1948, when General Tunner took command of the newly created Combined Airlift Task Force. The CALTF had complete control over the air corridors and Colonel Bettinger became chief of a new Air Traffic Control Office. Almost immediately, the new office reduced the altitude separation in the southern corridor from 1,000 to 500 feet and reduced the distance between aircraft in the pattern to a minimum of three minutes in good weather. This pattern was known as the "ladder" system, since each of the first five aircraft in a block entered the pattern three minutes behind and 500 feet above the

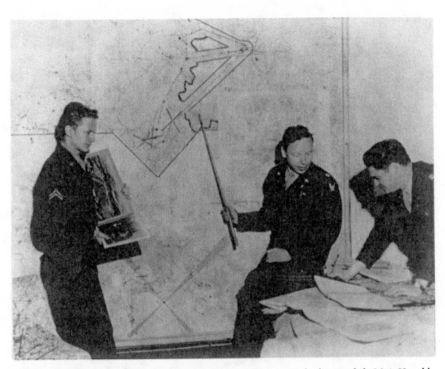

Figure 24. Cpl. Clyde J. Dhein (left) of Sheboygan, Wisconsin, looks on while Maj. Harold "Hal" Sims (center), chief of navigation and briefing, and Capt. Ray Towne (right), assistant chief of operations, discuss navigational problems in the air corridors. Courtesy U.S. Air Force

previous aircraft beginning at 4,000 feet through 6,000 feet. The sixth aircraft then entered the corridor at 4,000 feet three minutes behind number five at 6,000 feet, beginning the ladder again. Aircraft flying at the same level would thus be fifteen minutes from other aircraft at the same level. The ladder system successfully carried the airlift through the winter.

Additional improvement came in March, 1949. By then, the airlift had its maximum number of aircraft and the southern corridor was filled to capacity under the existing flight patterns. The problem of establishing and maintaining proper intervals during take offs and landings remained, however. In the ladder system, each aircraft reached its assigned altitude using its standard climbing airspeed and then established its standard cruising airspeed. Every extra 500 feet required an additional fraction of a minute before the airplane could assume its cruise speed. The number five aircraft at 6,000 feet was thus quite often behind its three-minute sepa-

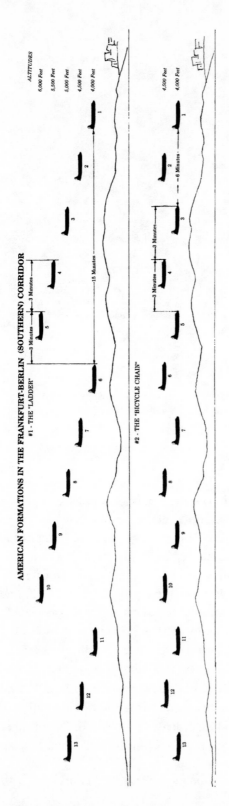

AMERICAN FORMATIONS IN THE FRANKFURT-BERLIN (SOUTHERN) CORRIDOR

#1 - THE "LADDER"

#2 - THE "BICYCLE CHAIN"

The key to increasing the amount of cargo delivered to Berlin lay in sending as many aircraft through the southern corridor as air traffic control capabilities and flight safety procedures allowed. USAFE quickly evolved a system called the "ladder," which separated aircraft by distance and altitude. By the time USAFE and BAFO established the Combined Airlift Task Force in September, 1948, aircraft flying under the ladder system in good weather were spaced three minutes apart at five different altitudes 500 feet apart beginning at 4,000 feet. The ladder system enabled CALTF to operate successfully through the winter of 1948–49. It was difficult, however, to maintain the spacing between aircraft #5 at 6,000 feet and #6 three minutes behind it at 4,000 feet as the aircraft descended to the landing altitude during the approach to Berlin. To eliminate this problem, in March, 1949, CALTF introduced the "bicycle chain" system in which the aircraft flew at two altitudes beginning at 4,000 feet. This system contributed greatly to the success of the "Easter Parade" in April, 1949.

ration from number six below it at 4,000 feet. Physical conflict between the two aircraft was mainly theoretic—it rarely occurred in practice— but the difficulty in maintaining the proper intervals complicated the process of letting the aircraft down to the standard 2,000-foot approach altitude where radar control took over. The descent from five levels to one level required extremely careful management by the air traffic controllers to avoid catastrophe. After studying the process carefully, Colonel Bettinger submitted a paper to General Tunner that recommended reducing the cruising altitudes in the corridor from five to two, at 4,000 and 4,500 feet, greatly simplifying control at both ends of the corridors. Tunner quickly authorized the system, which he called the "bicycle chain."

The final significant change in the southern corridor went into effect about April 1, 1949. Recognizing that Rhein-Main had about three times as many C-54s as Wiesbaden and that under the block system Wiesbaden had to wait for extended periods of time before its aircraft could depart, one of Bettinger's staff suggested that the block system be modified based upon the arrival times for the aircraft at the Darmstadt beacon, the first navigational beacon common to both bases. Because Rhein-Main had more aircraft and was closer to Darmstadt, it was given control of all take offs at both bases. In essence, the main flow of aircraft to Berlin came from Rhein-Main. When Wiesbaden had an aircraft ready, it notified the Rhein-Main controllers, who inserted it into the stream of aircraft from Rhein-Main and then resumed the flow at the proper intervals.

With this final modification in place, the airlift reached Tunner's goals. Under ideal conditions, aircraft in the southern corridor could take off at three-minute intervals, fly at three-minute intervals, and land at three-minute intervals, hour after hour, day after day. At Tempelhof, arriving aircraft alternated with those departing, thus C-54s were landing or taking off every ninety seconds. With one exception, the northern corridor continued to employ the block system because of the presence of different aircraft with significantly dissimilar performance operating from widely separated bases. The exception was the C-54s from the American bases at Fassberg and Celle. These adopted the "bicycle chain" system after Tegel opened, achieving separation from the British aircraft flying in the northern corridor by operating at different altitudes. By the beginning of April, therefore, airlift planners had developed a system that made the maximum use of available resources and techniques to deliver a maximum amount of cargo to Berlin through both the northern and southern corridors.

All of this precision required exceptional expertise, and this factor was complicated by the fact that airlift pilots came from different commands with different missions, especially troop carrier and MATS units. Major efforts went into thoroughly training each pilot in the standard procedures of the airlift and in maintaining his proficiency. This was a complex process since spare aircraft were unavailable for instruction and all training had to be done "on the job." The airlift adopted the chief-pilot system in each group. A "Crew Qualification Board," comprised of pilots with extensive instrument and precision flying experience, within CALTF headquarters developed standard techniques and operating procedures. The keys to the system, however, were the chief and check pilots within each group. The chief pilot was responsible for standardization within his group, and the check pilots under him ensured that the standard procedures were followed. Airlift leaders also selected and trained additional instructor pilots at squadron level, further spreading standardized training throughout the airlift. In the later stages of the operation, replacement crews arrived in Germany at the rate of about 17 percent per month. Most of these crews were comparatively inexperienced with an average of only about 1,750 flying hours apiece. Consequently, an average of about eight pilots per month per squadron required some training. At other times, however, crew turnover approached 80 percent within sixty days, placing a tremendous burden on the training system. The best indicator of the success of the chief pilot system was in the number of accidents per 100,000 flying hours: for the air force overall it was fifty-nine aircraft; for the Airlift Task Force, it was twenty-six.[61]

Communications and Control

Detachments and squadrons of the Airways and Air Communications System operated the extensive air control operation that underlay the airlift. Commanded by Lt. Col. Jess R. Guthrie, who had operated the communications system on the Hump in the China-Burma-India Theater, this system included ground controlled approach radar, which ultimately enabled the airlift to land aircraft around the clock under most weather conditions. In Berlin, disciplined operators staring at glowing green scopes in dark cramped rooms calmly talked the blind "Big Easies" down a steep glide path from which only a minor deviation could spell disaster. Often, the first the pilots saw of the ground at Tempelhof was a cemetery and the runway seconds ahead. GCA was more than equipment: it was a process that required steady nerves and mutual confidence both on the ground and in the air. T. Ross Milton later recalled a final approach controller "who could make you believe, by gentle corrections interspersed with compliments, that your rotten job of flying into Tempelhof was one of aviation's milestones." The extensive use of GCA at every airlift base, aided by the close relationship between the controllers and the aircrews, was probably the most important single technical factor in the success of the Berlin Airlift.[62]

The reduction of USAFE following the war had devastated air communications, and only the bare minimum of air traffic control equipment was in place in Germany prior to the airlift. Berlin had only one GCA set and one radar set for corridor control. Rhein-Main and Wiesbaden also had GCA. Beyond GCA, Rhein-Main, Fulda, Frankfurt, and Tempelhof had navigational aides in the form of radio ranges while Wiesbaden, Offenbach, and Tempelhof had radio beacons. Fixed beacons had been removed from the corridors, however, since these were in Soviet-controlled territory. The available equipment, it was immediately evident, was incapable of controlling heavy air traffic during IFR conditions. The problems faced were daunting. Controllers ultimately had to control aircraft taking off, flying, and landing three minutes apart through narrow corridors with a severely limited number of altitudes available. In Berlin, the bases were close together and the approach and let down patterns intersected in a vertical, plane, requiring rigid air traffic control both laterally and vertically.[63]

Tunner and his staff worked constantly to upgrade the airlift's radar capability, since they knew that this technology was vital to ensuring that the operation could continue through the winter. GCA equipment of the time was huge, bulky, and categorized as nontransportable by air. Air force communications experts broke these down anyway, packed them aboard aircraft, and rushed them to Germany from sites around the world. Ultimately, the U.S. Air Force operated two GCA sets continuously at each base. After the first week of September, communications failures proved a minor problem on the airlift, though they did still occur. On October 15, for example, the GCA system at Tempelhof broke, and in a twenty-four-hour period, thirty-one aircraft had to return to their home bases. By November, sufficient GCA units and beacons had been established at all American airlift bases. The most serious problem faced by GCA during the airlift was the fact that many units had been used well beyond the mandatory three-thousand-hour inspection and overhaul schedule. Some units, operating

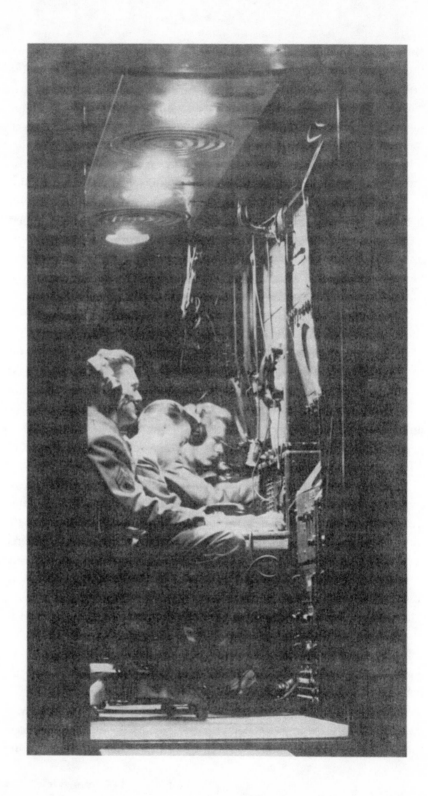

around the clock, were as many as four thousand hours past their requirement for major depot inspection, and it was not until April, 1949, that
depot overhaul of all GCA units began. The sheer bulk of GCA units was
also dealt with, and all GCA units were also made air transportable.[64]

Another important piece of equipment addressed the difficulties controllers faced in spacing aircraft entering the Berlin area. In August, USAFE
installed a "search radar system" on top of the eight-story administrative
building at Tempelhof. A "moving-target indicator" eliminated the clut-
ter caused by the surrounding buildings, and an "off-center radar" scope
was installed for Tempelhof, Tegel, and Gatow. The search radar showed
all traffic entering the area while the off-center scope showed air traffic at
the airfield to which individual aircraft were being directed. This system,
however, did not go into full operation until January, 1949.[65]

In December, the installation of the CPS-5 radar at Tempelhof enabled
operational personnel to detect aircraft over eighty-five miles from Berlin.
This capacity enabled them to space incoming aircraft fifty miles from
Berlin at ten-mile intervals not by adjusting their speed, but by directing
360-degree turns in specific directions. Tempelhof received enough of this
equipment to enable British controllers to give similar guidance to their
aircraft. Airlift headquarters also established six very high frequency (VHF)
ranges at airlift bases as additional navigational aides. The first was operational at Tempelhof by the end of November.[66]

Tunner's headquarters also studied the best airfield lighting arrangements for poor flying weather. Following his trip to Washington, D.C., in
October, 1948, USAF headquarters approved the installation of D-2 high-
intensity approach lights at the airlift bases and diverted to Germany some
scheduled for installation at bases in the United States and Alaska. Air
Matériel Command technicians supervised installation of the units beginning at Tempelhof. Tempelhof presented a special problem because tall
apartment buildings close to the field prevented installing the lights at
runway level; the best approach to the runway was over a cemetery. With
the permission of the city magistrate, engineers mounted the lights in the

Figure 25. (left) *GCA operators intently watch their scopes and give instructions while
acting as eyes for the airlift pilots landing at Tempelhof. Front to rear: S.Sgt. Darrel A.
Wright of Los Angeles, California; Sgt. Richard A. Pagonis of Pittsburgh, Pennsylvania;
and S.Sgt. James R. Gipson of Dallas, Texas, all from the 1946th Army Airways Communications Squadron.* Courtesy U.S. Air Force

cemetery on pylons welded together from pierced steel planking by German laborers. The lights, placed one hundred feet apart, started at ground level at the runway edge then rose in graduated heights away from the runway. The farthest pylon from the runway was seventy-five feet tall, enabling the lights to be visible to approaching aircraft.[67]

The C-54s also received modifications. On August 4, Tunner directed the airlift squadrons to strip the Long Range Air Navigation equipment and other communications gear from the cockpits. While removing superfluous equipment increased the aircraft's weight-carrying capacity, the practical result was a reduction in overall aircraft weight and, thus, a reduction in wear and tear. Subsequently, on August 18, airlift headquarters directed that modern eight-channel radios be added to the C-54s during the two-hundred-hour inspection.[68]

Tunner learned another important problem of airlift traffic control when he landed at Tempelhof during "Black Friday." There was a serious shortage of experienced GCA operators capable of handling the density of traffic flowing into Berlin. Most of those on hand, in fact, were operations officers rather than trained air traffic controllers. The problem went deeper than just the airlift—the air force seemed to have no air traffic controllers. The veteran air controllers from World War II had left the service after the war to work in civil aviation. The MATS Flight Advisory Centers in Europe, Tunner reported to Kuter, appeared to *follow* the traffic more than control it. Most of the controllers at Tempelhof were reasonably good, Tunner concluded, and he thought that the airlift could get along with them for the moment, but when bad weather set in, the lift could encounter trouble. He needed, he wrote Kuter, skilled, experienced operators.[69]

On September 2, Kuter wrote Tunner that the air force had acted on Tunner's request and had activated some experienced civilian traffic controllers. They were due to leave for Rhein-Main that day. Kuter went on to

Figure 26. A 200,000-watt system of high-intensity approach lights placed in a cemetery illuminated a 3,000-foot approach to the main runway at Tempelhof. Courtesy U.S. Air Force

acknowledge that the USAF lacked experienced air traffic controllers and that although Air Training Command had no training program for controllers, it was evaluating the situation. By September 10, nineteen veteran controllers were in place and Tunner expected a significant improvement in his air traffic control centers. He was also able to release some experienced controllers to his GCA units with pronounced improvement in their efficiency.[70]

Throughout the airlift, U.S. leaders feared that the Soviets would jam the communications and radar systems on which the airlift depended. On October 16, a Joint Chiefs of Staff study concluded that GCA could be easily jammed if the Soviets were willing to risk overt interference with the airlift. The instrument low approach (ILA) voice control system and the AN/APS-10 airborne search radar were also susceptible to the same type of interference. On October 19, air force communications experts reported that the Soviets would find it easy to cut ground communications cable systems with the Western occupation zones and to jam radio communications by introducing more powerful transmitters. The United States could do little to counter the jamming, they concluded, except to switch to alternate radio bands; however, the Soviets had also proven quite adept at chasing communications from one frequency to another. The experts recommended that consideration be given to the use of carrier pigeons.[71]

Weather Forecasting

Weather was probably the greatest natural hazard faced by the Berlin Airlift. Pilots faced fog, freezing rain, snow, turbulence, and heavy clouds, all of which posed major problems in Germany. Fog was the primary cause for interruptions to airlift operations, and it had its greatest impact in November, 1948, and February, 1949. The nature of airlift operations required the Air Weather Service to provide exact knowledge on ceilings and visibility for a minimum of three hours ahead of time, a state of accuracy beyond the equipment and ability of the day. At the beginning of the airlift, the 18th Weather Squadron handled all weather forecasting for the air force in Europe. The demand for an organization to accomplish forecasts, to brief aircrews on a twenty-four-hour basis, and to provide special attention to the requirements of the airlift led the chief of the Air Weather Service to authorize a special weather group to meet the increased demands. Ultimately, the 2105th Air Weather Group, headquartered at

Wiesbaden, included three squadrons in central Europe, England, and Tripoli in North Africa.[72]

The 18th Weather Squadron was persistently shorthanded during the late fall of 1948, forcing the organization to limit support to the rest of USAFE so that it could provide proper information to the airlift. By the end of the year, the shortage had been overcome. However, the airlift's insatiable need for weather information during the winter months led to the establishment of a separate unit, the 7169th Weather Reconnaissance Squadron, on November 25. Equipped with B-17s and based at Wiesbaden, the 7169th was responsible for transmitting reports on icing conditions and extreme turbulence in the air corridors.[73]

To develop a single "weather voice" and uniform forecast for the commander, the Air Weather Service developed a Master Control Weather Station at the Frankfurt Air Traffic Control Center with a substation at Tempelhof. Conference telephone capability enabled the Master Control

Station and the weather units at every airlift base to pool their information and to produce as accurate a forecast as possible. In August, the airlift could depend upon a system of six-hour weather forecasts. By the end of the month, however, it was apparent that the airlift required more frequent reports to keep up with rapid changes in the German weather. Tunner directed the Air Weather Service offices in Berlin and Frankfurt to update air controllers and operations officers hourly. This system ultimately proved to be such an asset that a similar arrangement was being developed with the British when the airlift ended.[74]

A more difficult challenge was keeping track of the fast-changing conditions along the corridors and relaying that data back to the originating bases. General Smith began the process on July 9 by arranging for a B-17 from Wiesbaden to fly the Frankfurt-to-Berlin corridor above the cargo aircraft to watch for thunderstorms and to provide immediate reports on bad weather. The first of these flights took place late that evening. In early August, Tunner's operations section concluded that two aircraft in every block should report the weather back to airlift headquarters, thus avoiding unnecessary use of radio facilities within the corridor.[75]

With a disciplined flying pattern established and taught, the necessary navigation and control equipment in place, some advanced notice of weather conditions available, and trained and skilled crews in the aircraft, Tunner's airlift was set to work. A typical flight to Berlin from Rhein-Main began with a loaded C-54 ready to depart. The pilot identified his aircraft to the Rhein-Main tower and requested taxi and takeoff instructions. In turn, the tower notified Frankfurt Flight Control Center, which assigned the airplane a departure time and altitude assignment that the Rhein-Main tower passed on to the pilot. Given his instructions, the pilot taxied to the take-off position, at which point the tower cleared him for departure and instructed him to follow standard climb and heading procedures. Following these instructions, the C-54 departed Rhein-Main and followed the take-off heading until it reached an altitude of nine hundred feet. It then turned south toward the Darmstadt beacon, climbing at three hundred–four hundred feet per minute at 155 m.p.h. At the Darmstadt beacon the aircraft turned east to the Aschaffenburg beacon and continued climbing until it reached the assigned cruising altitude and assumed a standard speed of 170 m.p.h. From the Aschaffenburg beacon, the aircraft turned north to the Fulda radio-range station, where the pilot had his first opportunity to check his position in the stream of aircraft flowing into Berlin. As each C-54 reached the Fulda station, its pilot broadcast the exact time, enabling the aircraft behind him to adjust its speed to maintain the three-minute interval. From the Fulda range, the C-54 entered the narrow corridor to Berlin navigating by dead reckoning since there were no beacons in the corridors. Forty minutes northeast of Fulda, the pilot contacted Tempelhof control, which cleared him to descend to the Wedding beacon and to two thousand feet at the standard speed of 140 m.p.h. At the Wedding beacon, the GCA system—known as "Jigsaw"—directed the aircraft to turn onto the downwind landing leg and descend to fifteen hundred feet. The final approach to Tempelhof was made over the Planter beacon.[76]

With the flight patterns and air routes in the corridors defined and improvements in navigation and air traffic control systems, ground-to-air communications, and weather forecasting, Operation Vittles prepared to face its greatest challenge—the winter weather in Germany.

chapter 4

The Airlift Meets "General Winter"

An enormous logistical endeavor in its own right, the Berlin Airlift was made possible by a massive logistical effort that stretched from the flight lines at the airfields in Germany, through the depots in Germany and England, and to the maintenance and supply facilities across the United States. The effectiveness of this system was critical to the success of the airlift. The most serious challenge faced by the airlift, other than flying under instrument conditions, was the servicing and maintenance of the airplanes that performed the work.[1]

Maintaining the C-54s presented serious problems. First, since the few Skymasters that had operated in Europe prior to the airlift were assigned to MATS, USAFE lacked the means to support them. Supplies and parts for the aircraft were not part of the USAFE supply system, maintenance facilities capable of handling them were in short supply, and few mechanics had experience with the big birds. Second, the squadrons deployed from the United States brought only a limited number of mechanics and few parts with them; most ground personnel and stocks of supplies arrived by ship, taking several weeks to reach Europe. Conditions on the airlift compounded these problems. The Skymaster had been designed and built to fly passengers over long distances, a mission that featured few take offs and landings and long hours at a standard cruising speed. Now, Tunner called upon them to make a large number of short flights carrying extremely heavy loads. Frequent take offs under maximum power strained engines and wore out parts; repeated landings stressed tires, brakes, and the C-54's fragile nose gear. The airlift placed a tremendous burden on engines and airframes and ate up spark plugs, brakes, and tires at an incredible rate. The pounding caused by the frequent landings loosened bolts and rivets and fractured metal fittings. The air force determined its stock levels by calculating the wear and tear on aircraft flying a standard number of hours per year. Skymasters on the Berlin Airlift used up a year's worth of flying hours in a month, placing demands on the system far in excess of anything that had been anticipated.[2]

The limited air force inventory of C-54 parts compounded the situation. There were simply too few parts to stock the supply pipeline and thus ensure a steady flow of immediately available replacements. This short-

Figure 27. Rhein-Main maintained a supply of thousands of tires ready for the C-54s. Inspectors checked them constantly for deterioration. Courtesy U.S. Air Force

age meant that standard practices, like delivery by ship, were insufficient to maintain supply levels, and thus thousands of tons of parts, equipment, and supplies had to be flown from the United States to Europe.[3]

USAFE letter 65-60, published on August 19, 1948, established basic supply and maintenance procedures for the Airlift Task Force (Provisional). Essentially, all common items of air force supply came from USAFE's primary supply facility, Erding Air Force Depot, in Bavaria. Erding also maintained the necessary stocks to support depot-level maintenance for C-54 engine accessories, instruments, surfaces, and electronic components. Task Force Headquarters designated Rhein-Main as the specialized supply depot for C-54 support, and Erding directed the establishment of a sixty-day supply level at that base for the big aircraft. Oberpfaffenhofen Air Force Depot, also in Bavaria, established electronics maintenance for radios and radars. The 7496th Air Wing at the British base at Fassberg requisitioned C-54 parts from Rhein-Main, and this arrangement served at Celle after that base began operations. Finally, Erding supplied equipment for the initial installation of AN/ARC-3 radios in the C-54s; replacement parts and spares for the radio came from Rhein-Main.[4]

In addition to its functions as a supply depot, Erding also accomplished sheet metal work, repaired aircraft instruments, and performed special work impossible at other bases (for example, the elimination of fuel-line leaks). Erding's direct support of the airlift was especially important during the summer of 1948, when it had to send many of its enlisted mechanics to reinforce the shorthanded maintenance crews servicing the C-47s at Wiesbaden.[5]

Maintenance on the C-54s required checks, or inspections, at carefully determined points—daily and at every fifty, two hundred, and one thousand hours of flying time—to ensure the integrity of the aircraft and its safe performance. Maintenance control personnel carefully scheduled these inspections and thoroughly documented the status of the airplane, the deficiencies identified, and the repair actions taken. Aircraft upkeep during the airlift was a continuous process that operated twenty-four hours a day, seven days a week, and precise scheduling followed accurately was the key to keeping the planes flying. The maintenance control unit within the airlift headquarters constantly updated a color-coded control board, displaying the status of each aircraft and providing the overall status of the airlift fleet at a glance.[6]

By the end of July, planning called for field maintenance to be a "theater" responsibility conducted at the individual flying bases in Germany. Oberpfaffenhofen would be responsible for the critical two-hundred-hour inspections until the air depot at Burtonwood in England opened for operations. The one-thousand-hour inspections would be the responsibility of Air Matériel Command and would take place at bases in the United States.[7]

It must be emphasized that mechanics at the bases and depots in Europe accomplished their work in terrible weather. Rain, fog, and cold—combined with poor facilities, long hours, and shortages of tools and parts—intensified by the tremendous pressure of keeping the airplanes flying, made maintenance a miserable, nasty job. The lack of amenities in the form of proper housing and, often, poor food did little to inspire the men. Maj. Vance Cornelius, a veteran maintenance officer at Rhein-Main, reported that the state of affairs was little different at his base than those that Eighth Air Force mechanics had faced during World War II, except that Eighth Air Force had a better supply of parts.[8]

In addition to the living and working conditions, maintenance on the airlift suffered severely from deficiencies in the number, experience, and ability of the mechanics and technicians available, especially early in the operation. Inexperienced personnel was a special problem; not only were they inefficient, but they could also double or triple the time required for even the simplest of repairs, which cost the airlift hundreds of flying hours. The situation gradually improved thanks to better screening of personnel sent to Germany and to an intensive on-the-job training program established by the CALTF. Nevertheless, as late as April, 1949, a newly arrived mechanic fresh from the C-54 course at Keesler Technical Training Center in Mississippi could encounter a sergeant mechanic who had never been taught to change the carburetor on the R-2000 engine. Further, the C-54 squadrons were not manned to support a round-the-clock operation, and the air force was unable to supply enough mechanics, especially trained ones, to provide all the support necessary. Personnel shortages ultimately forced USAFE to recruit German nationals, most former *Luftwaffe* mechanics, to serve with the airlift. Since few spoke English and all lacked experience with C-54s, this step required translating maintenance manuals, technical publications, and inspection checklists into German and establishing an intensive training program; these men made a substantial contribution to the maintenance effort.[9]

The best evidence of the progress made in developing a strong maintenance capability came between April and July, 1949, when the airlift averaged better than 190,000 tons of cargo per month, some 60,000 tons per month more than during the previous four months, although the number of aircraft assigned to Operation Vittles remained virtually unchanged.[10]

Airlift maintenance personnel assignments tended to follow standard USAF practices, but this often proved impossible. The shortage of personnel, especially early in the airlift, prevented dedicating a crew chief and crew to each aircraft at Rhein-Main. Consequently, maintenance planners had to alter techniques to make the most of the scarce mechanics.

Maintenance at the field level divided into three functions. First, each aircraft received a daily preflight check. Second, "turnaround" maintenance provided routine servicing when an aircraft landed and looked into pilot complaints. Third, maintenance personnel conducted routine checks at fifty, one hundred, and one hundred fifty hours. To accomplish these tasks, a squadron had 148 maintenance personnel assigned—often many less men were on hand—divided into three shifts working twelve hours on and twenty-four hours off. Each shift, in turn, was further divided into three crews. An "alert crew," usually twelve to sixteen men, carried out the preflight checks of the airframe, engines, landing gear, fluids, and electrical systems. They also inspected the radio and radar systems and conducted general turnaround maintenance. In this process, aircraft pilots notified the tower of any complaints or problems before they landed. If the problem was minor, the alert crew called for fuel, oil, another cargo load, and accomplished repairs on the flight line. If the work was beyond their capability, they turned the aircraft over to the appropriate crew that specialized in engines, electrical systems, hydraulics, radios, propellers, or other systems.[11] The third maintenance function, fifty-hour inspections, provided preventive maintenance designed to reduce the need for lengthy repairs by identifying and correcting problems before they became serious. This work included a thorough cleaning of the aircraft, the replacement of spark plugs, an oil change, and an inspection of the airframe, engines, and aircraft systems. The fifty-hour inspection usually took about five hours to complete.[12]

With each aircraft flying an incredible number of hours, the Skymasters reached the two-hundred-hour inspection mark quickly. This check was critical to the performance of the C-54 and the life of its airframe and could not be omitted. Since the aircraft had to be removed from the operation for several days, it rapidly became a major concern for airlift plan-

Figure 28. During unloading at Tempelhof, ground crew inspected engines and made minor adjustments. Here mechanics service the engine of a C-47, "The Fabulous Texan," at its hard stand. Courtesy U.S. Air Force

ners. USAFE planners centralized the two-hundred-hour inspections at one location to standardize and speed up the process. They determined to re-open a former World War II air depot at Burtonwood in northern England for that purpose because it had sufficient space and facilities for a complete inspection line. Opening Burtonwood and readying the facilities took time, however, and on August 6 Tunner wrote Kuter that two-hundred-hour inspections would take place at Oberpfaffenhofen near Munich until Burtonwood was ready.[13]

The 1421st Maintenance Squadron (Provisional) began operations at Oberpfaffenhofen during the first week of August and soon thereafter had 7 officers and 236 men on station. The first C-54 arrived at Oberpfaffenhofen on August 7. It should be emphasized that the two-hundred-hour inspection was much more than a casual evaluation of the airplane. It was a thorough review and repair of the aircraft that included a complete cleaning, overhaul, reconditioning, and replacement of worn parts and equipment. First, depot personnel removed all loose equipment, drained the oil, and conducted a general inspection. Second, the aircraft was thoroughly washed down with a chemical solution, scrubbed, and rinsed with water while other workers swept and vacuumed the inside of the aircraft. Third, personnel methodically completed the standard checklist of tasks and completed all necessary work on propellers, engines, ignition, and other systems ahead of the firewall. Fourth, they accomplished the same tasks on all other airplane systems. Fifth, maintenance personnel inspected the hydraulic system, wheels, brakes, and tires. Finally, they serviced the aircraft, replaced all equipment removed earlier, and conducted a final inspection. USAFE also took the opportunity provided by the two-hundred-hour inspection to make other changes and modifications to the aircraft. For example, Tunner ordered all unnecessary navigation equipment removed from the C-54s during the inspection to save weight and, in another case, depot personnel installed new deicer boots on all C-54s beginning in September.[14]

The demand for two-hundred-hour inspections soon forced the depot at Oberpfaffenhofen to divert 95 percent of its work force to the C-54s. Even this number proved insufficient, a problem compounded by conflicting instructions from airlift headquarters, which set the depot's quota at the completion of four inspections per day but would only allow thirteen C-54s at the depot at one time. Since the time required to repair deficiencies uncovered during the inspection varied substantially from airplane to airplane, the wash racks either had a line of aircraft waiting for service or stood empty. The labor force, accordingly, might have to work many hours overtime or might have to be laid off for several days. Recognizing the wash racks as the main problem, Oberpfaffenhofen hired sufficient local German workers in September to handle any influx of aircraft.[15]

In October, Airlift Task Force Headquarters increased the daily quota of aircraft from four to six and assigned Maj. Jules A. Prevost, a maintenance expert from Pan American Airlines recalled to active duty for sixty days, to Oberpfaffenhofen. Major Prevost established a "block system" that increased production slightly. However, this came at the same time the depot began preparations to close down the two-hundred-hour inspection program and transfer it to Burtonwood. In all, Oberpfaffenhofen completed 43 aircraft in August, 108 in September, 137 in October, and 96 in November. The last C-54 completed inspection at Oberpfaffenhofen on November 22.[16]

Figure 29. C-54s in the wooden inspection docks constructed at Oberpfaffenhofen Air Depot, Germany. Courtesy U.S. Air Force

During World War II, Burtonwood had served as one of the largest modification and repair centers in England. Reduced to a storage area for mothballed RAF bombers after the war, the site had been allowed to deteriorate: roofs leaked, buildings sagged, equipment rusted, and facilities decayed. A USAFE survey team went to England in August to inspect the installation, and by the end of the month the Air Ministry had informally agreed to the U.S. Air Force proposal to reopen the depot. Renovation necessary for reopening Burtonwood began on September 1, and Col. Paul B. Jackson, director of supply and maintenance at Oberpfaffenhofen, took command of the 303rd Air Repair Squadron at Burtonwood on November 2, giving the new operation veteran leadership. Personnel at Oberpfaffenhofen built thirteen wooden maintenance docks and six wing docks for the English facility and also supplied a cadre of experienced men, who applied the methods and techniques established at the depot in Germany within the enclosed hangars of Burtonwood.[17]

One measure undertaken at Burtonwood was a weight-stripping program for the D, E, and G series of the C-54s. When weighed, most C-54s were found to be about three hundred pounds lighter than listed in the aircraft data books. The maintenance crews removed roughly twenty-two hundred pounds of excess equipment during the renovation process. The aircraft thus emerged from the two-hundred-hour inspection with a payload capacity some twenty-five hundred pounds greater than before. However, since payloads on the airlift were limited to ten tons, this reduction in weight effectively translated into less maintenance and servicing requirements because of the reduced wear and tear on engines and airframes.[18]

The transfer of two-hundred-hour inspections from Oberpfaffenhofen to Burtonwood, however, severely affected the production program at a critical time. In November, when Oberpfaffenhofen produced 45 inspections, Burtonwood completed only 18. The shortfall was addressed by conducting two-hundred-hour inspections at the flying bases—9 at Fassberg, 6 at Wiesbaden, and 24 at Rhein-Main—a total of 102 aircraft all-round for the month. This situation, however, was highly unsatisfactory since the bases had to use scarce equipment and facilities, in addition to which the work was a severe drain on crews already committed to daily maintenance. The situation remained unchanged for several months and was a primary example of the problems Tunner's operation faced under USAFE. As discussed earlier, without direct control of Burtonwood, Tunner could not deal with the problems himself and had to depend upon USAFE, which, in his view, was unresponsive to the situation. In December, Burtonwood accomplished 49 inspections, just over a quarter of those required by the airlift fleet. Again, the flying bases had to make up the difference: Rhein-Main performed 47 inspections, Wiesbaden 16, and Fassberg 9. The situation was just as bad in January, when Rhein-Main had to conduct 70 of the 155 two-hundred-hour inspections required that month. By then, however, Secretary Symington had made his Christmas visit to Germany, and changes soon took place beginning with the arrival of additional personnel and equipment from the United States. Burtonwood conducted 85 inspections in February, then more than doubled the total to 177 in March, enabling USAFE to end two-hundred-hour inspections at the flying bases in April, although Rhein-Main continued to do a small number each month. Production at Burtonwood peaked in July, 1949, at 256 inspections.[19]

In support of the Berlin Airlift was the worldwide maintenance and supply capability of the United States and, in particular, Air Matériel Command, headquartered at Wright-Patterson Air Force Base, Ohio, with its system of depots at Sacramento, California; Ogden, Utah; San Antonio, Texas; Oklahoma City, Oklahoma; Mobile, Alabama; Middletown, Pennsylvania; and Warner Robins, Georgia. A steady stream of airplanes, engines, and subsystems flowed in and out of the depots as the airlift grew. The depot at San Antonio overhauled Pratt & Whitney engines while others there and at Middletown, Mobile, and Sacramento reconditioned starters. Generators were reworked at Sacramento, Ogden, Oklahoma City, and Mobile, and propellers repaired at Sacramento, San Antonio, and Warner Robins. The last three depots also overhauled communications equipment, and all repaired instruments.[20]

The C-54s themselves had to return to the United States periodically for cycle maintenance. Cycle maintenance was a major inspection and reconditioning accomplished at thousand-hour intervals. At one thousand hours, for example, personnel conducted a basic inspection of the airframe and systems. The two-thousand-hour inspection repeated the earlier review and also checked flaps, corrosion prevention, and tightened all bolts. At three thousand hours, personnel repeated the basic inspection and added reconditioning of valves and integral tank sealing. The thousand-hour inspections continued through eight thousand hours with changes in the components and systems addressed at each cycle.[21]

The depot at Middletown, Ohio, initially accomplished these inspections. The first two C-54s arrived there on August 11 and eight more were on hand by August 20. However, this was an interim measure. Early that same month, the U.S. Air Force made eleven million dollars available to Air Matériel Command to contract with civilian maintenance firms for cycle reconditioning of all C-54s assigned to the airlift (except the navy R5Ds). The contracts went to three civilian firms, Texas Engineering & Manufacturing Company at Dallas, Texas; Lockheed Aircraft Service Company at Burbank, California, and Sayville, New York; and Aircraft Engineering and Maintenance Corporation at Oakland, California. The first of these companies began operations about August 20. The navy accomplished its own cycle maintenance on its transport aircraft at Moffett Naval Air Station near San Francisco, California.[22]

Initial plans, based on 126 aircraft, called for 22 planes to be in the pipeline for thousand-hour inspections and 15 for two-hundred-hour inspections at any single time, and all would be carefully scheduled on a regular basis. The plan worked for thousand-hour inspections for the most part, but in November it became apparent that aircraft that had completed their inspections were not being returned to Europe as scheduled. Inspections expected to take an average of twenty-two days had actually averaged fifty-seven days. Shortages of spare parts, changing requirements for installation of equipment, and the generally poor condition of the planes were principal reasons for interruptions in the flow of aircraft through the inspection pipeline. Further, the shortage of aircrews also affected the return of aircraft. By October 8, for example, eight C-54s that had completed inspection were waiting for crews to fly them to Europe. The demands of the airlift precluded releasing aircrews for ferrying operations. As of November 26, sixty-seven C-54s had been sent to U.S. depots and only eighteen had returned. In the same time period, Skymasters on the airlift had flown 126,344 hours, meaning that 126 planes should have returned to the United States. Fifty C-54s had arrived in theater along with the eighteen returned, so the airlift had not suffered significantly. However, the situation was still of grave concern.[23]

The depot maintenance system gradually caught up with the demand for thousand-hour inspections. By early 1949, the arrival of additional mechanics and parts in Europe increased the number of aircraft on operational status, permitting more efficient utilization of aircraft and the prompt release of those scheduled for return to the United States. Tunner and his staff also brought the problem of delays with thousand-hour inspections in the United States to the attention of Secretary Symington, who focused high-level attention on the backlog. As a result, efficiency in processing the aircraft and accomplishing the repair work increased dramatically while the training of additional pilots and aircrews ensured that the C-54s returned to Germany on schedule. These measures began showing results by mid-February, and by May, 1949, the difficulties attending thousand-hour maintenance had been largely solved.[24]

Replacement Training

The need for additional pilots, aircrews, and maintenance personnel for the C-54s had become apparent during the late summer of 1948. To meet this need, the U.S. Air Force transferred the MATS training school at Fairfield-Suisun (later Travis) Air Force Base, California, to Great Falls Air

Force Base, Montana, in September. Training personnel built duplicates of the facilities at Rhein-Main, Wiesbaden, and Tempelhof. The replacement-training unit opened on October 1, 1948, with nineteen C-54s on hand at the base by October 15. Plans called for the program to produce one hundred crews per month, enabling the airlift to build its resources to

Figure 30. A Douglas C-54 Skymaster comes in low over the GCA van at the Replacement Training Unit at Great Falls Air Force Base, Montana. Courtesy U.S. Air Force

three complete crews per aircraft and to replace 16 percent of the flight crews every thirty days.[25]

Great Falls proved an ideal location for the replacement-training unit. The winter weather was similar to that in Germany, and planners made every effort to duplicate the conditions that the men would face on the airlift. The magnetic course used at Great Falls copied that on the approach to Berlin, and the aircraft had to land on the first part of the runway in order to simulate the short runway at Tempelhof. Sandbags gave the aircrew experience handling heavily loaded Skymasters, and each one had to make three landings at seventy thousand pounds gross weight before graduating. The three-week course provided preflight and flight training for all crewmembers, supplementary ground training for pilots, and on-the-job training for flight engineers. The trainees consisted mostly of former airmen recalled to active duty, few had flown in the previous three years and fewer still had any familiarity with Skymasters. The primary requirement was some experience in multiengine aircraft, thus most who went through Great Falls were experienced bomber crewmen, though not a few former fighter jocks found themselves wrestling the controls of a Skymaster. Construction difficulties and other problems prevented Great Falls from reaching its production goals immediately. Output during the first month was only about fifty crews. By the end of 1948, however, the program was graduating twenty-nine trained crews per week.[26]

The impact of the replacement-training unit on the Berlin Airlift cannot be underestimated. The greatest complaint by most men assigned to the airlift was that they had been uprooted from their homes and families on short notice and sent to Germany on temporary duty status that apparently had no end, since no one could be certain when the airlift would end. The darkest humor on the Berlin Airlift came from an anonymous document called "The Fassberg Diary," which circulated informally by hand in typescript. Ostensibly, it was the diary of a newspaper reporter sent to visit the "abandoned" airlift base sometime after the year 2100 who suddenly hears "weird, unearthly" singing:

> Around the corner of the Hangar came the singers of songs, a ghastly group of beings who may have been human, although the odds were all arrayed against such an eventually. . . . The ten or twelve creatures who came upon me were shrunken and shell-shocked. Their heads were bald, beards long and unkempt. Some wore tattered boots, most had

THANX TO LT. EUSTACE A.A.C.S.

"YEAH, ALL THE WAY FROM GREAT FALLS IN THEM DAMN BUCKET SEATS—"

their feet and legs bound with disreputable looking rags. Their only other garments were black stained coal-sacks, held together by tarnished metal pins in the shape of bars and oak-leaves. On the heads of two were torn, greasy snood-like caps with what must have once been leather visors. The device on these can only be described as a rusty eagle, rampant on a Weld of Wlth. All eyes were hollow and cruelly blood shot, faces painfully gaunt. . . . One of the circle, in a hoarse, creaking voice, said reverently: "A replacement!"[27]

The story of airlift personnel ignored, left behind, and forgotten for nearly two hundred years resonated with many men who felt much the same after only a few weeks in the primitive facilities at the airlift bases in Germany. Establishment of a rotational policy and the advent of replacements went far toward reassuring airlift personnel that they were remembered and that an end was in sight to service under the oppressive conditions they faced daily.

The Army Hauls the Freight

While the U.S. Air Force flew cargo from air base to air base, the U.S. Army moved all cargo to and from the bases. European Command furnished and hauled overland all material destined for Berlin and either provided or hired and supervised all of the truckers, transporters, and cargo handlers that supported the airlift. Its personnel managed the shipment from ports, depots, and other sources in the Western zones to terminal points at Rhein-Main and Wiesbaden; transported the cargo from the terminal points to the airplanes; and, once it reached Berlin, transported it from the airplanes to distribution centers in Berlin. In doing so, the army relied upon a coordinated rail and truck system developed largely through trial and error. EUCOM had learned many lessons during the Little Lift in April, 1948, and had continued to deliver tons of food and coal to Berlin in the interim between April and the June crisis. It thus proved easy to activate an "aerial port of embarkation" at Rhein-Main several days before the Berlin Airlift began and to begin forwarding supplies to that base. On June 21, the Logistics Branch at EUCOM headquarters learned of the need for food supplies in Berlin and ordered trainloads of flour from army depots to Rhein-Main. This supply was thus available a few days later when Colonel Howley in Berlin asked for flour in the first airlift deliveries. Concurrently, the European Quartermaster Supply Depot at Giessen sent additional supplies to Rhein-Main while the 6th Transportation Truck Battalion mobilized the 67th Heavy Transportation Truck Company. On June 29, the U.S. Army's Transportation Corps established a second traffic control point at Wiesbaden Air Base while the 66th Heavy Transportation Truck Company brought fifty-seven trucks and eighty-four ten-ton trailers to Wiesbaden from the Munich area on June 29 to move supplies.[28]

During the first five weeks of the airlift, EUCOM was responsible for procuring and transporting commodities from sources throughout the zone of occupation to the bases at Rhein-Main and Wiesbaden. It operated food trains from the port at Bremen to storage facilities at terminal points in the Frankfurt and Wiesbaden areas. From there, army trucks delivered the commodities to Rhein-Main or Wiesbaden as needed. The highest quality coal available from the mines in the Ruhr Valley was shipped by rail to dealers in Frankfurt, Hanau, Offenbach, and Mannheim, where merchants bagged it in regulation U.S. Army duffel bags. EUCOM's goal was to maintain a minimum supply of one day's airlift of vital commodities at the two

Figure 31. American trucks and their German crews waiting to load airlift aircraft at Wiesbaden, July 20, 1948. Courtesy U.S. Air Force

bases. The Transportation Corps also managed the delivery of aviation fuel from the ports to storage points in Germany. Ultimately, three ships and fifteen hundred railroad tank cars provided the necessary fuel, which amounted to 15.6 million gallons monthly.[29]

The Airlift Field Operations officer had a chart that listed all rail cars and the type of supplies each contained. Upon his request, the air base transportation officer notified local officials of the German railroad agency, the *Reichsbahn*, to make up a train with a specified cargo. Trains for Rhein-Main went to the railhead built at Zeppelinheim, just across the autobahn from the base, to support the airlift or to the air base railhead. At both locations, six-man teams of workers loaded the cargo on ten-ton trailers that hauled it to the control point near the aircraft loading area. This holding and consignment area was of absolute necessity to the smooth flow of the airlift because it ensured that cargo was always on hand for immediate loading on the aircraft. Rhein-Main lacked sufficient warehouse space nearly to the end of the airlift, so between two hundred and three hundred trailers were kept loaded at all times. The control point maintained its reserve of loaded trailers in three lines. The first was a "ready" line of loaded trucks and trailers that could be directed quickly to any aircraft ready for loading. The second "working," or "active," line was ready for loading at the railheads. The third, a "reserve" line, kept additional trucks and trailers on hand to fill any need that might arise.[30]

Army traffic control personnel directed trucks from the ready line at the control point to specific aircraft. When the control tower notified the control point that an empty plane was within ten minutes of landing, the lead truck was dispatched to the proper hardstand complete with a flight clerk and a crew of ten laborers. Officers in jeeps whizzed around the base ensuring that everything ran smoothly. Rhein-Main lacked a loading ramp almost to the end of the airlift, so the aircraft were loaded at their hardstands. Wiesbaden, in contrast, had a loading ramp as well as a more compact physical layout. Ultimately, centralization of cargo at each base by category facilitated the process. The loading of coal and food at Rhein-Main enabled an emphasis on speed and efficiency there. After July 26, Wiesbaden handled a wide variety of bulky, oversized, and heavy cargo that often required the use of forklifts or other mechanical loading equipment. Consequently, loading at Wiesbaden tended to take more time. Additionally, since such cargo was best carried by C-82s and the lone C-74, these aircraft usually flew out of Wiesbaden.[31]

The time factor dictated the use of hand labor at most bases. Sacks of coal and flour could be loaded, stowed, and unloaded more efficiently and quickly by hand. Consequently, most of the two million tons of cargo the airlift delivered to Berlin was carried at least part of the way on someone's back. Displaced persons from Germany or Eastern European nations did the majority of the loading work in the Western occupation zones. The first organized labor unit assigned to the lift, the 4060th Labor Service Company (Lithuanian), began work at Rhein-Main on June 22 but transferred to Wiesbaden on January 1, 1949. The 8958th Labor Service Company (Polish) started on June 30. Other labor service companies included the 2958th (German), 8957th (German) 4052nd (Polish), 4543rd (Polish), 7441st (German), 2905th (German), 8512th (Polish), and the 4041st (Polish). Each of the companies at Rhein-Main had 384 men on each shift, while those at Wiesbaden had 170 per shift. Ten-man teams loaded each aircraft, and each worker was expected to load one ton per hour. In exchange, the workers earned a daily ration of 2,900 calories, which included a hot meal at the air base. Initially, it took as long as five hours to load a C-47, but as the men gained experience and new techniques were developed, the time dropped substantially. Loading the big C-54s took more time, ultimately requiring an average of twenty-five minutes for standard commodities and about forty minutes for awkward cargo like pierced steel planking.[32]

Load checkers were a vital element in the airlift. They were responsible for ensuring that each aircraft carried no more than the maximum tonnage allowed. If they failed in their responsibility, the overburdened aircraft and its crew could be easily lost. Load checking was an air force responsibility, but due to the serious shortage of airmen available for this duty at first, enlisted men from the army's EUCOM School Center were initially pressed into service.[33]

At Tempelhof, the transportation officer for the garrison took charge of receiving and handling cargo at the aerial port of debarkation at Tempelhof Air Base and ensured that the incoming materials did not clog the airport, a practice that dated to the "Little Lift." When the Soviets halted military traffic through their occupation zone on April 1, 1948, Col. Lloyd D. Bunting, transportation officer of the Berlin Military Post, organized a Transportation Corps airhead at Tempelhof. The Transportation Corps airhead received all supplies flown into Berlin during the Little Lift and transported them to U.S. Army depots in Berlin. Colonel Bunting resumed airhead operations at Tempelhof about June 22, when the Soviets suspended land access to Berlin and air supply operations intensified. Trucking units delivered food from Tempelhof to OMGUS depots in the city and also to designated points in the French zone. By the end of July, the Transportation Corps had thirty tractors, forty "6 x 6" trucks, and forty-four ten-ton trailers at Tempelhof. The British provided all ground transport at Gatow, and the French did the same at Tegel.[34]

The mission of the transportation officer at Tempelhof was to provide a flexible organization capable of unloading cargo as quickly as possible without either destroying it or damaging the aircraft. The system as it evolved allowed for four eight-hour shifts with a field officer in charge of each shift. Under the field officer were three cargo directors and one warehouse supervisor, all officers. Each cargo director supervised a section of work crews consisting of one enlisted "boss checker" and twelve German laborers operating one truck and ten-ton trailer combination. Crews of six laborers and a two-and-a-half ton "6 x 6" truck handled the loads carried by C-47s, thus the transition to the C-54 on the airlift facilitated the efficiency of ground as well as air operations. The warehouse supervisor managed fifteen enlisted checkers and one hundred twenty German laborers. Colonel Bunting designed the tables of organization and equipment for the operation to be expandable, enabling the force to grow in increments each time the airlift increased cargo deliveries at Tempelhof by five hundred tons.[35]

At the receiving end of the airlift, it was important to clear the cargo off the base immediately and get it to city warehouses for distribution across Berlin. Timing, again, was the key. Empty trucks waited as each aircraft landed. The "boss checker" on each truck kept an eye on the "Follow Me" jeep and had already turned and begun backing his truck before the airplane had parked. When the aircraft's door opened, the truck with twelve laborers was waiting. If the cargo was coal, empty bags were first thrown into the aircraft, a process that took about two minutes. At the same time, a ramp was set up from the plane to the truck, and half the crew of laborers began sliding bags of coal down the ramp to the other half of the crew who stacked them in the vehicle. The truck then proceeded to the scale house, where it was weighed, and then to the railhead, where the same laborers emptied the sacks into freight cars. German rail personnel then delivered the freight cars to distribution points where the supplies could be dispersed throughout the Berlin economy. Problems at the receiving end of the lift were usually the result of unexpected surges in the number of aircraft arriving, which tended to break down the system.[36] The view of the airlift from the ground at Tempelhof was thus one of well-organized hustle and bustle. In Colonel Bunting's words: "The Air Force loaded planes and organized flights both from Rhein-Main and Wiesbaden bases, and consequently shot cargo to Tempelhof with a double barreled gun at the rate of one plane each 3 minutes arranged in flights echeloned at 500-foot horizontal levels. The sky over Tempelhof was always well dotted with planes circling to land or rising to take off, so that the 'boss checkers' and their work gangs were kept alert. Intermittent bad weather permitted some relaxation and time to better clean trucks and make minor repairs to equipment."[37]

The German magistrate in Berlin provided civilian labor at the airhead under U.S. Army supervision. Initially, these men assembled at Andrews Barracks some distance from Tempelhof, but as the operation grew this arrangement proved inefficient. The U.S. military government then estab-

THIS WAY, WE HAVE 'EM UNLOADED BEFORE THEY FINISH THEIR LANDING ROLL

lished next to the airfield a personnel office that handled time cards and pay for German civilians while the workers reported directly to the Transportation Corps truck center at Tempelhof. Some six hundred laborers began at Tempelhof on June 30, two hundred per shift for three shifts. This number rose steadily to five hundred per shift through November. (One of the great draws, as elsewhere on the airlift, was the hot meal provided to each worker.) Thereafter, the number began to decline gradually, thanks to more efficient handling techniques and equipment; in December, laborers handled 24 percent more cargo with 24 percent fewer trucks and 22 percent fewer workers. In addition to serving as laborers, German civilians at Tempelhof were employed as truck drivers. The EUCOM units at Tempelhof worked hard at reducing the unloading time for each aircraft. Transportation Corps specialists determined the optimum methods of handling the various types of cargo and taught the civilians through training materials and demonstrations. By the end of July, the unloading time per C-47 ranged from eight to forty-five minutes, with thirty minutes being a good average. This figure continued to drop, and at the peak of operations, the work gangs unloading C-54s averaged under ten minutes.[38]

Proper techniques were not always practiced by enthusiastic laborers, however, according to Colonel Bunting: "It was easy to get speed from the German workers, but they liked to carry sacks on their backs or toss them from one to another in bucket-line fashion because it looked more spectacular. Such handling was too slow, too fatiguing, and broke too many containers thus wasting precious contents."[39]

At its peak, the Transportation Corps had 55 officers, 295 enlisted men, 3,000 German laborers, and several truck companies providing the ground support necessary to enable the airlift to operate successfully. EUCOM formed provisional truck companies from combat and service units to meet the needs of the railheads supporting the Berlin Airlift. Each heavy truck company was equipped with 48 tractors and 96 trailers. Army support for the Berlin Airlift included 336 truck tractors and 672 ten-ton trailers. Of these, Transportation Corps units at Rhein-Main and Wiesbaden had 288 trucks and 476 trailers. The number of trucks at Tempelhof, however, declined throughout the airlift as the ground operations became more efficient. Tempelhof began the lift with 108 trucks in July. These had been reduced to 79 by December, 76 by January, 66 by February, 61 by March, and 59 by May. The average number of tons moved per vehicle per month rose from 905.2 in December to 1,225.5 in March. The factors that allowed the improvements at Tempelhof included the construction of better roads, utilization of a single ready line, increased warehouse space at Tempelhof eliminating the need to use trucks for the temporary storage of cargo, and construction of a land pier for handling most cargo other than coal.[40]

Fabrication of a railroad ramp parallel to the Tempelhof railroad switch line, an increase in the number of rail gondolas, and the addition of a *Reichsbahn* switch engine dramatically increased Tempelhof's ability to move coal. The switch engine—essentially a small locomotive—had to be moved from the Transportation Corps freight terminal at Anhalter Yards by truck through city streets. Transportation Corps personnel accomplished this mission in the face of opposition from Soviet military leaders in Berlin. By Four Power agreement, the Soviet occupation forces administered German railroads, including those in the Western sectors of Berlin, and they claimed that moving the engine was a misuse of *Reichsbahn* equipment. American military leaders promptly informed the Russians that interference with the move would be viewed as an unfriendly act, and the transfer took place without further incident.[41]

The Berlin Airlift was hard on truck equipment. Much of the army's wheeled equipment was old and had already seen much service. Axles, bearings, clutches, engines, tires, and batteries broke or wore out quickly. Shortages of parts "deadlined" many vehicles. The army also suffered from a shortage of truck mechanics and, like the air force, ultimately turned to a civilian source for personnel. Displaced men from Poland, overseen by military supervisors, provided much of the truck maintenance at Rhein-Main. The assignment of an additional truck company to Rhein-Main in January considerably reduced the maintenance burden while a new schedule lessened the tremendous demands on both equipment and personnel. Army personnel later concluded that vehicles subjected to round-the-clock operation in harsh weather and poor roads could be maintained indefinitely as long as personnel followed proper maintenance procedures, sufficient spare parts and tires were available, and enough rebuilt engines were on hand to support the machines. In Berlin, all Transportation Corps trucks were moved from Andrews Barracks to Tempelhof, where Transportation Corps and ordnance personnel conducted maintenance on a rotational basis that ensured minimum interference with operations.[42]

Some Problem Cargos

Cargo loading on the Berlin Airlift was both a science and an art form. Weight was everything. The goal was to deliver as much tonnage to Berlin as possible, but the amount of cargo carried by each aircraft had to be carefully determined and even more carefully controlled. A C-54 was capable of carrying fourteen-ton loads. However, one of the earliest decisions was to limit loads to ten tons, thus decreasing the wear and tear on engines and landing gear. The system developed on the airlift called for one trailer to contain the ten-ton load for one airplane. This goal was relatively simple when the cargo for an airplane consisted of a single commodity like coal. In the case of dissimilar cargo, however, army personnel had to properly mix high- and low-density loads to ensure the full use of each aircraft's tonnage capacity. Most bases had platform scales to weigh the trailers and their loads prior to parking them on the ready line. The army exercised additional control by weighing individual packages at the railheads. Without such checks, airlift personnel quickly learned, it was possible to overload an aircraft by as much as three tons, causing severe handling problems during takeoffs (and premature aging among pilots). Additionally, much care had to be given to the loading itself. Freight had to be balanced to maintain the aircraft's center of gravity, and preloading the trailers facilitated the process. In general, the heaviest cargo was placed at the rear of each trailer so that it could be loaded to the front of the airplane's fuselage, helping ensure that the aircraft would not be tail heavy. Additionally, light cargo could be loaded on top of heavier items to prevent crushing.[43]

In contrast to the Hump in China, where gasoline was the major cargo, the primary payload carried by the Berlin Airlift was coal. Many histories of the Berlin Crisis assert that the airlift began with a telephone call from General Clay to his air force commander, Curtis LeMay. In the words of one writer:

> "Curt," Clay asked, "have you planes there that can carry coal?"
>
> "Carry what?" LeMay asked incredulously.
>
> "Coal," Clay repeated.
>
> "General," LeMay apologized, "we must have a bad phone connection. It sounds as if you are asking whether we have planes for carrying coal."
>
> "Yes, that's what I said," Clay emphasized, his voice a shade higher. "Coal."
>
> Another pause, then LeMay rallied. "The Air Force can deliver anything," he promised.[44]

While this dramatic conversation probably took place at some point, it is unlikely that it occurred on the first day of the airlift. Clay's highest priorities for the first few days were food and the amount of tonnage the air force could deliver to Berlin immediately. According to the "Daily Diary" maintained by USAFE headquarters, the first telephone conversation about coal took place on June 29, when Clay called for information about USAFE's ability to deliver that commodity. This date makes sense, because by then the general and his staff knew that C-54s were on the way and had the time to consider Berlin's requirements beyond its immediate needs. LeMay's chief of staff, Maj. Gen. August W. Kissner, took General Clay's phone call. LeMay had left headquarters earlier in the day for a personal meeting with Clay and was stuck at the controls of a Gooney Bird in a long line of C-47s waiting to take off from Rhein-Main. When LeMay reached Berlin and met with Clay later that day, delivering coal was a major topic of the conversation, however, and the first planeload of coal reached the city on July 7.[45]

The significance of the story about the phone call between Clay and LeMay is that it dramatically emphasized the critical nature of coal during the blockade. Ultimately, coal made up about 65 percent of all cargo flown and proved to be a dirty, miserable cargo that caused all sorts of hazards for the airplanes and aircrews. The fundamental problem was coal dust, which filled the cabins and coated everything that it touched, permeating every nook and cranny. The dust corroded control cables, eroded electrical connections, and added additional weight to the plane. It seemed to have a special affinity for damaging radios and navigational equipment but also caused endless trouble for other sensitive gear and could be highly explosive in enclosed spaces.[46] However, the aircrews suffered most and complained of headaches and breathing problems. "Oh, gee, did those aircraft get dirty—filthy," pilot Harry D. Immel Jr. remembered. "Everything you touched was coal black."[47] One of Jake Schuffert's popular cartoons showed a chimney sweep outfitted with top hat and brush sitting in an airlift dispensary, while a corporal announces to the flight surgeon: "He's the new nose and throat specialist for the coal fliers, sir!!"[48]

Attempts to control the dust were many and often ingenious. USAFE initially considered using the B-29's bombing capability to drop coal. The idea had great merit. The aircraft could carry ten tons of bombs and dropping the coal would provide immediate turnaround time for deliveries. On the other hand, the size and speed of the B-29 would make it difficult to operate in the narrow corridors, and suitable "coal bombing" sites in Berlin were limited. Further, operating a strategic bomber in the Berlin area might prove highly provocative and escalate the crisis. Perhaps most significantly, LeMay opposed committing the air force's major combat striking force to a mission outside that role. He agreed, however, to conduct tests on the feasibility of delivering coal in sacks hooked to the bomb shackles. The tests proved that bombing with coal was not the answer—the coal disintegrated into powder when it hit the ground.[49]

USAFE turned to bags and the Quartermaster Corps provided almost 500,000 canvas duffel bags for use as coal sacks. Additionally, EUCOM also procured jute bags in England and in Switzerland, although these would last only from three to five trips compared to ten for the duffel bags. Based upon these figures, planners figured that the airlift required about 850,000 sacks per month at a cost of about $250,000 each month. The answer ultimately lay in the development of inexpensive, multi-ply paper sacks manufactured specifically for the airlift. These were successfully tested in

Figure 32. A loading crew transfers bags of coal destined for Berlin from a British lorry to a U.S. C-54 at Fassberg. Courtesy U.S. Air Force

March, 1949, and were in extensive used by May. Manufactured by German companies for a penny each, the sacks reduced the cost of packaging to about $12,000 per month.[50]

Whether the airplanes carried bags made of canvas, jute, or several layers of paper, dust still escaped and seeped into nooks and crannies of the aircraft, coating equipment, damaging systems, and adding unnecessary weight. Loading crews tried to wet down the coal, but this step only added extra weight without solving the problem. Airlift crews even made some attempt to seal off the cargo hold to no avail. "[A]t present," minutes for the Airlift Task Force staff meeting on August 14 reported, "it is estimated that between three and four hundred pounds of coal are being carried back from Berlin."[51] Tunner's staff directed that every aircraft be swept in Berlin, and that EUCOM be requested to provide personnel for the job. German civilians swept the airplanes carefully after unloading, often collecting several pounds of dust. Still the problem remained. Finally, an imaginative airman created a system that used a hose and the vacuum created by the airplane's slipstream to suck coal dust out during the return trip. Even this setup was imperfect, and well into the 1960s mechanics servicing Skytrains and Skymasters could find deposits of coal dust in inaccessible sections of the aircraft.

Mention also must be made of some thirty-eight C-54s that MATS had modified specifically to carry coal. Stripped of all excess equipment and designated C-54Ms, these planes could carry an additional twenty-five hundred pounds of coal.[52]

Two special cargos became the responsibility of the Royal Air Force, which had access to specially equipped aircraft. Shipping fuel by air had always been a major difficulty. On the Hump, gasoline had been transported in cumbersome and inefficient fifty-five-gallon drums, and the Americans resorted to this technique at the beginning of the airlift. The British, however successfully addressed the problem by chartering a fleet of civilian tanker aircraft equipped to carry fuel in internal storage tanks and able to load and unload the cargo with hoses. From that point on, the delivery of liquid fuel became a primary responsibility of the Royal Air Force. The RAF also came to the rescue in the airlift of salt, an extremely corrosive substance capable of eroding many critical aviation-related metal alloys. The British first made deliveries in their big Sunderland flying boats. The Sunderlands had control systems that ran along the upper spine of the aircraft, whereas in most aircraft these ran along the bottom

"JUST OUR LUCK, A DAMN COAL PLANE!!"

of the fuselage, making the latter vulnerable to salt filtering down from the cargo hold. Additionally, the Sunderland's hull was anodized to prevent corrosion from salt water. Later, when winter froze Lake Havel, the RAF turned to Halifax bombers equipped to carry salt in a pannier slung under the fuselage, much in the same way that it had been transported via camel along the ancient trade routes of the Middle East.[53]

For carrying the heavy equipment required for runway construction in Berlin, the C-82 Packets and giant C-74 Globemaster proved especially useful. Even these, however, were unable to carry some items, and the Pentagon sought out airfield engineer H. P. Lacomb, who had learned his trade in South America, for crucial assistance. A maestro with an acetylene torch, Lacomb cut up everything from caterpillar tractors to road graders, numbered the parts, and had them flown into Berlin, where he welded them together. The rapid construction of additional runways at Tempelhof and the airfield at Tegel, which were instrumental in the growth of the airlift, owed much to this technique.[54]

A final difficulty with cargo had nothing to do with any of the freight itself. Pilferage, while understandable, proved a rather serious problem, especially at Tempelhof, where workers were exposed to commodities that had been rationed for years if available at all. The temptation was too great for some workers, who proved ingenious in their methods of siphoning off and hiding sugar, flour, butter, and other food items, a large quantity of which ended up on the black market. Theft of clothes and, especially, shoes was also a problem; in the latter case, OMGUS directed that only left or right shoes be shipped for several days, ending that particular problem. During the airlift, about one hundred laborers were fired from their jobs at Tempelhof for pilfering.[55]

"General Winter" Arrives

The influx of aircraft, personnel, and supplies, the expanding construction programs in Berlin, and the operational improvements instituted by Tunner and his staff made their mark and the tonnage delivered by the airlift increased steadily. In September, 1948, the combined airlift delivered 139,622.9 tons of cargo to Berlin, an average of 4,655.4 tons per day. During the following month, it delivered 147,580.8 tons, an average of 4,760.7 tons per day. As of the end of October, the airlift had delivered a cumulative total of 332,467 tons of cargo composing 97.9 percent of the city's food requirements, though only 73.77 percent of the coal requirement. The previous week had seen a drop in deliveries due to deteriorating weather conditions, however, and forecasts for the next week projected little improvement. Because of anticipated problems with weather and maintenance and an expected 66 percent availability rate for the C-54s, this trend promised to continue. Berlin had reserve stocks for forty-two days for food, fifty-three days for coal dedicated to utilities, and fifty-two days of coal for other uses. Despite the foreboding situation, military personnel in OMGUS planned to increase the daily food ration in the Western sectors of Berlin by 250 calories and improve food quality with additional amounts of oats, milk, and sugar.[56]

The Combined Airlift Task Force now faced its most serious obstacle: the weather conditions that Soviet leaders, and not a few Western leaders, believed would bring the Berlin Airlift to a halt. "General Winter, the unconquerable Russian general, positively frowned on us," the embattled American commandant in Berlin, Colonel Howley, later wrote, "and we

Figure 33. A line of C-54s from Fassberg being unloaded at Gatow in the early morning mist and fog. The piles of coal along the taxiway are swept-up residue from the unloading process and were later bagged for distribution in Berlin; nothing was wasted. Courtesy U.S. Air Force

could almost hear the Russians guffawing through the Iron Curtain."[57] The major flying hazard was the thick, heavy fog that blanketed the bases.[58] In early November, Lucius Clay flew into Tempelhof through miserable German skies and later wrote: "Thanks to the effectiveness of GCA and its well-trained operators, we landed without accident but with our brakes hot. When the tower directed us to the taxiway we found the visibility so poor that we dare not move farther down the runway. We were unable to follow the jeep that was sent to guide us and finally reached the unloading ramp guided by an airman under each wing signaling with flashlights."[59] Clay's words, "Thanks to the effectiveness of GCA and its well-trained operators," could have been the mantra of the Berlin Airlift that winter. The establishment of GCA units along with high-intensity landing lights and other navigational aides enabled the Skymasters to operate in all but the worst weather and gave the airlift a chance.

The other prerequisite to success was additional aircraft. Soon after his arrival in Germany, Tunner had written General Kuter that "the key to the whole problem is big airplanes and lots of them." The only limit, he reported, was the number of aircraft that the facilities in Berlin could handle. Based on those available and those planned, 225 C-54s based at Rhein-Main, Wiesbaden, and Fassberg—the decision to open Celle would come later—would saturate the corridors into Berlin. On August 13, Kuter replied that plans for augmenting the airlift to 225 aircraft were being drawn up and MATS would be in a position to take immediate action as soon as it received approval from the National Security Council.[60]

At the end of September, American airlift forces consisted of the 60th and 61st Troop Carrier Groups and 1420th and 1422nd Air Transport Groups. The 60th flew its last C-47 mission on September 30 and was replaced by the thirty-six C-54s of the 317th Troop Carrier Group that began arriving at Wiesbaden from Tachikawa, Japan, that day. Pilots from the 60th either joined the 317th or were distributed among Wiesbaden, Rhein-Main, and Fassberg to correct an imbalance between pilots and copilots. Subsequently, in mid-October, twelve of the 317th's aircraft went to Fassberg, where, because of the distances involved, a single C-54 was the equivalent of 1.6 C-54s based at Wiesbaden.[61]

But this force was insufficient, and Clay continued to press for enough C-54s to reach the projected goal of 225 planes. He specifically requested 116 aircraft on September 10 and again on September 23, enough, he believed, to raise the airlift capacity to eight thousand tons daily in good flying weather and an average capacity of forty-five hundred tons in poor weather. As a result, the U.S. Air Force prepared a plan that called for the U.S. Navy to furnish thirty R5Ds, the navy version of the C-54, and sixty crews and for MATS to provide thirty-six C-54s as soon as crews were trained and USAFE facilities prepared to receive them. The air force furnished fifty of the aircraft in September. However, there were continued delays in delivering the C-54s to Germany. Ordered to increase the C-54 maintenance pool in the United States with thirty-six additional planes, for example, General Kuter complied but protested that "MATS cannot provide additional C-54 aircraft to support Operation VITTLES without further reductions in our long-line regularly scheduled air transport operations." Determined to keep MATS aircraft from being siphoned off, Kuter recommended that the Air Staff establish a policy of taking C-54s from commands and that the navy provide additional R5Ds. Then and only then, he advocated,

Figure 34. A line of C-54s at Celle. Additional Skymasters are parked at their hard stands while others undergo inspection and maintenance in the hangars at the bottom. Trucks and trailers parked side-by-side on the ready line are visible at the bottom left between the C-54s and the trains on the railroad spurs. Two C-47s are parked on the turf below the runway. Courtesy Lewis Dale Whipple, Benton, Louisiana

should the Air Staff ask for additional MATS aircraft.[62] Kuter's protest was in vain. Two days later on September 24, General Vandenberg announced his policy to "reorient MATS as completely as practicable to the support of and direct participation in 'Vittles.'"[63] Vandenberg did agree to request additional R5Ds from the navy, but he determined not to take additional C-54s from the troop carrier units assigned to overseas commands for the time being.[64]

Even with this approval, delays in getting Skymasters to Germany continued. Clay, with winter weather approaching, protested the delays on October 4 and again ten days later. *"We have proved that given the airplanes we can meet needs,"* Clay emphasized. *"Please send us the right airplanes now."*[65] He visited Washington again in October and asked for sixty-six additional C-54s to give the airlift a total of 224. Augmentation, however, continued to pose serious problems for the Joint Chiefs, who remained concerned about the nation's vast, worldwide commitments and limited resources. The drain of aircraft had already seriously affected air transport support around the world, aircraft dedicated to emergency operations had already been siphoned off, and the sixteen thousand men sent to Germany had reduced several technical specialties throughout the air force to a critical level.[66] In the view of the Joint Chiefs of Staff: "With increases in personnel and funds the Berlin air lift can be continued indefinitely. Our present military power cannot effectively support the supply of Berlin by air lift on an indefinite basis, however, without such a diversion of military effort as has affected and will continue to affect the ability of the National Military Establishment to meet its primary national security responsibilities."[67]

The question for the Pentagon to answer was the affect of the loss of C-54s on critical global responsibilities. Sending sixty-six aircraft would require taking fifty-one aircraft from MATS, eleven from Caribbean Command, three from Air Matériel Command, and one from Tactical Air Command. The major impact of diverting these resources would be a severe reduction in MATS's ability to support a major contingency operation, "Fleetwood," which called for the transfer of a reinforced combat team to Egypt, a reinforced marine battalion to Iceland, and B-29 bomber groups to Egypt, the United Kingdom, and Okinawa within thirty days in case of war with the USSR. An assessment of the problem by the Plans and Operation Division of the General Staff concluded that enough civilian C-54s could be made available to support Fleetwood, thus the release of the sixty-six C-54s, while it might increase the time phasing of airlifted elements slightly, would not significantly degrade the movement if it occurred. Separately, Caribbean Command protested the diversion of eleven of its remaining C-54s because it would reduce the command's ability to safeguard Venezuelan oil fields and refineries, one of its primary responsibilities.[68]

Despite concerns over the air force's worldwide commitments, the National Security Council approved the request for additional aircraft on October 18, and the Pentagon notified General Clay the next day. On October 22, 1948, President Truman formally authorized an increase in airlift strength by sixty-six C-54s.[69]

On September 18, 1948, the U.S. Air Force celebrated its first birthday. In recognition of "Air Force Day," Tunner determined to set a record in tonnage delivered within a twenty-four-hour period between noon on the seventeenth and noon on the eighteenth, and Clay directed that all air-craft deliver coal for distribution among the German public as a special ration. In those twenty-four hours, Skymasters delivered 5,000.4 tons, C-47s 417.6 tons, C-82s 50.3 tons, and the lone C-74 114.4 tons for an official total of 5,582.7 tons. Added to the British delivery of 1,405.3 tons, the total delivery for the period was 6,988.7 tons of cargo. Much of the success of the Air Force Day lift was attributable to the rapid turnaround times in Berlin, with C-54s being unloaded in as little as seven-and-a-half minutes and C-47s in three-and-a-half. Additionally, the C-74 made six round trips. During one of these deliveries, German ground crews un-loaded just over nineteen tons of coal from the huge transport in twelve minutes.[70] The day-long effort was a potent demonstration of things to come. "I feel . . . sure that the record lift of 5,500 tons of coal carried by your planes on Air Force Day, with all its implications, did not escape the attention of our Russian friends," Secretary Royall wrote Symington in congratulations.[71]

Sir Brian Robertson, however, took the opportunity to express his doubts about the ability of the airlift to continue through the winter. While Robertson remained committed to maintaining the position of the Western allies in Berlin, he believed that operating the airlift through the winter on a scale necessary to supply the city was impractical. He had ex-pressed this view in a long memorandum to his government as early as July 12, and his opinion had not changed by September. Tunner's demon-stration had reinforced Clay's confidence, however, and he replied to Robertson that the best answer to his concerns was the record tonnage delivered on Air Force Day. Clay also told Robertson that he believed the airlift could average eight thousand tons each day in good weather, more with the completion of Tegel. "At present we are holding our own," he concluded, "and my records show that food and total coal reserves equal the quantities available at the start of the airlift." When the additional aircraft requested arrived, Clay was confident that the airlift could carry the city through to spring. Robertson found little comfort in Clay's reply, knowing that Air Force Day had required an extraordinary effort.[72]

Meeting later with the French and British foreign ministers in Paris, General Clay also found deep reservations about the West's ability to main-tain the airlift during the coming months. Again, Clay cited the Air Force Day statistics as proof that the airlift could land over 800 aircraft per day in Berlin (they actually landed 861 planes in eighteen hours), and with that number of C-54 landings, the airlift could deliver more than eight thousand tons of cargo per day on good days, almost as much as had been delivered by train and truck before the blockade. Even with a loss of 30 percent of flying days to bad weather, the general concluded, the airlift would still meet the forty-five-hundred-ton minimum requirement.[73]

But the key was the Skymasters. Clay knew that he had to have the planes requested on September 10 to meet minimum needs and build up reserves for the winter, and by early November he was still seriously concerned over the glacier-like speed of their arrival. Reports on November 9 listed 258 C-54s assigned to Operation Vittles, but only 169 were actually available for operations; the others were either returning to or coming from Germany for overhaul, in stateside repair depots, or training aircrews in Great Falls, Montana. The Pentagon had difficulty finding the aircraft and crews and interpreted the requirement for 66 C-54s approved by the president to include aircraft in the maintenance pipeline as well as those operating on the airlift. Only 44 Skymasters would be sent to Germany under this interpretation while the balance would be placed in overhaul pools in the United States without crew: their availability would depend on the advent of crews and spare engines. In response, Clay emphasized that when he talked about 225 aircraft, he meant those in the corridors, not stuck somewhere in the maintenance pipeline. General Cannon weighed in, supporting Clay and stressing the need for 225 Skymasters in Germany by January 1.[74]

Ultimately, the last 19 aircraft reaching Europe in January, 1949, 3 less than that authorized by the NSC, for a total of 201 air force and 24 navy aircraft in Germany and 67 air force and 8 navy aircraft in the maintenance and inspection pipeline. Counting the additional 16 C-54s at the replacement-training unit and 3 in the pipeline, the air force had 287 C-54s assigned to the Berlin Airlift by the end of January, 1949. Only 169 C-54s remained to service critical air transport routes, aided by 40 C-54s leased from the U.S. Air Force by civilian air carriers. Subsequent experience in January and February, 1949, showed the need for an additional 25 aircraft in the maintenance pipeline, and these had been assigned by April. At its greatest strength, subtracting for attrition, the airlift had 312 C-54s out of the total of 441 C-54s then in the air force inventory.[75]

It should also be recognized that the movement of aircraft was only part of the story, and the 317th Troop Carrier Group's deployment to Celle in the fall and winter of 1948 provided a prime example. The flying personnel traveled with their aircraft, but the all-important ground-support teams had to take a winter ocean voyage. These troops, about one thousand men strong, left Yokohama on December 2, 1948, in a U.S. Army transport ship, *Sgt. Sylvester J. Antolak*. During the 13,200-mile, forty-day trip, personnel from the 317th set foot on solid land twice, once for eight hours in Hawaii and again for dockside Christmas services while transiting the Panama Canal. The *Antolak* reached Bremerhaven on January 9, 1949, where the sea-weary men boarded a train for the rest of the trip to Celle.[76]

"Anchors Aweigh"

Among the new arrivals in November were two squadrons of U.S. Navy cargo planes. On October 19, Secretary Symington asked the secretary of the navy for twenty-four R5Ds, the navy version of the C-54, each with three aircrews. Symington preferred that these be taken from units outside MATS, but this arrangement proved impracticable. Two units assigned to MATS routes in the Pacific, VR-6 based at Guam and VR-8 at Honolulu, were selected for duty in Germany. Marine Transport Squadron 352, with fifteen transports, took over the MATS duties performed by the two squadrons. Additionally, a third navy squadron, VR-3 with fifteen aircraft, provided trans-Atlantic support for the Berlin Airlift, and VR-44, a transport training squadron, provided pilot training for replacement crews.[77]

Initially, USAFE officials were concerned about the decision to send navy R5Ds to Germany, because they feared that step would unnecessarily complicate logistical support. It turned out, however, that most R5D parts and equipment were interchangeable with C-54 parts. Additionally, the navy brought its own stocks and supplied its own R-2000-9 engines using navy transportation. In other arrangements, the air force agreed to furnish parts to the navy from its stocks on the same basis as the C-54s and to repair navy equipment in Germany on the same basis as it repaired air force parts. Navy equipment not reparable in Europe was returned to navy depots in the United States through naval supply channels.[78]

VR-6 and VR-8 began the long trip from the Pacific to Germany by flying to Moffett Field, California, where they traded their high-mileage aircraft for newer R5Ds, installed the latest radar, stocked up on spare parts, and secured winter gear. From Moffatt they flew to the East Coast and then staged to Germany through Lajes in the Azores. Fog, however, socked

Figure 35. Navy crews fuel their R5Ds at dawn. Courtesy Barry Conklin, Denver, Colorado

in their destination, Rhein-Main, and the aircraft ended up at airfields throughout France and Germany. The first R5D, from VR-8, reached Rhein-Main on November 9, 1948, landing in a pouring rain that saturated the base and covered the tarmac with eight inches of water. It was weather typical of Germany in November, but seemed to have been provided especially to welcome the navy. Tunner met the airplane, and he later wrote that it was difficult to tell who was more embarrassed, the navy officers in dress uniforms and spit-polished shoes concerned about stepping onto the flooded ground or the air force general standing calf-deep in water trying to maintain his dignity. The R5D flew its first mission into Berlin four hours after its arrival. The last aircraft from VR-8 reached Rhein-Main on November 15; VR-6 completed its movement a week later. The CALTF headquarters attached VR-6 to the 513th Troop Carrier Group and VR-8 to the 61st Troop Carrier Group for administrative purposes.[79]

Despite early planning, spare engines proved a significant problem. On

November 20, General Cannon reported that the navy squadrons at Rhein-Main lacked facilities for engine buildup. Accordingly, the navy had only one reserve engine but required ten. He wanted the navy to ship nine engines immediately and two more each week. Failing that, Cannon wanted the navy to deliver unassembled engines to Rhein-Main and authorize the assembly, or buildup, of engines by the navy squadrons. Naval leaders, in reply, pointed out that ten engines had been shipped with the R5D squadrons and ten more sent by sealift were due to arrive in Frankfurt by December 5. All engines sent in the future, they reported, would be shipped by air. Further, engine buildup would continue to be accomplished in the continental United States, but engines returned to the West Coast would be given a higher priority. Despite such measures, the shortage of engines for the navy aircraft remained, ultimately forcing mixed installations of air force and navy engines—which had slightly different performance characteristics—on some R5Ds.[80]

The great strength of the two navy squadrons lay in the fact that they were overmanned, by air force standards, and that the units had high-quality personnel. U.S. Navy aircrews proved well trained, and the pilots had considerable experience with GCA, which served them well in the winter conditions in Germany. The first navy flights to Berlin took place in poor weather, and when the weather changed, some were shocked. "I was just a dumb ensign flying copilot," Alfred N. Cave remembered later, "and with the fog I had no idea where we were landing. Then one afternoon the fog lifted a bit as we were coming in. I glanced to my side and saw people looking back at me from fifth floor apartment windows. It was not until then that we realized our approach was down a corridor lined on both sides with apartment houses. Where we stopped was only a stone's throw from more tall buildings in front of us. It was a revelation."[81]

The navy squadrons were also manned with a large number of experienced mechanics. Unlike their air force counterparts, the navy squadrons were expected to accomplish two-hundred-hour inspections themselves, thus VR-6 and VR-8 had more maintenance personnel assigned than air force squadrons, including a high concentration of skilled technicians. In addition, since Burtonwood in England was scheduled to conduct two-hundred-hour inspections for all airlift aircraft, these ground crews were available now for day-to-day servicing of their aircraft. In general, VR-6

Figure 36. R5D number 110 receives a new engine at Rhein-Main. Courtesy Barry Conklin, Denver, Colorado

and VR-8 hauled more tonnage per aircraft and maintained a higher rate of aircraft utilization than their air force counterparts. The two units made an important contribution to Operation Vittles.[82]

Airlift: November, 1948–May, 1949

November was the worst month for the Berlin Airlift. The amount of cargo delivered had risen steadily through the end of October. During that month, the American and British effort had delivered 147,580.8 tons, an average of 4,760.7 per day. But in November the weather closed in on the Berlin run. To deal with some of the winter conditions, Tempelhof had five thousand cubic yards of sand that could be spread in case of ice, and, if necessary, the airfield could call on Berlin's administration for the five pieces of snow removal equipment available. These, added to the equipment already at the field, proved sufficient to deal with snow.[83] However, nothing available could remove the fog. Colonel Howley, the American commandant in Berlin, provided a dramatic description of the situation: "The worst enemy of air operations is not cold, but fog, and we had plenty of that, too—thick impenetrable fog. November and December were bad months. During November, fifteen of the thirty days were almost impossible for flying, and December wasn't much better. . . . Fog-bound November and December were the acid test of the airlift. If we could put these two normally bad flying months behind us without serious disaster to the people we were feeding, and could get well into January, we should know that we had the blockade licked."[84]

It was a close run thing. Deliveries by the Combined Airlift Task Force dropped from 147,580.8 tons in October to 113,587.9 tons in November, the lowest monthly total since July. This averaged out at 3,786.3 tons per day, well below the 4,500-ton minimum Berlin required.[85]

CALTF met the challenge with new techniques. Some worked, others did not. Most successful was the airlift's ability to take advantage of good weather. When favorable conditions appeared on November 6, for example, General Tunner called all of his commanding officers and the RAF's No. 46 Group and directed them to make a maximum effort to take advantage of the situation. On the other hand, the plan to temporarily operate C-54s normally based at Rhein-Main and Wiesbaden from Fassberg and Celle, which averaged better flying conditions, yielded mixed results. On November 10, eighteen C-54s transferred to the British zone bases for several days.

During the twenty-four hours ending at noon on the twelfth, aircraft from Fassberg were the only ones to deliver cargo to Berlin. On the surface, that fact seemed to justify the temporary transfer. However, it proved difficult to service the additional aircraft or provide the necessary field mainte-nance: Fassberg was neither manned nor equipped to handle the extra planes, and it was impractical to transfer additional equipment, person-nel, and parts with them. This experiment was considered a success, in general, and would be repeated, but it was apparent that it was a limited solution to the problems posed by poor weather and was unprofitable un-less conditions elsewhere remained below minimum flying conditions for longer than twenty-four hours.[86]

Ironically, despite the lost flying time and extreme hardships, the main lesson of November was increased confidence in the airlift. While true that the overall tonnage delivered had declined severely, "there was a growing certainty on the part of Task Force Headquarters that the mission could be successfully accomplished throughout the winter."[87] On November 22, General Clay increased the daily airlift requirement to 5,620 tons begin-ning in January. This figure included 375 tons of military supplies for the American, 285 for the British, and 113 for the French garrisons. Coal re-mained the major cargo, 2,534 tons for industrial use and 550 for heating. Based upon these figures, the airlift was running an average of 1,490 tons of coal per day below the requirement. However, Clay expected to reach his goals by the beginning of the new year.[88]

The primary reasons for increased confidence was the success of GCA, the opening of Tegel and the new runways at Tempelhof, the arrival of additional personnel, and the appearance of more aircraft. The airlift had 177 C-54s on November 24, would have 206 by December 1, and would reach 225 by January, 1949. The American forces in the airlift at the end of November consisted of the 7480th Air Force Wing at Celle; the 61st Troop Carrier Group (Heavy) and 513th Troop Carrier Group at Rhein-Main; the 7169th Weather Reconnaissance Squadron, 7150th Air Force Composite Wing, and 317th Troop Carrier Group at Wiesbaden; the 313th Troop Carrier Wing (Heavy) at Fassberg; and the 7350th Air Base Group at Tempelhof with a detachment each at Gatow and Tegel. Two Air Traffic Control Centers were at Tempelhof and Frankfurt am Main. Later, the 317th moved to Celle when that base became operational. The 313th at Fassberg consisted of the 513th Maintenance Supply Group and 313th Troop Carrier Group. At Rhein-Main the navy's VR-8 Transport Squadron functioned as one of the 61st Troop Carrier Group's four squadrons while VR-6 Transport Squadron reported to the 513th.[89]

General Vandenberg visited Germany in early December and found that the men were generally doing well. However, he also heard that in many cases they were suffering greatly because they had been separated from their families on short notice, and many of their dependents were at overseas locations like Guam, the Philippine Islands, and Alaska. In its efforts to establish the airlift and make it succeed, the air force had overlooked the welfare of these wives and children. Husbands and fathers had been whisked off to Germany with little notice, leaving families confused, lonely, and, in some cases, in dire circumstances. Famous was the story of the C-54 squadron winging east from Hawaii to California—the first stop on its way to Germany—that flew over a ship carrying the squadron's families heading west to Honolulu. Vandenberg ordered all overseas commanders to give special attention to this situation. Also, he initiated "Project Sleighbells," a special airlift of letters and packages between overseas dependents and airlift personnel; delivery took place by Christmas Eve.[90]

December saw a significant improvement in tonnage. The weather proved less severe than November, and total tonnage increased to 141,438.1 tons, an average of 4,562.5 tons per day. While the total was still below that delivered in October, it reflected considerable improvement over the November effort and moved the daily average above the minimum required by Berlin once again although it was short of the new minimum set by Clay. On the last day of 1948, 526 flights delivered 5,120.4 tons of cargo to Berlin. At the same time, the RAF delivered an additional 1,007.4 tons for a total airlift of 6,127.8 tons.[91]

At the end of 1948, the airlift was more than meeting the requirements of western Berlin for food and living up to its codename "Vittles." Liquid fuels also had been delivered in amounts far greater than required thanks to the RAF's superb tanker fleet. Coal was a different matter. Deliveries through the end of December proved insufficient to meet the requirements as set by OMGUS; however, enough had arrived to meet most essential requirements. Despite serious supply shortages and maintenance difficulties, the logistical infrastructure that supported the airlift had proven effective enough to keep sufficient aircraft flying.[92]

Nevertheless, coal remained the most serious concern. A news dispatch in December caused a flurry of concern in the Pentagon by forecasting a coal crisis in January. Clay reported that as of December 24 Berlin had a nineteen-day reserve of utility coal and a twenty-day reserve of heating coal. Based on a daily average delivery of 5,141 tons of cargo overall, approximately 3,073 tons of this would be coal, enough to maintain current reserves without reducing allocations to bakers, hospitals, and essential industries. Any increase over the quantities delivered would be added to the Berlin stockpiles. In short, unless there was a major crisis with the airlift, Clay saw no need for concern.[93]

The fact that most of the coal delivered by the airlift went to industry and utilities limited that available to households. As of early January, this allocation totaled 27,000 tons for a population of 2,100,000, giving each family from twenty-five to thirty pounds of coal. Although this supply was supplemented with firewood from various sources, it was still a cold, hard winter for most Berliners. The food supply, on the other hand, appeared to be less of a problem. On the average, Berliners received 2,300 calories per person per day, about 10 percent of which was "scrounged." Nutrition had generally improved during the blockade despite a shortage of fresh vegetables, especially potatoes, thanks to the use of vitamin pills and dehydrated foodstuffs. However, if Berliners had a serious complaint about the airlift, it was that it should bring in a greater variety and quantity of food.[94]

The Soviet blockade also severely reduced the availability of electricity. Most Berliners received power for no more than four hours each day at extremely odd hours on a weekly rotation. The few substitutions available were extremely expensive, and one dentist's wife pedaled a bicycle to generate the electricity for her husband's drill. The vast majority of Berliners, though, had to adjust their daily habits. For some, this meant that all meals for a day might have to be cooked after midnight. The blockade reduced streetcar service by 40 percent and subway service by 50 percent. The Soviets did not cut service to the elevated railway, the S-Bahn, because they had to use it themselves, so most Berliners shifted to that mode of transportation wherever possible. Social life almost ended after dark, except in certain quarters. Possibly most important was the crippling effect of the blockade on the rebuilding of Berlin. The shortage of materials almost ended the construction of residential housing for the time being. Unemployment was a serious concern, not only to the Berliners without a paycheck, but to the Western authorities as well. Of some 900,000 Berliners gainfully employed, the blockade threw some 10 percent out of work. Since the unemployed received a ration card, this factor had little effect from a nutritional perspective. However, enforced idleness posed a serious morale problem and threatened public and political stability.[95]

Yet, the vast majority of the Berliners, showing the tremendous strength and will that had enabled them to survive the devastating Allied bombing campaign against the city just a few years earlier, refused to buckle. It would be wrong to write, as many have, that "morale remained high." However, it is fair to say that, despite everything, the population of the Western sectors of the city exhibited a resilient, hard-bought toughness that rejected surrender to the Soviet Union and ensured the success of the airlift. An army intelligence summary on January 13, 1949, observed: "Faith in the airlift and in the willingness of the Western Powers' determination to remain in the city has increased since the beginning of the winter." This assessment accurately concluded that "unless the situation becomes definitely worse, the population of the West sectors of Berlin may be relied upon to support the policy of the Western Powers through this winter."[96]

January promised victory as milder winter weather held, more C-54s arrived and the maintenance system improved, the supply of spares and parts continued to grow, and the management principles Tunner had instituted took firm hold. The cargo totals for the month jumped to 171,959.2 tons, an average of 5,547 tons per day.[97]

The weather in February returned to the conditions that had made November so difficult, and thus total tonnage dropped somewhat. However, the strength of the airlift was such that it still delivered 152,240.7 tons, an average of 5,437.2 per day. The recovery in March was spectacular, though. Tonnage jumped dramatically to 196,160.7 tons, an average of 6,327.8 tons each day—from then on the airlift never faltered. The amount of cargo delivered to Berlin increased each month through July, reaching a total during that month of 253,090 tons, an average of 8,164.2 tons daily.[98]

On February 18, the airlift delivered the one millionth ton of cargo to Berlin. Dean Acheson, who had replaced George C. Marshall as secretary of state, recognized the feat and the importance of Operation Vittles. The airlift had "sustained the physical existence and elemental human rights of more than two million Berliners," he wrote General Clay. In doing so: "The success of the Airlift has enabled the Western Powers to maintain their rights and discharge their obligations as prescribed by solemn international agreement and has given encouragement to the efforts of the

Democratic peoples of Europe to resist the use of lawless force. Our Government offers its grateful commendation, in particular to the personnel of the Air Forces and to all units civilian and military. We are gratified that German citizens have given their unstinted help."[99]

Challenges still remained, however. A crash on March 17 and another airplane undergoing major repairs reduced the airlift fleet below the 225 Skymasters required to maintain the air bridge. Consequently, the Joint Chiefs considered the transfer of two additional C-54s per month from Far East Air Force (FEAF) beginning in April to cover attrition. FEAF immediately transferred two C-54s undergoing depot repair in the United States and planned to provide the additional aircraft through the same mechanism. This decision reduced FEAF to twenty C-54s, the minimum number, FEAF's commander figured, needed to meet essential requirements.[100]

The success of the airlift amazed and appalled Soviets leaders. They had counted on "General Winter" to bring the bridge of airplanes to a halt. The strategy had failed, and, after the problems of November had been overcome, the steady drone of Pratt & Whitney engines at three-minute intervals was about as welcome to them as acid rock to the ears of a connoisseur of Mozart. Indeed, it appeared to some of Marshal Sokolovsky's staff that the C-54 traffic pattern, which passed over the Soviet headquarters building, was a calculated measure designed to thumb the American nose at them. A former Soviet officer remembered years later, "One would appear overhead, another would disappear over the horizon, and a third emerge, one after another, without interruption, like a conveyor belt."[101]

The airlift continued to meet the minimum requirements of the civilian population. Public health records for Berlin documented a consistent improvement in the people's health since 1945, and despite Soviet actions, the population in the Western sectors was better off in terms of communicable diseases than during the previous winter. OMGUS concluded that, "On the premise that the airlift tonnage request is met, the loss of supplies from surrounding Soviet areas would not materially reduce the standard of living now existing in Berlin's western sectors during the winter months."[102]

The "Easter Parade"

The most dramatic twenty-four hours of the airlift took place on April 15–16, 1949. By April, Tunner's conveyor belt was humming like a finely tuned machine. The general had 154 assorted British aircraft and 200 Skymasters operating in the corridors. Fifty charts in his headquarters, continuously maintained, provided a clear picture of the airlift around the clock. "Things were going too well," he later wrote. "It was necessary, I thought, to do something to shake up the command." Competition, once again would provide the answer. Tunner determined to pit his units against each other in a full-scale assault on the Berlin Airlift's tonnage record.[103]

The CALTF staff planned in great secrecy. If they had announced a quota and failed to achieve it for any reason, the Soviet propaganda machine would have trumpeted that failure to the world. They selected the weekend of April 15–16, because of the promise of ideal weather, and concentrated their efforts on one cargo, coal, although some mixed loads of other commodities were also transported. The Army's Transportation Corps assured Tunner's staff that well over ten thousand tons of coal had been stockpiled and would be readily available to the loading bases. Other planners massaged the maintenance schedule, ensuring that the largest number of aircraft possible were available on the target dates.

At noon on Saturday, April 15, sergeants from the operations offices at each base posted the quotas for the next twenty-four hours. Since the quotas were divided among the squadrons, the ultimate goal was not readily apparent, but rumors had gotten out and everyone on the airlift sensed that something big was taking place. Everyone, Tunner later wrote, from the colonels in command down to the laborers loading aircraft for little more than a hot meal, put all their efforts into driving up the tonnage figures. Tunner first flew into Tempelhof to watch the operations from that end. He then went from base to base in the American and British zones observing, cajoling, prodding, and pushing.

The intense effort by everyone on the airlift succeeded. Seconds before the last aircraft left Rhein-Main on Sunday, April 16, someone totaled the final figures and, with a brush and bucket of red paint, inscribed "RECORD TONNAGE 12941 FLTS 1383" on the Skymaster's nose. The Easter Parade was a spectacular success, showcasing airlift's capacity to deliver huge amounts of cargo and demonstrating conclusively the ability of Tunner's system to manage an unprecedented density of traffic. The Easter Parade also had a side benefit. Some worried that the extra strain of setting this record would affect the subsequent performance of the aircrews. In fact, as Tunner anticipated, the opposite occurred. For the ten days prior to the record, the airlift averaged 6,729 tons per day. The average beginning after the Easter

Figure 37. On April 16, 1949, the airlift established a new record for delivering cargo to Berlin, a feat known as "The Easter Parade." Courtesy U.S. Air Force

Parade, however, was 8,893 tons per day.[104] Tunner and his staff had known for months that the airlift would succeed. The Easter Parade provided dramatic demonstration of that fact.

Contingency Planning: Airlift to 1952

As of early December, 1948, American leaders could see little evidence that the Berlin Blockade would end soon. On December 7, Secretary Forrestal directed the Department of the Army to take the lead in developing plans to continue the airlift if the Soviets maintained the blockade for up to three years. Secretary of the Army Royall asked General Clay to provide data projecting the average daily tonnage requirements, the additional funds required beyond normal requirements, the type of ground equipment needed, and the number of additional military personnel required.[105]

The most important point was that the amount of tonnage had to be increased. One way to increase tonnage had already been explored. In mid-September, Air Commodore Waite—who had proposed an airlift to

Berlin in June—concluded that with the existing organization, basing, and operations, the airlift would fail and all stocks in Berlin would be exhausted about January 28, 1949. Waite calculated, however, that if the airlift was equipped with 240 C-54s, then the airlift could "scrape through" provided that the rate of flow into Berlin could be increased. To attain this increased rate of flow, Waite proposed to base U.S. aircraft in the British zone of occupation and retire the less-efficient British aircraft from the airlift. American planners reached the same conclusion separately at about the same time. On September 28, Clay wrote Vandenberg that to reach the maximum tonnage possible, it would be best to use one standard airplane, the C-54, flying from bases in the British zone. The same number of C-54s flying the shorter corridor from the British zone could deliver 50 percent more cargo than those operating through the southern corridor. Mathematically, operating the C-54s out of British bases and reducing the British operation to ground support for the U.S. planes was a logical plan. Ultimately, however, CALTF continued to increase tonnage through other measures, and the idea of making the airlift an exclusively American effort proved unnecessary. The CALTF did base Skymasters at Fassberg and Celle to take advantage of the shorter distance and better weather furnished by the British zone, but the Royal Air Force continued to make its important contribution to the operation.[106]

In response to Secretary Royall's December request, CALTF planners projected Berlin's needs between April 1, 1949, and June 30, 1950, to determine the requirements necessary to ensure a significant improvement in Berlin's living conditions and a reasonably high level of employment for Berliners. The planners concluded that both goals would be possible within a daily average delivery of 8,685 tons of cargo. This increased tonnage would allow the basic ration to be raised from 1,990 to 2,100 calories and food stocks in Berlin to be increased from forty-two to forty-five days. More variety could be provided by such measures as delivering one-third of the potato ration in the form of fresh potatoes during winter months. The greater tonnage also allowed for a substantial increase in coal for domestic heating, a measure important for morale. Additional coal could be devoted to increased electrical production, enabling the domestic electricity ration to be increased from four to five hours daily, and eventually to six hours. The rest of the tonnage would go primarily to commercial use, including gasoline for industrial users, electricity for longer running hours for streetcars, and diesel fuel for buses. More tonnage would also be devoted to importing raw materials and consumer goods into Berlin. Beginning in July, 1949, airlift tonnage would have to increase to 11,249 tons daily.[107]

Over the next few months, the CALTF planners concluded that meeting these demands with the existing airlift would require the complete commitment of the air force's entire C-54 fleet. Further, their figures were based upon a 65 percent in-commission rate. The existing rate was 52.77 percent, so a major expansion of maintenance and support facilities would be necessary along with a huge addition of parts, equipment, and spares. The need for additional aircrews and support personnel was equally dramatic. CALTF planners also recommended further rationalizing the airlift by establishing standard bases of sixty aircraft. Experience had shown that sixty was the ideal number of planes that could be serviced with maximum efficiency at one location. In January, the airlift was operating from seven bases in the British and American zones; one more would have to be opened to support the expanded lift. Based on its studies, CALTF planners concluded that the airlift could be sustained as long as the C-54s lasted.[108]

The end of the Skymasters' useful life, however, was fast approaching. By November, 1952, they would reach 14,400 hours, exceeding their "second line life." Flying them beyond that date could be done only with excessive operational risks. New aircraft on the horizon—but not yet in the inventory—would have to begin reaching Germany in 1950 to continue the airlift beyond 1952. The "48 Group Program," then in effect for fiscal year 1949, included the delivery of fifty four-engine Boeing C-97 Stratofreighters between July, 1949, and March, 1950, and if Congress approved the air force's proposed "57 Group Program," a further fifty-four C-97s would be purchased. More significantly, the "48 Group Program" also authorized the purchase of giant Douglas C-124 Globemaster IIs, a development of the C-74. The procurement schedule called for the first of these aircraft to reach the flight line in May, 1950. CALTF planners concluded that delivery of the two new planes on schedule with a minimal amount of "teething problems" along with a major construction program on runways, taxiways, and other infrastructure beginning in the summer of 1949 would enable the airlift to continue through at least 1952 and possibly indefinitely should that unlikely event become necessary.[109]

Planning for an extended airlift went far enough that on December 20, Maj. Gen. Robert W. Douglass, Jr., General Cannon's chief of staff at USAFE headquarters, asked the Air Staff for one engineer aviation group head-quarters and service company, two engineer aviation battalions, and one engineer maintenance company. These were required, he reported, to construct the runways, parking facilities, and other ground infrastructure necessary as the C-54s were phased out and replaced by larger aircraft during 1950 and 1951.[110]

Additionally, on January 1, Tunner submitted a proposal to modify the organization and deployment of the CALTF in preparation for a long-term effort. Organizationally, he wanted further integration and collocation in his headquarters. The British and American staff sections responsible for operational planning and control were completely integrated, and he wanted that integration extended to the sections dealing with traffic, communications, and air installations (works). He also recommended unification of command in the Berlin area through the appointment of a single officer to coordinate activities at all three bases and the Berlin approach control center. Operationally, Tunner proposed taking advantage of the shorter distance between the British zone of occupation and Berlin by shifting all but sixty American C-54s to British bases. This step would require opening and manning an additional base in the north. Further, if most of the airlift operated out of that zone, he should be there also, and Tunner proposed relocating Combined Airlift Task Force headquarters to a British base. Finally, Burtonwood remained a problem; Tunner believed that his aircraft lost too much time when it came their turn to undergo inspection at the base in England. Moving most of the C-54s to the British zone would open up the American bases, and Tunner proposed transferring two-hundred-hour inspections back to Rhein-Main.[111]

Tunner's proposals were largely stillborn, however. General Cannon approved the unification of command in Berlin and greater integration of the CALTF staff, except for an air installations (works) section. However, Cannon opposed the proposal to move most airlift operations out of the American zone and the use of Rhein-Main, an active operational base, for two-hundred-hour inspections. He preferred to make Burtonwood more efficient, but if that failed and a depot had to be developed in Germany, he wanted it at some location other than the primary airlift base.[112] Of more significance, though, were events early in 1949 that seemed to indicate the airlift might not have to continue much longer.

chapter 5

"Blockade Ends, Airlift Wins"

By December, 1948, Joseph Stalin appears to have recognized that his policies in Germany had failed. His actions had contributed to and even hastened the death of his goal of a united Germany within the Soviet orbit. Throughout the fall and winter of 1948–49, the Western powers and German leaders continued the process of creating a separate West Germany, and there was simply nothing that the Soviet Union could do to halt, slow, or divert the process. Beyond Germany, the establishment of the Western Alliance through the North Atlantic Treaty Organization (NATO) was firmly on track, and neither Soviet threats nor offers could alter the process. The determining factor in the USSR's failure was the Berlin Airlift. It had succeeded, leaving the Soviet dictator with only the options of direct, brute force or a diplomatic settlement. Direct action risked war with the United States, something Stalin refused to consider. Negotiation was the only alternative. The Berlin Airlift, however, ensured that the Western allies could negotiate without haste or undue pressure.[1]

The Western counterblockade (mentioned earlier) of eastern Germany imposed in response to the USSR's isolation of Berlin hurt the eastern occupation zone and Soviet standing in Germany more than the Soviet blockade hurt the western zones of occupation. Eastern Germany lacked sufficient quantities of essential industrial materials like coal and steel, and there was no equivalent to the airlift that could supply these necessary commodities. Western Germany further benefited from its access to the industrial resources of the West and, indirectly, from the aid provided through the Marshall Plan. From the beginning of the Berlin Crisis, Clay firmly believed that this situation would ultimately force Soviet leaders to put an end to the blockade. Others expressed that opinion as well. In December, a key advisor on Germany to the French government, François Seydoux de Clausonne, in a speech monitored closely by Soviet intelligence, conjectured that the Berlin Blockade was worse than a failure—it was a positive embarrassment to the Soviet Union. Lack of coal from the Ruhr alone would place the Soviet zone in a disastrous economic condition that would contrast dramatically with economic success in Western Germany. After the blockade ended, a telegram from the American ambassador in Moscow concluded, "Berlin blockade backfired, airlift was a phenomenal practical and political success and counter-blockade pinched seriously."[2] By early 1949, the economy of the Soviet zone in Germany had stagnated and rumors soon spread that the blockade would be lifted.[3]

Stalin had already begun to retreat from his stance on Germany by then. In mid-December, 1948, he counseled German communist leaders to temper their anti-Western activities. He lost little in doing so, because their efforts at rabble-rousing and intimidation had accomplished little more than to alienate noncommunist German leaders, harden Western resolve, and further emphasize the divisions between East and West in Germany and Berlin. Stalin offered the German communists solace, emphasizing that Germany could be united at the proper time once the Berlin problem was resolved. Six weeks later, on January 30, 1949, Stalin signaled his intentions to the West when he told Kingsbury Smith, European director of the American International News Service, that the blockade could be lifted in exchange for a Western promise to refrain from establishing a West German state and for negotiation of a USSR–US nonaggression pact. He made no mention of the currency issue. The Western powers took note of the exchange but preferred to wait for a more specific proposal. Again, waiting was an option thanks to the Berlin Airlift.[4]

The break began in the United Nations in February, 1949, when the U.S. delegate, Philip Jessup, asked the Soviet delegate, Jacob Malik, whether Stalin's omission of currency as an issue in the statement to Kingsbury Smith was accidental. Malik responded that he did not know but would inquire. A month went by. On March 5, Stalin replaced his two top policy officials, Foreign Minister Vyacheslav Molotov and Minister of Foreign

Trade Anastas Mikoyan, with Andrey Vishinsky and Mikhail A. Menshi-kov, a drastic change that Moscow watchers saw as indicative of a significant shift in the course of Soviet foreign policy. Ten days later on March 15, Malik told Jessup that Stalin's omission had been deliberate. At Jessup's request, Malik agreed to ask for further information concerning the Soviet leader's views on lifting the blockade and convening a meeting of the Council of Foreign Ministers. Malik returned on March 21 with details that suggested an agreement was possible. During subsequent talks, the Soviets proposed that the blockade could end in exchange for a meet-ing of the Council of Foreign Ministers that would discuss the future of Germany. Initially, Soviet diplomats demanded that the West refrain from creating a separate German state out of the western zones until after any meeting of the Council of Foreign Ministers concluded; however, they later abandoned even this requirement.[5]

Lucius Clay also observed the changes in Soviet policy, punctuated on March 29 when General of the Army Vassily Chuikov replaced Marshal Sokolovsky, who returned to Moscow and a succession of higher posts that would eventually see him become the Soviet equivalent of chairman of the Joint Chiefs of Staff. When Chuikov, who had commanded Soviet forces in the battle for Berlin in 1945, arrived in Germany, he sent Clay a personal letter, a courtesy so unexpected that Clay concluded it represented a possible prelude to a settlement of the Berlin Blockade.[6]

On May 4, 1949, in exchange for a meeting of the Council of Foreign Ministers that would "consider questions relating to Germany" and the lifting of the counterblockade of eastern Germany, the Soviet negotiators reached an agreement with the Western allies. The USSR lifted the block-ade on May 12, 1949.[7] The announcement of victory to the secretary gen-eral of the United Nations was simple, yet impressive: "We, the Represen-tatives of France, the United Kingdom and the United States of America on the Security Council, have the honor to request that you bring to the attention of the members of the Security Council the fact that our Gov-ernments have concluded an agreement with the Union of Soviet Social-ist Republics providing for the lifting of the restrictions which have been imposed on communications, transportation and trade with Berlin."[8]

In automatic, face-saving mode, Soviet propaganda brazenly declared that the end of the Berlin Blockade was a victory for the USSR. Soviet or-gans proclaimed that the will of the German people had proven too strong for the "planners and inciters [of a] new war," that the talks between Jessup

Figure 38. At Rhein-Main, an aircrew from the 330th Troop Carrier Squadron celebrates news of the official lifting of the Berlin Blockade while their aircraft is loaded for another trip to the German city. Left to right: S.Sgt. Claude Richeson, San Antonio, Texas, a veteran of 62 missions; 1st Lt. James R. Davis, Los Angeles, California, a veteran of 110 missions; and Capt. Alfred Rumberg, Phoenix, Arizona, a veteran of 90 missions. Courtesy U.S. Air Force

and Malik in the United Nations were "a reversal of attitude on [the] part of [the] U.S.," and that the "warmongers had proven uncertain in the face of the growing popular peace movement." It was standard rhetoric that would become commonplace during the next forty years.[9]

Clay, for one, refused to celebrate too early. "There is one important thing to remember," he wrote Assistant Secretary of the Army Tracy Voorhees, "The blockade was broken by airpower, and the airpower should be maintained in full until the Council of Foreign Ministers has completed its deliberations."[10] It was well that he took this stance. Despite their defeat, Soviet leaders sought to continue the option of blockading Berlin as a threat to the West. The Council of Foreign Ministers meeting, held in Paris between May 23 and June 20, 1949, failed to reach an agreement on

Western transportation rights, and interference with overland transport continued over the next months. The Soviets began imposing new restrictions even before the meeting in Paris began: for example, all rolling stock on the railroads had to be pulled by Soviet engines, West German vehicles could not travel on the autobahns, and Soviet officials refused to issue permits for barge traffic. On May 20, fifteen thousand West German railroad workers went on strike against the Russian authorities controlling the railroads. The strikers demanded payment of wages in West German currency, the rehiring of fired workers, and recognition for their union. The protest halted rail traffic and led to bloody confrontations between strikers and Soviet-sponsored strikebreakers. With the railroads paralyzed, the airlift stepped into the breach once again.[11]

Clay, Robertson, and Koenig were determined to continue the Berlin Airlift until all transport systems between the Western zones and Berlin were completely open and a substantial reserve had been built up in Berlin. The military governors agreed that a stockpile of 1.1 million tons of essential supplies would provide a four- to five-month reserve for the Western sectors, and that this goal would be achieved around mid-August. The airlift would continue at least until then. The military governors further recommended that two U.S. Air Force troop carrier groups and two Royal Air Force heavy transport squadrons remain in Germany and that all three Western powers maintain the facilities in their zones and sectors in such a condition that they could be activated easily in case of an emergency.[12]

Clay, however, had little time left in Germany. Exhausted and worn out by January 5, 1949, but knowing that the airlift was a success, he had requested a retirement date. He felt it his duty to remain until the blockade was lifted, however, to ensure continuity of policy and avoid adversely affecting German morale with a premature departure. A final parade was held on May 4 after which Clay departed Germany, retiring from the U.S. Army on May 15. He left Germany as a popular and respected commander and perhaps the best friend that the German people had in the early postwar era. As in the case of Douglas MacArthur in Japan, perhaps no single individual did more to shape modern Germany than Lucius DuBignon Clay. Yet, in many ways it had been a bittersweet experience. According to his biographer, Jean Edward Smith: "For Clay, the Occupation of Germany was a tragic international failure, and a significant personal success. Wartime harmony had given way to Cold War rivalry. But an independent West German state was in the offing, and Berlin had been defended successfully. If competition with the Soviet Union was inevitable, Clay had reversed the odds in the West's favor."

Dismantling the Airlift

On July 28, 1949, President Truman directed that the Berlin Airlift begin phasing out its operations on August 1 provided that arrangements were made so that an airlift could be reestablished and brought to full capacity within ninety days in the event of an emergency. On the following day, the United States and Great Britain issued a press release announcing that the airlift would end but affirming that sufficient air forces and installations would remain in Germany to reestablish the airlift on short notice.[13]

The airlift disappeared almost as rapidly as it had appeared. The phased plan called for the U.S. units operating in the British zone and those from the navy to close operations and return to the United States. The remaining air force units would continue operations on a reduced scale based out of Rhein-Main. On August 1, the two U.S. Navy squadrons at Rhein-Main and the air force group at Celle terminated operations and prepared to return to the United States. Officers and men from Erding Air Depot supervised the disposition of vehicles and supplies, completing their work at Celle on August 26, which officially closed as an airlift base on September 16. The contingent from Erding then set up shop at Fassberg, accomplishing their tasks there by September 26. The Royal Air Force ceased to fly official airlift missions into Berlin on August 31. The next day, the Combined Airlift Task Force headquarters dissolved, leaving operational matters in the hands of the commanding general, 1st Airlift Task Force, and the air officer commanding, No. 46 Group. The U.S. Air Force retained one heavy troop carrier group in Germany in case of emergencies. This was the 61st Troop Carrier Group based at Rhein-Main. The 61st supervised the reassignment of the C-54s no longer required in Europe to bases in the United States.[14]

On September 30, 1949, a C-54 took off from Rhein-Main with a planeload of coal, the most common cargo delivered by the CALTF. Piloted by Capt. Harry D. Immel, chief pilot of the 61st Troop Carrier Group, who had made one of the first airlift flights into Berlin fifteen months earlier, this was the last official flight of Operation Vittles. The takeoff ceremony included a flyover by a formation of Douglas C-54 Skymasters, the airplane made famous by the airlift. On that day, William Tunner, the man who did so much to perfect the airlift and make it a success, worked alone in his Wiesbaden office.[15] Officially, the airlift went out of existence at midnight. The history of the 1st Airlift Task Force provided a simple and concise epitaph: "At 0001, October 1, 1949, the Berlin Airlift came to an end—undramatically, without fanfare. As the Command wrote 'mission accomplished,' it could look back on the 15 turbulent months of operations with the satisfaction of having steered an unprecedented organization of men and aircraft through the most significant peacetime air transport operation in the history of the United States and British Air Forces."[16]

In the end, perhaps it was most appropriate for the Royal Air Force to have the last word on the Berlin Airlift. Air Commodore Waite had first proposed an airlift, RAF leaders had committed to the airlift fully, and, despite flying a smaller number of mismatched and generally less satisfactory aircraft than the U.S. Air Force, British airmen had earned a distinguished record during the successful effort to save the city. On September 23, 1949, an RAF C-47 Dakota touched down at Gatow Airfield in the

Figure 39. The crew of the last flight of Operation Vittles enjoyed a royal ceremony before taking off for Berlin on September 30, 1949. Brig. Gen. Edward H. Alexander, commander, 61st Troop Carrier Wing, shakes hands with instructor pilot Capt. Harry D. Immel of Pittsburgh, Pennsylvania. The rest of the crew are (left to right): 1st Lt. Charles N. Reece, Athens, Texas; 1st Lt. James C. Powell, Fort Worth, Texas; S.Sgt. Jerry G. Cooksy, Chicago, Illinois; and T.Sgt. Matthew M. Terenzi, Lynn, Massachusetts. Courtesy U.S. Air Force

British sector of Berlin. Written on its nose were the words: "Psalm 21, verse 11."[17] For those who knew their Bible or who took the time to look, the Dakota's message proclaimed victory: "For they intended evil against thee: they imagined a mischievous device, which they are not able to perform."

The Berlin Airlift: A Tally and Legacy

Statistics on the Berlin Airlift vary from source to source. The official USAFE account of the airlift, *Berlin Airlift: A USAFE Summary*, provides perhaps the most complete and accurate data available. According to that source, the Berlin Airlift delivered a total of 2,325,509.6 tons of cargo to Berlin. Of this amount, Operation Vittles delivered a total of 1,783,572.7 tons, while Operation Plainfare delivered 541,936.9 tons. American deliveries included 1,421,118.8 of coal, 296,319.3 tons of food, and 66,134 tons of miscellaneous cargo. British deliveries included 164,910.5 tons of coal, 240,386 tons of food, and 136,640.4 tons of miscellaneous cargo. Among other commodities, the miscellaneous category included 92,282 tons of liquid fuels, most delivered by British civilian aircraft operating under contract. Civilian aircraft also delivered 146,918 tons of the cargo included in the British statistics. In terms of percentages, the U.S. Air Force contributed 76.7 percent of the total tonnage, the Royal Air Force transported 17 percent, and the British civil airlift carried the remaining 6.3 percent.[18]

In addition to the cargo flown into the city, the CALTF transported 81,730.8 tons of cargo out of Berlin during the airlift. Of this freight, 45,887.7 tons went in U.S. aircraft, while the British flew out 35,843.1 tons. Much of the outbound cargo comprised small manufactured items produced by Berlin industry under incredibly difficult conditions and labeled *"Hergestellt im Blockierten Berlin"* ("Manufactured in Blockaded Berlin"). The airlift also carried a total of 227,655 military and civilian passengers to and from the beleaguered city.[19]

The total number of flights made by the airlift varies somewhat from source to source. The USAFE summary concluded that the total was 277,569 flights, 189,963 flown by the U.S. Air Force and 87,606 by the Royal Air Force; the civilian airlift contributed 21,121 sorties to the RAF total.[20] The incredible number of flights in fifteen months certified the intensity of the Berlin Airlift and the efficiency with which it operated.

The number of ground-control-approach landings attested to the poor weather conditions faced by the airmen of the Berlin Airlift. GCA conducted 33,180 landings under visual flight rules and 42,205 under instrument flight rules. Further, GCA directed an additional 3,960 landings under conditions considered to be "below IFR."[21] Again, the Berlin Airlift was a victory by people, not technology, but if there was a technological "hero" on the airlift, it was GCA.

Over all, safety on the Berlin Airlift was generally good. Measured in lives, the airlift was expensive, but in the number of accidents, less so. The Royal Air Force lost eighteen airmen killed: fifteen RAF personnel, one army sergeant, one Royal Australian Air Force pilot, and one South African Air Force flying officer. The British civil airlift lost an additional twenty-one men. American casualties totaled thirty-one men: twenty-two U.S. Air Force pilots, six U.S. Air Force airmen, one U.S. Navy petty officer, one U.S. Army private, and one civilian. Thirteen German civilians perished: five Berliners, seven passengers on an RAF Dakota that crashed at Lübeck on January 24, 1949, and one truck driver who drove into the propeller of a Hastings at Schleswigland on January 15. USAFE counted 70 major and 56 minor accidents on Operation Vittles, a total of 126. The RAF listed a total of 46 accidents requiring salvage to aircraft on Operation Plainfare.[22]

The Berlin Blockade proved a disaster for Joseph Stalin and his foreign policies by providing graphic evidence of Soviet ruthlessness and inhumanity. Frightened by Russian cynicism and brutality, Western European leaders took a long close look at the "red menace" and turned to each other and the United States for protection. Soviet policies drove these nations to seek safety within a unified defense system, and the Berlin Crisis of 1948 led directly to the creation of the North Atlantic Treaty Organization in April, 1949, and the creation of the Federal Republic of Germany the following month.[23] According to distinguished historian John Lewis Gaddis, the irony of the Berlin Crisis was that "Through his own policies ... Stalin brought about many of the things he most feared: an American commitment to defend Western Europe; a revived West German state closely tied to his adversaries; the beginnings of fragmentation within the international communist movement; and a conviction on the part of Western leaders that, because the Soviet Union could not be trusted, negotiations with it on the resolution of outstanding differences could only be approached with the greatest caution and from positions of strength, if they were to take place at all."[24]

Washington's viewpoint also changed during 1948. Originally, most

U.S. leaders saw the balance of power in Europe as a political and economic problem, or at least one that could be addressed in those terms. The Berlin Blockade, along with the earlier coup in Czechoslovakia and, later, the loss of China and the development of the Soviet atomic bomb, forced upon most an increased awareness of Soviet military power. It became clear that the Marshall Plan would not guarantee the ability of Europe to defend itself from Soviet aggression. The answer to this threat was a formal military alliance that assured the commitment of the United States to the defense of Europe.[25]

American public opinion had already begun to favor some kind of alliance with the European nations that had participated in the Marshall Plan. In January, 1948, Ernest Bevin and George Marshall agreed on the need to consolidate western Europe, and Bevin suggested that the first step should be a mutual defense treaty between Great Britain, France, and the Benelux nations (Belgium, the Netherlands, and Luxembourg). On March 17, these nations signed the Treaty of Economic, Social, and Cultural Collaboration and Collective Self Defense—better known as the Brussels Pact—which among other provisions established a collective security organization, the Western European Union (WEU). Shortly afterward, the National Security Council began to consider participation in some kind of alliance with this organization in an Atlantic security system. The USSR's machinations in Germany and its threats to Berlin during the summer of 1948 drove the WEU and United States together. Congress, however, refused to provide funding for an organization its members considered too European for isolationists to accept. Other U.S. leaders believed that the WEU was too small and lacked the depth necessary for the defense of Europe and wanted to include Portugal, Iceland, and Denmark in any security arrangement. Subsequent Soviet threats convinced Norway to participate as well. Backed by bipartisan support and favorable public opinion, Secretary of State Marshall began negotiations with the WEU in mid-1948.[26]

In the meantime, the basic outline for the military command structure of the alliance was worked out on the ground in direct response to the Soviet threat in Germany. By early July, Generals Clay, Robertson, and Koenig and their staffs had worked out an emergency plan for withdrawal to and defense of the Rhine River. The Western governments needed to establish an Allied Force Headquarters and designate a single commander. On July 12, the British element of the Combined Chiefs of Staff proposed that the first stage of implementation of the Brussels Treaty should have a British supreme commander, a French ground commander, a British naval commander, and a French air commander. Ultimately, the supreme command would go to an American, who would have a French ground commander, British naval commander, and American air commander under him.[27]

On July 16, the British, French, and American occupation commanders agreed that a single commander in chief should be appointed to conduct the defense of the Rhine River barrier and that a planning staff be assembled to select a location and establish a joint land and air headquarters. Clay recommended an American commander with a British air commander as deputy. The Rhine front would be divided into a northern sector commanded by a British officer and a southern sector commanded by either an American or French officer. The U.S. Army chief of staff, General Bradley, authorized General Clay to establish a joint planning staff with the British and French to develop contingencies for a withdrawal of forces to the Rhine River and the occupation of defensive positions along the river. However, Bradley cautioned him, decisions at his level would have to be tentative, since military talks then taking place in London might supersede his agreements. Allied planners met at Wiesbaden beginning on September 2 and started work on the coordination of the individual allied war plans.[28]

Ultimately, command of the unified force went to Field Marshal Viscount Montgomery, who held a meeting with the Allied military governors and senior ground and air commanders at Melle, Belgium, on November 8, 1948. Montgomery's plans were to set up his headquarters at Fontainebleau outside Paris with an advanced headquarters near Rheims. Planners began to prepare three strategies: a short-term emergency plan based on the work of the joint staff at Wiesbaden, a two-year plan based on the WEU's planned strength as of January, 1951, and a five-year plan based on the forces expected to be available by January, 1954. What would ultimately become, with modifications, the military command structure of a Western military alliance was, thus, brought into being by the Berlin Crisis and made possible by the Berlin Airlift.[29]

In the spring of 1949, Secretary of State Dean Acheson completed negotiations for an Atlantic-region military alliance. On April 4, the Western allies drove another nail into the coffin of Stalin's hopes for the future when twelve nations—Belgium, Canada, Denmark, France, Iceland, Italy,

Luxembourg, the Netherlands, Norway, Portugal, the United Kingdom, and the United States—signed the North Atlantic Treaty, which declared that an attack on any one signatory nation would be regarded as an attack on all. The U.S. Senate ratified the treaty on July 21, 1949, breaking for good the American isolationist tradition. The North Atlantic Treaty established the North Atlantic Council, which held its first meeting in September, the last month of the Berlin Airlift. In October, Congress appropriated one billion dollars for military assistance to Europe. Once the North Atlantic Treaty Organization was a fact, Stalin could do little to prevent the rise of American stature and strength in Western Europe. He could only increase his hegemony over Eastern Europe and retreat from the position where he had played for high international stakes and lost—Berlin.[30]

NATO represented an unprecedented, long-term commitment by the United States to remain in Europe, and its importance was far reaching. The existence of NATO and the presence of the United States ensured the longest period of peace in recent European history. Extended into the eastern Mediterranean, with the addition of Greece and Turkey, and eastward in Europe, with the addition of West Germany, the alliance ultimately formed a solid barrier to Soviet and communist aspirations west of the Iron Curtain. Forty years later, when the communist empire fragmented and the USSR collapsed, NATO still stood as a source of strength, unity, and stability in Europe.

All Soviet haggling and efforts to pressure the allies also failed to prevent the establishment of West Germany. The role of the airlift in the process was subtle but significant. For the Western powers, the German enemy now became an ally in the confrontation with a Soviet Union bent on subjecting Germany to a hostile and pernicious form of government. Lucius Clay saw the Berlin Airlift as a collaborative effort between the Western allies and the German people and later wrote that, in their steadfastness, the Germans, and particularly the Berliners, had redeemed much in their past: "The determination of the people did not falter. They were proud to carry their burden as the price of their freedom, and though the price was high it had brought them something in return that had become dear. They had earned their right to freedom; they had atoned for their failure to repudiate Hitler when such repudiation on their part might have stopped his rise to power."[31]

For Germans, the dedication of American and British resources and the nations' willingness to sacrifice lives succoring Berlin represented an

Figure 40. Berliners crowd around to view the ceremonies commemorating the end of the Berlin Blockade, May 12, 1949. Courtesy U.S. Air Force

unexpected commitment by enemies and conquerors. "The German people, who had been somewhat apathetic ever since their defeat, came back to life during the Airlift," Robert Murphy, General Clay's political advisor, recalled. "For the first time since the war, all their organizing genius was needed in this unprecedented attempt to feed and maintain two and a half million Germans in addition to the Western military and diplomatic communities."[32] The airlift thus made a massive contribution to pro-Western thought among the German population. "In the end," scholar Vojtech Mastny wrote recently, "the certitude of their commitment to Western democracy . . . was what made the Berlin airlift such a memorable success."[33]

The need for economic growth and stability in Europe and the collapse of efforts to operate the Eastern and Western zones of occupation as a single economic unit caused the United States and Great Britain to merge their zones into a single economic and administrative unit in February,

1948. The introduction of a new currency in June led to increased separation from the Eastern zone and served as the pretext for the blockade of Berlin. In September, a parliamentary council chaired by Konrad Adenauer, a devout Catholic and staunch democrat who had spent World War II in a concentration camp, began meeting in Bonn.[34]

On Monday, May 12, 1949, the day the Berlin Blockade ended and trucks and trains began carrying food and coal to the city once again, General Clay flew to Frankfurt to meet with his colleagues from Great Britain and France. There they approved the Basic Law, which led to the establishment of a West German state. On May 23, 1949, the day that the Council of Foreign Ministers meeting demanded by the Soviets convened, the West German constitution was adopted effective at midnight. In rapid sequence and with Western blessings, German leaders proclaimed the formation of the Federal Republic of Germany and in August elected a free parliament. In September, 1949, the federal parliament met for the first time.[35]

Thereafter, under the leadership of Chancellor Adenauer and his successors, the Federal Republic of Germany emerged as a strong, stable democratic keystone in the belt of European security. The status of Berlin and its relationship with West Germany remained in limbo for some time, though. On October 21, 1949, the Western powers decided that Berlin would be treated as part of the Federal Republic. The Soviets, in response, created their own German Democratic Republic out of the eastern zone. Berlin, a dagger pointed at the heart of communist Eastern Europe, remained a bone of contention throughout the next forty years. When the East German government collapsed and the barbed wire fences and concrete walls came down, the Federal Republic quickly united with the former East Germany and emerged from the Cold War as a powerful democratic nation.

For the U.S. Air Force, in its underlying lessons, the Berlin Airlift demonstrated the need to throw off the "milk run" mentality of the airlines and earlier military air transport operations. Modern airlift required professional organization and exceptional precision in all aspects of transportation, communications, maintenance, and supply. Above all, the airlift validated the need for large cargo airplanes designed specifically for use as military transports. No longer could the U.S. Air Force rely on modified civilian airliners for its strategic and tactical airlift capability. The drive now was to move the maximum amount of goods in as few missions as possible.[36] Further, an official USAFE study of the airlift in 1948 concluded that future personnel had to be "selected and trained rather than merely assigned and utilized"; in other words, a modern airlift should not be run by amateurs and part-time workers.[37] Strategic air transport required dedicated, trained professionals, and these would best be developed and promoted under a central command like MATS. These lessons, however, were by no means obvious to everyone.

Air force leaders who believed in the importance of air logistics viewed the Berlin Airlift as an opportunity to spread the gospel of global air transport. In particular, the carefully chosen officers from Military Air Transport Service assigned to the Combined Airlift Task Force had believed that "Perhaps [the airlift's] most immediate value was to bring to those responsible for the public defense a quickened awareness of the need for a logistical air fleet."[38] Chief among these men was the commander of CALTF, General Tunner. A series of letters between Tunner and the MATS commander, Maj. Gen. Laurence S. Kuter, in August and September, 1948, provides a good picture of their views and aspirations. Essentially, they concentrated on two goals: First, they wanted to unify strategic air transport under one command, MATS, and eliminate the troop carrier groups. Second, they, and especially General Tunner, pushed the development of huge transport aircraft designed specifically for military use.

Propaganda played a major role in their campaign. On August 31, Kuter took part in a conference of MATS and USAFE personnel that convinced him, he wrote Tunner, "that we should make every effort to have the VITTLES story told by qualified aviation writers who can appreciate the implications of such strategic air transport and who can explain both the techniques of the effort and its essential place in any plan for national defense."[39] To that end, Kuter arranged for several aviation journalists to visit Germany and survey the airlift. Tunner reciprocated on the potential value of the airlift. "As you know," he assured Kuter on September 3, "no one is more aware than I of the terrific public relations potential in this operation—that this is the greatest opportunity we have ever had, or probably ever will have, to tell the air transport story and make certain that people will pay attention to us." Thanks to the wide variety of air force and congressional leaders visiting Germany, Tunner could get his message out: "You may be sure," Tunner assured Kuter, "that I am taking every opportunity to point out the significance of the relationship between a project of this kind and military air transport, of the kinds and types of aircraft we should have, and what our organization should look like."[40]

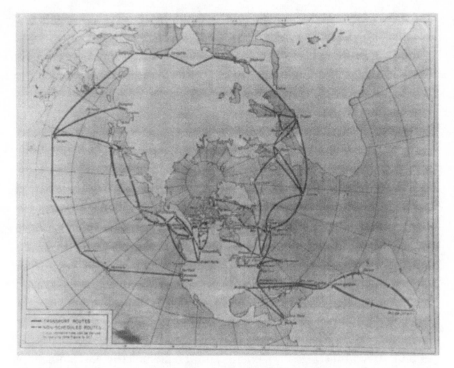

Figure 41. Maj. Gen. Laurence S. Kuter, commander, MATS, made every effort to ensure that the Berlin Airlift did not compromise the worldwide schedule flown by MATS.
Courtesy Laurence S. Kuter Papers, Special Collections, Air Force Academy Library

The division of air transport between MATS and the troop carrier groups assigned to other commands distressed both generals. This consideration partly explains Kuter's concerns over the source of the contingent of fifty C-54s sent to Germany in late August, 1948. He found that most senior air force leaders in the Pentagon as well as in the other major commands wanted to take all fifty Skymasters from MATS. His position, Kuter explained, was that no more C-54s should be removed from his command while any remained with the troop carrier groups. He recognized that (to borrow a phrase) possession was nine-tenths of air force regulations. "It seems obvious," Kuter wrote Tunner, "that MATS will wind up in a very strong position if you have in your command all troop carrier C-54s when VITTLES terminates." The flip side of the coin was unpalatable: "On the other hand, as a global air transport agency, MATS will have in fact been destroyed if we wind up with our resources in VITTLES and the troop carriers doing the global job."[41] Kuter continued making every effort to ensure that augmentation of the Berlin Airlift came from Troop Carrier Command resources, thus maintaining MATS's remaining long-line overseas service and putting troop carriers out of that business. Additionally, he reported, his allies on the Air Staff had dusted off and planned to update an earlier proposal to consolidate Troop Carrier Command and Air Transport Command vetoed earlier.[42]

In turn, Tunner provided Kuter with ammunition, reporting that he had observed MATS transport personnel and personnel from the troop carrier groups closely and had "come to the conclusion that it was now time to put out some long-range propaganda, looking toward the consolidation of the troop carrier units with MATS."[43] Tunner reminded Kuter, as if he had to do so, of the inefficiency in having two separate transport operations in the U.S. Air Force, a luxury the service could not afford as economic pressures reduced the size of the resources at its disposal. Tunner also firmly believed that there were practical, operational reasons for unifying air transport. He found the MATS squadrons assigned to the airlift uniformly efficient, he reported, while the caliber of the troop carrier units varied a great deal depending upon the ability and drive of the individual commanders. Curtis LeMay reported similar discrepancies. On August 30, 1948, he complained to Lt. Gen. Elwood R. "Pete" Quesada, commander of Tactical Air Command, that the C-54s arriving in Europe were well prepared for their mission except for some of those from troop carrier units.[44]

The lack of standardization between the two types of units posed problems. The troop carrier units lacked the traffic administrators and technicians necessary for sustained airlift operations and were overmanned in other technical specialties. The fact that troop carrier squadrons and groups were organized, equipped, and manned as table-of-organization units contributed to some of the inefficiency. Pete Quesada's response to LeMay's complaint was to blame the troubles on air force headquarters, which was sending aircraft and bodies rather than units to Europe. Instead of airplanes in twos and threes, Quesada told LeMay, he wanted to send complete squadrons. Instead of a small number of C-82s, for example, Quesada hoped to send a fully trained and equipped squadron of Packets to Germany. LeMay agreed in principle with Quesada's point of view, but the airlift, he replied, was a special case. The motivating factor behind his requests was tonnage. It made more sense to ask for the number of aircraft needed to meet a delivery goal than to request squadrons. In addition, eliminating nonessential personnel was extremely important because of the limited resources and facilities available. Complete squadrons would bring along many men in overly redundant roles.[45] MATS, which could assign individual aircraft and the personnel required or complete squadrons if necessary, provided a much more flexible and responsive organization.

The lessons about the need for a unified air transport organization, thus, would seem clear for anyone who looked closely at the Berlin Airlift. Yet, as historian Robert Owen has argued, Tunner and his men had done their job too well. Tunner expounded at length on the inefficiency of having two separate transport organizations, but, in fact, he had successfully accomplished the airlift by integrating those two organizations and making them work together. On the surface, then, the lessons of the Berlin Airlift concerning air transport organization were not as obvious as Tunner and Kuter believed. Ultimately, MATS gained control of troop carrier assets, aircraft, and aircrews but not until 1957. Military Air Transport Service finally became the single manager for military air transport in 1962, thirteen years after the airlift ended.[46]

Likewise, Tunner's success vitiated to a great degree his views that the Berlin Airlift should have been a MATS operation and that the Combined Airlift Task Force should have been outside the command of USAFE. When General Cannon curtailed Tunner's ability to deal directly with air force agencies outside USAFE and forced him to deal with supporting bases like Burtonwood through the USAFE staff, he significantly reduced the independence that Tunner believed he required to accomplish his mission. But, in fact, Tunner did succeed in his mission despite having to report to USAFE. It is clear that many problems might have been dealt with more quickly and the airlift might have proceeded somewhat more smoothly, but, once again, it proved difficult to argue with success.[47]

The argument for larger transport aircraft faced a similar challenge in the wake of the airlift's success. In the push for a large strategic transport designed especially for military use, Tunner had pried loose from MATS one giant Douglas C-74 Globemaster for a few weeks' service early in the airlift to demonstrate the larger plane's superiority over the smaller C-54s and C-47s. This test, though, provided both an opportunity and a risk, and Kuter was extremely concerned about the airplane. Failure to meet expectations might compromise efforts to purchase big military transports. "The adverse consequences of a little bad luck with this particular airplane," he wrote Tunner in August, 1948, "are obviously broad in nature and could be most serious."[48] He cautioned Tunner not to let the airplane get "bogged down" on an airfield with an inadequate runway and expressed special concern about the need to carry a spare engine on all flights in case the aircraft experienced an emergency in Berlin. Having to tote an extra engine around was a poor way to demonstrate efficiency, however, so Kuter talked Col. Albert Boyd, chief of the Flight Test Division in Dayton, Ohio, into compiling data on the C-74's takeoff performance with three engines. This data convinced MATS officials that the C-74 could operate safely on the airlift without lugging around a spare engine.[49]

General Kuter need not have worried. The C-74 proved its effectiveness, especially on September 18, when it flew six round-trips into Berlin and delivered 150 tons of cargo. When Sen. Chan Gurney, the powerful chairman of the Senate Armed Services Committee, visited Berlin, Tunner was able to present statistical data demonstrating the tremendous superiority of the C-74 over the C-54 and the cost effectiveness of operating an airlift with larger rather than smaller airplanes.[50]

In addition to the C-74, the airlift served as a test for another giant aircraft. On May 1, 1949, the Strategic Air Command's Boeing YC-97A Stratofreighter arrived in Germany. The transport version of the B-29, the YC-97A first flew in January, 1948. Along with the airplane came one SAC aircrew, seven maintenance personnel, and over ten tons of specialized parts. Later, additional maintenance personnel and enough people to make up three full crews arrived. Service tests of the YC-97A proved somewhat anticlimactic. Initial assessment of the aircraft showed several problems, including the length of the fuselage, which caused both fatigue and confusion for loaders, and the difference in height between trucks and the aircraft's deck, which necessitated borrowing a conveyor belt from a German company. The Stratofreighter flew twenty-three missions, delivering 444.8 tons of cargo to Berlin. It also experienced the failure, however, that Kuter had feared earlier for the C-74. On May 24, engine problems forced the YC-97A to make an emergency landing in Berlin during which the giant aircraft blew four tires and caused enough damage to close Gatow's runway for over seven hours. The plane remained at the British base until three new engines arrived on June 17, after which it returned to the United States.[51]

As the airlift continued, Tunner and his staff increasingly argued the need for a military transport capable of carrying a twenty-five-ton cargo based primarily upon the performance of the C-74. A transport capable

Figure 42. The YC-97A Stratofreighter, along with the C-124, was part of the next generation of U.S. Air Force transports. It was more successful, though, as a tanker for air-to-air refueling. Courtesy U.S. Air Force

of carrying twenty-five tons promised huge economies of scale. Sixty-eight C-74s could do the work of 178 C-54s or 899 C-47s. It would only have to fly 5,400 trips per month to the C-54's 13,800 or the C-47's 39,706. The C-74 would require 180 aircrews to do the same amount of flying as 465 for a C-54 operation or 1,765 on a C-47 operation. Only 2,700 maintenance personnel would be required for the C-74 compared to 4,674 for the C-54 or 10,588 for the C-47. Finally, 68 C-74s would deliver this cargo equivalent using only 6,804,000 gallons of gasoline compared to 8,577,600 for the C-54s and 14,294,00 for the C-47s. Each giant transport would do the work of three C-54s and would reduce dramatically most of the problems of scheduling, maintenance, and support. The number of crews and maintenance personnel would be reduced correspondingly as would all of the attendant housing, feeding, and administrative problems caused by a huge work force.[52] Recognizing the economies of scale, Tunner became a passionate advocate of the big military transport:

[A]s we flew more and more tonnage into Berlin, the superiority of the twenty-five ton transport became more and more obvious. With one plane which could do the work of three, all of our major problems would have been proportionally reduced. With only one-third of the flight crews and ground crews to house, quarters would not have presented such a problem. With a third of the airplanes to maintain, the situation at Burtonwood would have been less desperate. . . . If we had had a full fleet of the Douglas C-74's [sic] for the Airlift we would have been able to deliver eight thousand tons daily using only two bases in West Germany and one field in Berlin. Imagine the saving! Using more bases and two fields in Berlin, we could have increased the tonnage up to twenty-four thousand tons a day, far more than the city required, and . . . this could have been done at considerably less expense than the actual operation with ten-ton planes.[53]

In August, 1948, General Kuter met with senior Department of the Air Force leaders who expressed "sympathetic interest" in the proposal by MATS to replace C-54s with a combination of C-97s and Douglas C-124 Globemaster IIs beginning in fiscal year 1949. The navy was expected to make a similar proposal for the replacement of their R5Ds. In addition, CALTF's long-range plans for prolonging the airlift beyond 1950, if that proved necessary, were predicated on the advent of the C-97 and C-124.[54]

Tunner worked on his superiors shamelessly. When he learned that Secretary Symington was coming to visit the airlift in December, Tunner seized the opportunity to brief his vision to the receptive air force secretary. Thoroughly convinced of the importance of the big transport to the air force mission, Symington returned to Washington and pushed development of the C-124. Tunner gave the same treatment to Secretary of Defense Forrestal in December, 1948, and, following his visit to Berlin, Forrestal asked Air Force Chief of Staff General Vandenberg for information on the development of strategic transport aircraft. Vandenberg reported that the C-124, a modified version of the C-74 capable of a 73,000-pound payload, was waiting in the wings while the C-97 with its 55,000-pound payload was already on the ramp.[55] Yet ironically, as Owen concludes, once again Tunner's success with the Berlin Airlift made it easy to ignore the need for the larger aircraft. Tunner's arguments in favor of larger military air transports could be ignored by the superficial recognition that he and his men had accomplished the mission using smaller aircraft designed for civilian use and for hauling passengers instead of cargo.[56]

Ultimately, the big transports that Tunner sought so desperately would arrive in the air force inventory. The C-97 would serve as a satisfactory strategic transport but achieve its greatest fame and most valuable role as an aerial tanker refueling aircraft in flight. The C-124, nicknamed "Old Shaky," would serve as the backbone of strategic air transport for the U.S. Air Force for the next decade. Old Shaky and its kind were just the beginning, though. The Lockheed C-130 Hercules, Lockheed C-141 Starlifter, Lockheed C-5 Galaxy, and McDonnell Douglas C-17 Globemaster III used by the air force at the beginning of the twenty-first century are the direct descendants of the C-47s and C-54s that performed so brilliantly during the Berlin Airlift.

Berlin Airlift Summary

Tonnage Delivered
26 June 1948–30 September 1949 (short tons)

	US Tonnage	British Tonnage	Total Tonnage	US Flights	British Flights	Total Flights
Jun 48	1,199.0	205.0	1,404.0	474	26	500
Jul 48	39,971.0	29,034.7	69,005.7	7,550	5,978	13,528
Aug 48	73,658.1	45,344.5	119,002.6	9,770	8,372	18,142
Sep 48	101,846.7	37,776.2	139,622.9	12,904	6,825	19,729
Oct 48	115,792.2	31,788.6	147,580.8	12,135	6,100	18,235
Nov 48	87,979.3	25,608.6	113,587.9	9,047	4,305	13,352
Dec 48	114,567.2	26,870.9	141,438.1	11,660	4,832	16,492
Jan 49	139,218.8	32,740.4	171,959.2	14,095	5,397	19,492
Feb 49	120,394.6	31,846.1	152,240.7	12,043	5,043	17,086
Mar 49	154,475.0	41,685.7	196,160.7	15,530	6,633	22,163
Apr 49	189,957.2	45,406.5	235,363.7	19,130	6,896	26,026
May 49	192,271.4	58,547.1	250,818.5	19,366	8,352	27,718
Jun 49	182,722.9	57,602.1	240,325.0	18,451	8,094	26,545
Jul 49	201,532.2	51,557.8	253,090.0	20,488	7,104	27,592
Aug 49	55,940.0	21,818.6	77,758.6	5,886	3,098	8,984
Sep 49	12,047.1	4,104.1	16,151.2	1,434	551	1,985
Total	1,783,572.7	541,936.9	2,325,509.6	189,963	87,606	277,569

Not included above are French deliveries for their garrison of 800 metric tons (881.8 short tons) in 424 flights.

Inbound Cargo

	Food	Coal	Other	Total
US	296,319.3	1,421,118.8	66,134.6	1,783,572.7
UK	240,386.0	164,910.5	136,640.4	541,936.9
Total	536,705.3	1,586,029.3	202,775.0	2,325,509.6

Outbound Cargo

US	UK	Total
45,887.7	35,843.1	81,730.8

Passengers Flown

	Inbound	Outbound	Total
US	25,263	37,486	62,749
UK	34,815	130,091	164,906
Total	60,078	167,577	227,655

The French also carried 10,000 passengers, inbound and outbound

Berlin Airlift Fatalities

A. U.S. Fatalities during the Berlin Airlift

Date	Name	Grade	Service No.	Location	Aircraft	Tail Number	Remarks
8 Jul 48	HAGEN, Carl von	DA Civ	None	NE of Wiesbaden	C-47	43-48256	Crashed into hill on approach
	SMITH, George B.	1Lt	AO 794 711				
	WILLIAMS, Leland V.	1Lt	AO 686 293				
25 Jul 48	KING, Charles H.	1Lt	AO 27 501	Handjerystraße 2 Friedenau, Berlin	C-47	43-49534	Crashed on final approach to Tempelhof
	STUBER, Robert W.	1Lt	AO 56 312				
24 Aug 48	DEVOLENTINE, Joel M.	Capt	AO 53 549	Ravolzhausen, NE of Hanau	C-47	43-16036	Midair
	LUCAS, William T.	1Lt	AO 715 565				
24 Aug 48	DILTZ, Edwin C.	Maj	AO 423 920	Ravolzhausen, NE of Hanau	C-47	43-15116	Midair
	HOWARD, William R.	Capt	AO 789 573				
2 Oct 48	ORMS, Johnnie T.	PFC	RA 37 222 718	Rhein-Main	C-54	45-520	Ground accident
18 Oct 48	ERICKSON, Eugene S.	1Lt	AO 568 053	Near Rhein-Main	C-54	42-72688	Hit trees on approach
	VAUGHAN, James A.	Capt	AO 862 809				
	WINTER, Richard	Sgt	AF 39 203 365				
29 Oct 48	BURNS, George S.	Cpl	RA 34777365	Tegel	None	N/A	Killed in construction accident

Date	Name	Rank	Service No.	Location	Aircraft	Tail No.	Cause
5 Dec 48	HARGIS, Willis F.	1Lt	AO 760 457	Fassberg	C-54	42-72698	Crashed on takeoff
	PHELPS, Billy E.	Capt	AO 55 141				
	WELLS, Lloyd G.	TSgt	AF 7 060 860				
11 Dec 48	CRITES, Harry R., Jr.	AMM3	USN 2945 831	N of Rhein-Main	R5D	USN 5602	Crashed on approach
7 Jan 49	RATHGEBER, William A.	Capt	AO 65 187	15 mi NE of Blackpool, England	C-54	45-5543	En route to Burtonwood
	STONE, Ronald E.	Pvt	AF 15 199 071				
	THEIS, Norbert H.	Cpl	AF 17 191 076				
	WATKINS, Bernard J.	Sgt	AF 15 101 399				
	WHEATON, Lowell A., Jr.	1Lt	AO 677 371				
	WURGEL, Richard M.	1Lt	AO 826 341				
12 Jan 49	BOYD, Ralph H.	1Lt	AO 691 225	Near Rhein-Main	C-54	42-72629	Crashed on approach
	LADD, Craig B.	1Lt	AO 687 483				
	PUTNAM, Charles L.	TSgt	AF 17 146 457				
18 Jan 49	WEAVER, Robert P.	1Lt	AO 527017	6 mi E Fassberg	C-54	45-563	Crashed on approach
4 Mar 49	STEPHENS, Royce C.	1Lt	AO 680 754	S corridor E of Fulda	C-54	44-9086	No.3 engine fire
12 Jul 49	HEINIG, Herbert F.	TSgt	AF 15 061 938	Rathenau, N corridor	C-54	42-72476	Crashed en route from Celle to Tegel
	LEEMON, Donald J.	2Lt	AO 929 355				
	VON LUEHRTE, Robert C.	1Lt	AO 757 344				

B. British Military Fatalities during the Berlin Airlift

Date	Name	Grade	Crew Position	Aircraft	Location	Remarks
19 Sep 48	GILBERT, L. E. H.	Nav II	Navigator	York, MW 288	Wunstorf	Engine failure on takeoff
	KELL, G.	Flt Lt	Co-pilot			
	THOMSON, H. W.	Flt Lt	Pilot			
	TOWERSEY, S. M. L.	Sig II	Signaller			
	WATSON, E. W.	Eng II	Flt Engr			
17 Nov 48	DOWLING, F.	Sgt	Passenger	Dakota, KP 223	Russian zone, near Lübeck	Bad weather; night
	LOUGH, B. A.	Sig III	Navigator			
	TREZONA, F.	Pilot I	Pilot			
	WILKINS, J. G.	Flt Lt	Co-pilot			
24 Jan 49	GROUT, J. D.	Sig II	Signaller	Dakota, KN 491	Russian zone, near Lübeck	7 German passengers killed
22 Mar 49	PENNY, A.	M Sig	Signaller	Dakota, KJ 970	Lübeck	
	QUINN, M. J.	Flt Lt	Pilot (RAAF)			
	REEVES, K. A.	Flying Ofcr	Nav (SAAF)			
16 Jul 49	DONALDSON, I. R.	Flying Ofcr	Pilot	Hastings, TG 611	Tegel	Faulty trim on takeoff
	DUNSIRE, A.	Sig II	Signaller			
	GIBBS, R. R.	Engr II	Engineer			
	PAGE, W. G.	Nav I	Navigator			
	TOAL, J.	Sgt, Army Glider Regt	Co-pilot			

Note: The Berlin Airlift memorials list another British military member, Signalman R. C. Marks, as an airlift fatality. British records indicate Marks died in a traffic accident near Hamburg on 2 June 1949. The archives unfortunately contain no details regarding the accident and do not indicate whether Marks was performing duty related to the

Date	Name	Crew Position	Aircraft	Company	Location	Remarks
23 Nov 48	BURTON, Alan John	Nav Off	Lancastrian, G-AOJW	Flight Refueling, Ltd.	Thruxton, UK	Crash returning to UK
	CASEY, Michael Edwin	Nav Off				
	CUSACK, William	Captain				
	HEATH, Reginald Merrick Watson	Captain				
	ROBERTSON, Dornford Winston	Radio Officer				
	SEABORNE, Kenneth Arthur	Flight Engr				
	TAYLOR, Cyril	Captain				
8 Dec 48	UTTING, Clement Wilbur	Captain	Ground accident	Airlift, Ltd.	Gatow	Hit and run
15 Jan 49	GRIFFIN, Patrick James	Grd Engr	Ground accident	Lancashire Aircraft Corp.	Schleswigland	Truck drove into propeller of RAF Hastings TG 521
	O'NEIL, Edward	Grd Engr				
	SUPERNATT, Theodor	Grd Engr				
15 Mar 49	EDWARDS, Peter James	Radio Officer	York, G-AHFI	Skyways, Ltd.	Gatow	
	GOLDING, Cecil	Captain				
	NEWMAN, Henry Thomas	1st Officer				
21 Mar 49	FREIGHT, Robert John	Captain	Halifax, G-AJZZ	Lancashire Aircraft Corp.	Schleswigland	
	PATTERSON, Henry	Engr Off				
	SHARP, James Patrick Lewin	Nav Off				
30 Apr 49	ANDERSON, John	Engr Off	Halton, G-AKAC	World Air Freight	N. of Tegel	
	CARROLL, Edward Ernest	Nav Off				
	LEWIS, William Richard Donald	Captain				
	WOOD, Kenneth George	Radio Officer				

D. German Fatalities during the Berlin Airlift

Date	Name	Location	Remarks
15 Jan 49	NEUMANN, Richard K. O.	Schleswigland	Truck collided with RAF Hastings TG 521 at night; 3 British ground engineers (passengers) also killed and one injured.
24 Jan 49	GASHOFF, Ursula GIESDLER, Gundrun KELCH, Emanuel KELCH, Irmgard LERCHER, Johann ZIMMERMAN, Gerti ZIMMERMAN, Silvia	Russian zone, 10 mi E of Lübeck	Passengers killed in crash of RAF Dakota KN 491
11 Mar 49	ZÜLSDORF, Kurt	Gatow	Policeman from Berlin-Spandau. Walked into prop of York MW 189 at night
Apr 49?	Unknown	Rhein-Main	Truck driver killed when drove gas truck into propeller of parked aircraft. (May be garbled report of 2 Oct 48 accident that killed PFC Johnnie Orms.)
Unknown	DÜHRING, Willi	Unknown	Transport worker, Berlin-Kreuzberg
Unknown	FIEDLER, Hans	Unknown	Transport worker, Berlin-Moabit

| 9 Apr 49 | SCHLINSOG, Kurt | Tegel | Transport worker, Berlin-Luebars. Died of head injuries suffered in windstorm the previous day. |
| Unknown | SCHWARZ, Hermann | Unknown | Transport worker, Berlin-Kreuzberg |

Appendix 2 Sources: Rpt, "Berlin Airlift Fatalities," n.d. Rpt, "Airlift Fatalities," n.d., and Ltr, Army Records Ctr to CINC-USAFE, 9 Oct 56, all on microfilm reel Z-0038, USAFE/HO; USAFDE Press Release 4497-A, 28 Jul 49, microfilm reel Z-0039, USAFE/HO; *New York Times*, 8 Jan 49, p. 4; Rpt, BAFO, "A Report on Operation Plainfare (The Berlin Airlift)," [AP 3257], Apr 50, pp. 33—36, 239, 542, AIR 10/5067, PRO; Robert Jackson, *The Berlin Airlift* (Wellingsborough, UK, 1988), 151—54; *Hist of USAFE, Apr 49*, p. 50; [Berlin Magistraf], *Airlift Berlin: A Report with Pictures* (Berlin, 1949); Rpt, RAF, "List of Civilian Occupants," n.d. (24 Jan 49); FAX, AFHRA to USAFE/HO, 9 Feb 98; FAX, RAF AHB to USAFE/HO, 13 Mar 98; Hirst to author, 21 Mar 98; Cox to author, 23 Apr 99.

Notes

Chapter 1. Crisis in Germany

1. Quoted in Mikhail M. Narinskii, "The USSR and the Berlin Crisis, 1948–1949," (paper presented at a conference on the Soviet Union and Europe in the Cold War, 1943–53, Cortona, Italy, Sept. 23–24, 1994), p. 14. Milovan Djilas, a leader of the Yugoslavian Communist Party who knew Stalin, described him as "a dark, cunning, and cruel individual." Milovan Djilas, *Conversations with Stalin*, trans. Michael B. Petrovich, p. 187.
2. Frank Ninkovich, *Germany and the United States: The Transformation of the German Question since 1945*, pp. 20–23.
3. U.S. Department of State, *Germany, 1947–1949: The Story in Documents*, pp. 42–57; Lucius D. Clay, *Decision in Germany*, pp. 11–13, 40–41.
4. Steven L. Rearden, *The Formative Years, 1947–1950*, vol. 1 of *History of the Office of the Secretary of Defense*, p. 276.
5. Quoted in Ninkovich, *Germany and the United States*, p. 24.
6. Richard Crockatt, *The Fifty Years War: The United States and the Soviet Union in World Politics, 1941–1991*, p. 52.
7. Winston S. Churchill, *Triumph and Tragedy*, vol. 6 of *The Second World War*, p. 674.
8. Ibid., pp. 514–15, 654–67; Clay, *Decision in Germany*, p. 121.
9. Jean Edward Smith, *Lucius D. Clay: An American Life*, pp. 255, 257, 279.
10. Chuck Pennacchio, "Origins of the Berlin Blockade Crisis: New Evidence from the East German Communist Party Archive" (paper presented at the Conference on the Soviet Union, Germany, and the Cold War, 1945–62: New Evidence from the Eastern Archives, Essen and Potsdam, Germany, June 28–July 3, 1994), p. 1.
11. Clay, *Decision in Germany*, p. 21.
12. Ibid., pp. 25–26; Rearden, *Formative Years*, p. 276; Ann Tusa and John Tusa, *The Berlin Airlift*, pp. 12–14.
13. Tusa and Tusa, *Berlin Airlift*, pp. 31–33, 46–47.
14. Allied Control Authority Coordinating Committee, "Report of the Air Directorate Concerning the Creation of a System of Air Corridors to be Used for Flights in the Respective Zones of Occupation in Germany [w/atch.]," Nov. 22,

1945, no. CORC/P(45)170, Box 806; Excerpt, "Paragraph No. 110 from the Minutes of the 13th Meeting of the Control Council [w/atch.]", Nov. 30, 1945, no. CONL/M(45)13, Box 806, Allied Control Authority, Air Directorate, "Flight Rules for Aircraft Flying in Air Corridors in Germany and Berlin Control Zone," Oct. 22, 1946, no. DAIR/P(45)71, Box 806, Record Group (RG) 341, National Archives (NA).

15. William C. Wohlforth, *The Elusive Balance: Power and Perceptions during the Cold War*, pp. 88–89; Crockatt, *Fifty Years War*, pp. 70–71.

16. Mikhail M. Narinskii, "The Soviet Union and the Berlin Crisis, 1948–49," in *The Soviet Union and Europe in the Cold War, 1943–1953*, eds. Francesca Gori and Silvio Pons, pp. 58–59; Robert Murphy, *Diplomat among Warriors*, pp. 283–85; Rearden, *Formative Years*, p. 278; Department of State, *Germany, 1947–1949*, pp. 22–41.

17. Richard Collier, *Bridge across the Sky: The Berlin Blockade and Airlift, 1948–1949*, p. 2.; Smith, *Lucius D. Clay*, pp. 400–401. The quote is from Murphy, *Diplomat among Warriors*, p. 289.

18. Churchill, *Triumph and Tragedy*, p. 241.

19. Quoted in Djilas, *Conversations with Stalin*, p. 114.

20. Pennacchio, "Origins of the Berlin Blockade Crisis," pp. 5–6, 12–16.

21. Norman N. Naimark, *The Russians in Germany: A History of the Soviet Zone of Occupation, 1945–1949*, pp. 10, 107; Vladislav Zubok and Constantine Pleshakov, *Inside the Kremlin's Cold War: From Stalin to Khrushchev*, p. 147; Gerhard L.Weinberg, *A World at Arms: A Global History of World War II*, pp. 266–68; Pennacchio, "Origins of the Berlin Blockade Crisis," pp. 19–20, 23; Clay, *Decision in Germany*, p. 12.

22. David E. Murphy, Sergei A. Kondrashev, and George Bailey, *Battleground Berlin: CIA vs. KGB in the Cold War*, pp. 13–15.

23. Zubok and Pleshakov, *Kremlin's Cold War*, p. 147; Narinskii, "Soviet Union and the Berlin Crisis," pp. 58–59; Djilas, *Conversations with Stalin*, pp. 153–54.

24. John Lewis Gaddis, *We Now Know: Rethinking Cold War History*, pp. 44–45; Zubok and Pleshakov, *Kremlin's Cold War*, p. 147.

25. Pennacchio, "Origins of the Berlin Blockade Crisis," pp. 19–20, 23.

26. Ibid., p. 4.

27. Gaddis, *We Now Know*, p. 31; Zubok and Pleshakov, *Kremlin's Cold War*, p. 45.

28. Crockatt, *Fifty Years War*, pp. 72–74.

29. John Lewis Gaddis, *Russia, the Soviet Union, and the United States*, pp. 184–86; Vojtech Mastny, *The Cold War and Soviet Insecurity: The Stalin Years*, p. 25; Naimark, *Russians in Germany*, p. 304.

30. Smith, *Lucius D. Clay*, p. 405.

31. Ibid., p. 410.

32. Ibid., pp. 411–14; Ninkovich, *Germany and the United States*, p. 58.

33. Ninkovich, *Germany and the United States*, pp. 59–60; Department of State, *Germany, 1947–1949*, pp. 57–63.

34. Norman N. Naimark and Leonid Gibianski, eds., *The Establishment of Commu-*

nist Regimes in Eastern Europe, 1944–1949, pp. 267–90; Gaddis, *We Now Know,* p. 43; Crockatt, *Fifty Years War,* pp. 77–79.

35. Quoted in Mikhail M. Narinskii, "Soviet Policy and the Berlin Blockade, 1948" (unpublished paper in author's files), p. 1.
36. Quoted in ibid., p. 2.
37. Walter Millis, ed., *The Forrestal Diaries,* pp. 353–54; Clay, *Decision in Germany,* pp. 346–48.
38. Secretary of State Marshall to AMEMBASSY, Feb. 20, 1948, no. 597, Box 7, RG 218, NA.
39. Ibid.; Gaddis, *Russia, the Soviet Union, and the United States,* pp. 184–86.
40. Mastny, *Cold War and Soviet Insecurity,* p. 41.
41. Gaddis, *Russia, the Soviet Union, and the United States,* pp. 184–86; Crockatt, *Fifty Years War,* pp. 78–79; Tony Judt, "Why the Cold War Worked," *New York Times Book Reviews,* Oct. 9, 1997, p. 40.
42. Millis, *Forrestal Diaries,* p. 382.
43. The Brookings Institution, *Major Problems of the United States: Foreign Policy, 1949–1950* (Washington, D.C.: The Brookings Institution, 1949), p. 99.
44. Alexander L. George and Richard Smoke, *Deterrence in American Foreign Policy: Theory and Practice,* p. 110; Gaddis, *We Now Know,* p. 47.
45. Gaddis, *We Now Know,* p. 47.
46. Victor M. Gobarev, "Soviet Military Plans and Activities during the Berlin Crisis, 1948–1949" (paper presented at the Conference on the Soviet Union, Germany, and the Cold War, 1945–62: New Evidence from the Eastern Archives, Essen and Potsdam, Germany, June 28–July 3, 1994), p. 4; Zubok and Pleshakov, *Kremlin's Cold War,* p. 51; Mastny, *Cold War and Soviet Insecurity,* p. 43; Collier, *Bridge across the Sky,* pp. 4–5; George and Smoke, *Deterrence in American Foreign Policy,* p. 113.
47. Clay, *Decision in Germany,* p. 356.
48. Smith, *Lucius D. Clay,* pp. 464–65.
49. "Chronology of Developments in Berlin Situation," n.d., Box 14, RG 335, NA; Millis, *Forrestal Diaries,* pp. 407–409; Clay, *Decision in Germany,* pp. 360–61; Smith, *Lucius D. Clay,* p. 471.
50. DeWitt S. Copp, *A Few Great Captains: The Men and Events that Shaped the Development of U.S. Air Power* (Garden City, N.Y.: Doubleday, 1980), pp. 418–24; and *Forged in Fire: Strategy and Decisions in the Airwar over Europe, 1940–1945* (Garden City, N.Y.: Doubleday, 1982), pp. 313–14, 331–32; Alvin D. Coox, "Strategic Bombing in the Pacific, 1942–1945," in *Case Studies in Strategic Bombardment,* ed. R. Cargill Hall (Washington, D.C.: Air Force History and Museums Program, 1998), pp. 316–22.
51. Gordon Swanborough and Peter M. Bowers, *United States Military Aircraft since 1909,* pp. 266–74.
52. Hist, "USAFE and the Berlin Airlift, 1948: Supply and Operational Aspects," Apr. 1, 1949, Box 809, RG 341, NA, pp. 3–7; Hist, "Rhein/Main and Eschborn Air Bases, 1 June 1948–30 June 1948," Air Force Historical Research Agency,

Maxwell AFB, Ala., pp. 8–10 (microfilm); Stewart M. Powell, "The Berlin Air-lift," *Air Force Magazine*, June, 1998, p. 52.

53. Quoted in Powell, "Berlin Airlift," p. 53.
54. Lt. Col. Lester H. Gallogly, et al., "Report of Department of the Army Observer Group Concerning Study of Operation VITTLES," Feb. 16, 1949, History Office, United States Air Forces in Europe, Ramstein AB, Germany (microfilm #Z-0038).
55. Quoted in Narinskii, "Soviet Policy and the Berlin Blockade," p. 9.
56. Gobarev, "Soviet Military Plans and Activities," p. 17.
57. Quoted in Narinskii, "Soviet Policy and the Berlin Blockade," p. 9.
58. Murphy, Kondrashev, and Bailey, *Battleground Berlin*, pp. 54, 62–63, 65–67.
59. Narinskii, "Soviet Union and the Berlin Crisis," pp. 64–65; Gobarev, "Soviet Military Plans and Activities," p. 4.
60. Smith, *Lucius D. Clay*, pp. 478–80.
61. "Chronology of Developments in Berlin Situation," Box 14, RG 335; Memorandum, "Use of Fighter Escorts in the Berlin Airlift Air Corridors," Sept. 8, 1948, Box 103, RG 319, NA; George and Smoke, *Deterrence in American Foreign Policy*, p. 123; Robert Jackson, Berlin Airlift, p. 37; David Williamson, *A Most Diplomatic General: The Life of General Lord Robertson of Oakridge*, pp. 1, 120.
62. Quoted in Narinskii, "Soviet Union and the Berlin Crisis," p. 62.
63. Quoted in Murphy, Kondrashev, and Bailey, *Battleground Berlin*, p. 56.
64. George and Smoke, *Deterrence in American Foreign Policy*, pp. 123, 125; Mastny, *Cold War and Soviet Insecurity*, pp. 48–49.
65. George and Smoke, *Deterrence in American Foreign Policy*, p. 123.
66. "Chronology of Developments in Berlin Situation," Box 14, RG 335; Narinskii, "Soviet Union and the Berlin Crisis," pp. 64–65; Gobarev, "Soviet Military Plans and Activities," p. 4; Clay, *Decision in Germany*, p. 363.
67. Murphy, Kondrashev, and Bailey, *Battleground Berlin*, p. 52.
68. "Soviets Harass Western Allies in Berlin," *Intelligence Review*, Apr. 11, 1948, p. 59.
69. Ibid., p. 56.
70. MFR, "Shipment of Freight into Berlin," June 21, 1948, P&O 381 TS, P&O Division Decimal File; Hist, "The Berlin Air Lift," part 1, p. 7–9.
71. H.G.S. to General Wedemeyer, "Planning Information Concerning Berlin Situation," June 15, 1948, Box 118, RG 319.
72. Millis, *Forrestal Diaries*, pp. 375, 377; Clay, *Decision in Germany*, p. 230; Smith, *Lucius D. Clay*, pp. 400–402. The quotation is from ibid., p. 401.
73. "Summary of the Military Situation in Germany [w/atchs.]," July 19, 1948, JCS 1907/1, Box 177, RG 218, NA.
74. Lt. Gen. [Curtis] LeMay to [Muir S.] Fairchild, attached to staff summary sheet for Maj. Gen. F. H. Smith Jr., asst. for programming, DCS/O, HQ USAFE, June 22, 1948, Box 1, Muir S. Fairchild Papers, Library of Congress (LC); "Summary of the Military Situation in Germany [w/atchs.]," July 19, 1948, Central Decimal File; "Rotation Plan for SAC VHB Groups," Mar. 26, 1948, "Blitz Book," DCS/Ops, Box 38, Hoyt S. Vandenberg Papers, LC; Patricia Parrish, *Forty-Five Years of Vigilance for Freedom: United States Air Forces in Europe, 1942–1987*, pp. 26, 30.

75. Lt. Gen. Clarence R. Huebner, chief of staff, EUCOM, to Lt. Gen. Albert C. Wedemeyer, director, Plans & Operations, May 18, 1948, Box 103, RG 319, NA.

76. Gobarev, "Soviet Military Plans and Activities," pp. 11–12.

77. Ibid., p. 4; Narinskii, "Soviet Union and the Berlin Crisis," pp. 61, 64–66; George and Smoke, *Deterrence in American Foreign Policy*, pp. 114–15; Smith, *Lucius D. Clay*, p. 480.

78. CINCEUR to CSUSA (for Gen. Omar Bradley and Lt. Gen. Albert C. Wedemeyer), "Berlin Situation Report, Events of Period 18–23 June," June 23, 1948, Box 118, RG 319; Hist, "USAFE and the Berlin Airlift, 1948," p. 10.

79. Quoted in Narinskii, "Soviet Policy and the Berlin Blockade," p. 11.

80. CINCEUR to CSUSA (for Bradley and Wedemeyer), "Berlin Situation Report," June 23, 1948, Box 118, RG 319; Memorandum, Maj. Gen. Ray T. Maddocks (deputy director, Plans & Operations) to General Bradley, "The Berlin Situation," June 27, 1948, Box 103, RG 319; Frank Howley, *Berlin Command*, p. 200.

81. Memorandum, Maddocks to Bradley, "The Berlin Situation," June 27, 1948, Box 118, RG 319; Hist, "Berlin Air Lift," 1:8–9; Narinskii, "Soviet Union and the Berlin Crisis," pp. 66–67.

82. Mastny, *Cold War and Soviet Insecurity*, pp. 48–49.

83. Amb. Alexander S. Payushkin to U.S. Secretary of State, July 14, 1948, p. 5. Truman Presidential Library Website/Digitalization: Project Whistle Stop, Berlin Airlift/Papers of Clark Clifford. http:www.whistlestop.org/study_collections/berlin_airlift/large/clarkcliff/bal37-1.htm (Apr. 21, 1999).

84. Narinskii, "Soviet Union and the Berlin Crisis," pp. 67–68.

85. Memorandum, Maddocks to Bradley, "The Berlin Situation," June 27, 1948, Box 118, RG 319; Smith, *Lucius D. Clay*, pp. 506–25; George and Smoke, *Deterrence in American Foreign Policy*, p. 108; Tusa and Tusa, *Berlin Airlift*, p. 53.

86. Clay, *Decision in Germany*, p. 270.

87. Murphy, Kondrashev, and Bailey, *Battleground Berlin*, p. 57.

Chapter 2. The Airlift Begins

1. Except where noted, the following discussion is based on Robert Charles Owen, "Creating Global Airlift in the United States Air Force, 1945–1977: The Relationship of Power, Doctrine, and Policy," pp. 12–65. See also Roger G. Miller, "Air Transport on the Eve of Pearl Harbor," *Air Power History*, summer, 1998, pp. 26–37.

2. Wesley Frank Craven and James Lea Cate, eds., *Army Air Forces in World War II*, vol. 7 of *Services around the World* (Washington, D.C.: Office of Air Force History, 1983), pp. 6–7.

3. Quoted in Owen, "Creating Global Airlift," p. 61.

4. Hist, "Berlin Air Lift," 1:7.

5. Quoted in Hist, "USAFE and the Berlin Airlift, 1948," p. 11.

6. LeMay to Fairchild, June 22, 1948, General Correspondence File (May 17–July 31, 1948), Box 1, Fairchild Papers.

7. Ibid.; Parrish, *Forty-Five Years of Vigilance*, p. 30. The acronym for the European Air Transport Service was "EATS," a coincidence that led some veterans to believe the codename "Operation Vittles" came from that acronym. For example, see Shelley Davis, "The Human Side of the Berlin Airlift," *The Retired Officer Magazine*, Dec., 1998, p. 70. No evidence supporting this belief, however, has been located.

8. J. B. McLaughlin, "Berlin Airlift: Plus Fifty," *IFR*, June, 1998, pp. 6–7.

9. LeMay to Fairchild, June 22, 1948, General Correspondence File (May 17–July 31, 1948), Box 1, Fairchild Papers; Hist, "USAFE and the Berlin Airlift, 1948," p. 166.

10. Hist, "Berlin Air Lift," 1:7–8.

11. Curtis E. LeMay (with MacKinley Kantor), *Mission with LeMay: My Story*, p. 415.

12. Smith, *Lucius D. Clay*, pp. 495–96.

13. Ibid., pp. 495–97; Williamson, *A Most Diplomatic General*, p. 127; Collier, *Bridge across the Sky*, pp. 54–56, 59–61. The quotation is from Collier, p. 55. Williamson states that Waite went with Robertson to meet with Clay.

14. Collier, *Bridge across the Sky*, p. 60.

15. Smith, *Lucius D. Clay*, p. 502.

16. Howley, *Berlin Command*, p. 204; HQ USAFE Daily Diary, June 26, 1948, Box 47, Curtis E. LeMay Papers, Library of Congress.

17. Howley, *Berlin Command*, pp. 204–205.

18. Patrick E. Murray, "An Initial Response to the Cold War: The Buildup of the U.S. Air Force in the United Kingdom, 1948–1956," in *Seeing Off the Bear: Anglo-American Air Power Cooperation during the Cold War*, ed. Roger G. Miller, p. 15–17.

19. Memorandum of conversation, British Ambassador, Secretary of State Marshall, Mr. Lovett, July 14, 1948, Box 177, RG 218, NA; Walton S. Moody, *Building a Strategic Air Force*, pp. 141–42, 207–209; Phillip S. Meilinger, *Hoyt S. Vandenberg: The Life of a General*, p. 96; Robert Frank Futrell, *Ideas, Concepts, Doctrine: Basic Thinking in the United States Air Force, 1907–1960*, p. 236.

20. Moody, *Building a Strategic Air Force*, pp. 141–42.

21. Ibid., pp. 207–209; Meilinger, *Hoyt S. Vandenberg*, pp. 97, 233–34, n. 234.

22. Gobarev, "Soviet Military Plans and Activities," pp. 7, 10, 16.

23. Memorandum for the President, July 16, 1948, Box 220, President's Secretary's Files, Harry S. Truman Papers, Harry S. Truman Library, Independence, Mo.; Mastny, *Cold War and Soviet Insecurity*, p. 49.

24. Memorandum, "Military Implications of Continued Supply of Berlin by Air," July 13, 1948, Box 103, RG 319, NA.

25. Ibid.; Millis, *Forrestal Diaries*, pp. 459–60.

26. Memorandum, [Lt. Gen. Albert C.] Wedemeyer to CSA, "Plan for the Supply of Berlin by Armed Convoy [w/atchs.]," Sept. 22, 1948, ICS 1907/3, Box 103, RG 319; CSGPO to CINCEUR, Aug. 9, 1948, no. WARX-87296, Box 177, RG 218; memorandum for the secretary, Joint Chiefs of Staff, "Plan for the Supply

of Berlin by Armed Convoy [w/atch.]," Sept. 28, 1948, JCS 1907/3, Box 177, RG 218.

27. Memorandum for Admiral Leahy, et al., "Memorandum for Record of Conversations between U.S. Chiefs of Staff and Representatives of the British Chiefs of Staff," July 9, 1948, Box 7, RG 218, NA; memorandum for the president, July 23, 1948, Box 220, President's Secretary's Files, Truman Papers; Memorandum, Brig. Gen. T. S. Timberman (chief, Operations Group, P&O) to [Lt.] General [Albert C.] Wedemeyer, "Matters for Discussion with Mr. Royall at the Conference on Courses of Action in the Berlin Situation," Aug. 23, 1948, Box 103, RG 319; memorandum, Wedemeyer to CSA, [Gen. Omar Bradley] "Plan for the Supply of Berlin by Armed Convoy," Sept. 22, 1948, Box 103, RG 319; CSGPO to CINCEUR, Aug. 9, 1948, Box 177, RG 218; memorandum for the secretary, Joint Chiefs of Staff, "Supply of Berlin by Armed Convoy," Sept. 28, 1948, Box 177, RG 218.

28. Gobarev, "Soviet Military Plans and Activities," pp. 14–15.

29. *Berlin Airlift: A USAFE Summary, 26 June 1948–30 September 1949*, pp. 110, 112; Jackson, *Berlin Airlift*, pp. 32–33.

30. Jackson, *Berlin Airlift*, p. 32; Dudley Barker, *Berlin Air Lift: An Account of the British Contribution*, pp. 12–13; John Provan and R. E. G. Davies, *Berlin Airlift: The Effort and the Aircraft, the Greatest Humanitarian Airlift in History*, pp. 35–39.

31. Hist, " Berlin Air Lift," 1:17.

32. Barker, *Berlin Airlift*, pp. 9–10.

33. Aviation Operations Magazine, *A Special Study of Operation Vittles*, pp. 13–15; Barker, *Berlin Airlift*, pp. 9–10; Howley, *Berlin Command*, p. 207.

34. William Stivers, "The Incomplete Blockade: Soviet Zone Supply of West Berlin, 1948–1949," *Diplomatic History*, fall, 1997, p. 569.

35. Office of Military Government for Germany (US), "Weekly Intelligence Report No. 128," Oct. 23, 1948, Box 118, RG 319; CINCEUR to CSUSA (for General Bradley and Lieutenant General Wedemeyer), June 26, 1948, no. CC-4883, Box 118, RG 319.

36. Howley, *Berlin Command*, pp. 210–11.

37. Ibid., p. 240.

38. Military Government for Germany (US), "Weekly Intelligence Report No. 128," Oct. 23, 1948, Box 118, RG 319; HQ EUCOM to CSUSA for CSGID, Jan. 31, 1949, Box 14, RG 335, NA; Murphy, Kondrashev, and Bailey, *Battleground Berlin*, p. 58; Stivers, "Incomplete Blockade," p. 570.

39. Robert H. Ferrell, *George C. Marshall*, vol. 15 of *The American Secretaries of State and Their Diplomacy*, p. 154.

40. CINCEUR to CSUSA (for Bradley and Wedemeyer), June 26, 1948, no. CC-4883, Box 118, RG 319.

41. Intelligence Report, "Problems of the Western and Soviet Zones of Germany," May 18, 1949, OIR Report No. 4966, Box 365, RG 341, NA.

42. MFR, "United Kingdom Air Lift to Berlin (RDC 5/1)," June 29, 1948, P&O 381 TS, P&O Division Decimal File; HQ USAFE Daily Diary, June 25, 1948, Box 47, LeMay Papers; Hist, "USAFE and the Berlin Airlift, 1948," pp. 28–29.

43. COMGENUSAFE to Chief of Staff Air Force, June 27, 1948, no. UA-8561, Office of Sec Air Staff, Message Division (#23), TS Msgs., Box 2, RG 341, NA; HQ USAFE Daily Diary, June 27, 1948, LeMay Papers; [Gen. Lucius] Clay to [Gen. Omar] Bradley, June 27, 1948, no. CC-4910, Box 177, RG 218; Hist, "USAFE and the Berlin Airlift, 1948," p. 12.

44. COMGENUSAFE to Chief of Staff Air Force, June 27, 1948, Air Staff Message Division (#23), TS Msgs., Box 2, RG 341; Hist, "USAFE and the Berlin Airlift, 1948," p. 167; Swanborough and Bowers, *United States Military Aircraft since 1909*, pp. 289–93.

45. CSUSA to CINCEUR, June 27, 1948, Box 103, RG 319; Hist, "USAFE and the Berlin Airlift, 1948," pp. 13–14; Millis, *Forrestal Diaries*, pp. 454–55.

46. COMGENSAC to 301st Bomb Group, June 28, 1948, no. 282320Z, Box 7, RG 218; MFR, "Movement of Aircraft to Europe," June 29, 1948, Box 103, RG 319; David McCullough, *Truman*, p. 630; Hist, "Berlin Air Lift," 1:17; Millis, *Forrestal Diaries*, pp. 454–55.

47. HQ USAFE Daily Diary, June 29, 1948, Box 47, LeMay Papers; LeMay, *Mission with LeMay*, pp. 416–17.

48. Hist, "USAFE and the Berlin Airlift, 1948," pp. 14–15, 30–31; Owen, "Creating Global Airlift," p. 111; Obituary, "Gen. Smith Dies: Organized Berlin Airlift," *Washington Post*, May 22, 1993.

49. As quoted in William H. Tunner, *Over the Hump*, p. 159.

50. Col. William R. Large, Jr., (USAF Ret.) to Air Force Historical Research Agency, Aug. 3, 1948, copy in author's possession. Colonel Large's story is plausible but cannot be substantiated at this time from contemporary sources. If the messages that ordered the movement of the 17th, 19th, 20th, and 54th Troop Carrier Squadrons to Germany two days before General Smith was appointed provisional airlift commander—HQ USAF to CG, Alaskan Air Command, June 27, 1948, WARX-84756; and HQ USAF to CG-TAC, June 27, 1948, WARX-84772—contain the term "Operation Vittles," they would substantiate the story. Copies, however, have yet to be located. Interestingly, on July 2, 1948, when HQ MATS drafted the subsequent plan to move fifty additional C-54s from Westover AFB, Massachusetts; Fairfield-Suisun AFB, California; Brookley AFB, Alabama; and Great Falls AFB, Montana, to Germany, the planning name was "Operation Manna." HQ MATS to Cmdrs., ATLD, PACD, CNTLD, July 2, 1948, no. MATS EN-8009 F29, Berlin Airlift Files, History Office, Air Mobility Command, Scott AFB, Ill.

51. HQ USAFE Daily Diary, July 1, 1948, Box 47, LeMay Papers; Hist, "USAFE and the Berlin Airlift, 1948," pp. 15–16, 18, 21–22, 32–33; Hist, "USAFE and the Berlin Airlift, 1948," pp. 6–7, table G.

52. Hist, "USAFE and the Berlin Airlift, 1948," p. 15, table G; Hist, "Rhein/Main Air Force Base, from 1 July 1948 to 31 July 1948," Air Force Historical Research Agency, Maxwell AFB, Ala., pp. 12–13 (microfilm).

53. Hist, "USAFE and the Berlin Airlift, 1948," pp. 15–16, 18, 34–35.

54. Ibid., p. 13, table G.

55. Ibid., pp. 34–35.

56. Ibid., pp. 25–26.
57. ALREP no. 4, parts 2–2a, Box 57, RG 260, NA; *Berlin Airlift: A USAFE Summary*, p. 12.
58. Chaz Bowyer, *History of the RAF*, pp. 188, 193–94. See also Malcolm Postgate, "Operation Firedog: Air Support in the Malayan Emergency," in Miller, *Seeing Off the Bear*, pp. 181–90.
59. Barker, *Berlin Air Lift*, p. 41; Jackson, *Berlin Airlift*, pp. 44, 51; A. B. Stephens, "The RAF Contribution to the Berlin Airlift, 1948–1949" (paper presented at Freedom through Air Power: A Historical Symposium Commemorating the Berlin Airlift, 1948–49, Berlin, Germany, July 7–8, 1998), p. 4.
60. Tusa and Tusa, *Berlin Airlift*, p. 152.
61. Barker, *Berlin Air Lift*, pp. 16–19; Jackson, *Berlin Airlift*, pp. 44–45, 48; Tusa and Tusa, *Berlin Airlift*, pp. 150; Stephens, "RAF Contribution to the Berlin Airlift," pp. 4–5.
62. Jackson, *Berlin Airlift*, pp. 45–46. Stephens, "RAF Contribution to the Berlin Airlift," pp. 11–12. Cross is quoted in Stevens, p. 8.
63. Jackson, *Berlin Airlift*, pp. 46, 53, 55; Barker, *Berlin Air Lift*, pp. 46, 53; Stephens, "RAF Contribution to the Berlin Airlift," p. 6.
64. Jackson, *Berlin Airlift*, pp. 60–61; Barker, *Berlin Air Lift*, pp. 6, 46, 53.
65. Jackson, *Berlin Airlift*, p. 143.
66. Quoted in Stephens, "RAF Contribution to the Berlin Airlift," pp. 10–11.
67. Barker, *Berlin Air Lift*, pp. 52–53; Provan and Davies, *Berlin Airlift*, p. 54; Tusa and Tusa, *Berlin Airlift*, pp. 168.
68. Jackson, *Berlin Airlift*, p. 143; Tusa and Tusa, *Berlin Airlift*, pp. 310–11; Stephens, "RAF Contribution to the Berlin Airlift," pp. 20–21.
69. Stephens, "RAF Contribution to the Berlin Airlift," p. 21.
70. Jackson, *Berlin Airlift*, pp. 12–13.
71. Barker, *Berlin Air Lift*, pp. 19–20, 52–53.
72. Clive Richards, "Whitfield's Circus: The British Civil Contribution to the Berlin Airlift, August 1948–August 1949" (paper presented at Freedom through Air Power: A Historical Symposium Commemorating the Berlin Airlift, 1948–49, Berlin, Germany, July 7–8, 1998), pp. 2–5
73. Jackson, *Berlin Airlift*, pp. 98–100.
74. Barker, *Berlin Air Lift*, p. 41.
75. Jackson, *Berlin Airlift*, pp. 100–102, 115–16; Tusa and Tusa, *Berlin Airlift*, pp. 414–19.
76. Jackson, *Berlin Airlift*, pp. 113–15, 118–19.
77. Ibid., pp. 99–100, 147–49, 124.
78. Barker, *Berlin Air Lift*, pp. 39–40.
79. Ibid., pp. 23–25; Jackson, *Berlin Airlift*, pp. 47–51.
80. Provan and Davies, *Berlin Airlift*, p. 32.
81. Arthur Pearcy Jr., *Berlin Airlift*, pp. 55–60; Bill Morrissey, "Over Berlin Thirty Years Ago: The Tree Grows," *Phi Delta Kappa Magazine*, Aug., 1978, pp. 6–7.
82. Quoted in Morrissey, "Over Berlin Thirty Years Ago," p. 7.

83. Tusa and Tusa, *Berlin Airlift*, pp. 183–85.

84. Charles Christienne and Pierre Lissarrague, *A History of French Military Aviation*, p. 436; Daniel F. Harrington, *"The Air Force Can Deliver Anything!"* 109–10; P. St. John Turner and Heinz J. Nowarra, *Junkers: An Aircraft Album, No. 3* (New York: Arco Publishing Company, 1971), p. 62; Gen. Jacques Mutin, "The French Air Force in the Berlin Airlift," typescript furnished by Lt. Col. J. W. Bradbury (USAF Ret.), San Antonio, Tex.

85. Christienne and Lissarrague, *French Military Aviation*, p. 436; Mutin, "French Air Force in the Berlin Airlift." Arthur Pearcy states that two of the three Ju-52s collided and were destroyed on the ground at Wunstorf. Pearcy, *Berlin Airlift*, p. 40. Robert Jackson, who has written the best book describing the British airlift, does not mention such an incident.

86. Provan and Davies, *Berlin Airlift*, p. 44.

87. Ibid., pp. 44–45; "A Special Study of Operation 'Vittles,'" *Aviation Operations*, Apr., 1949, p. 115.

88. "Airlift to Berlin," *The National Geographic Magazine*, May, 1949, pp. 610–11.

89. Erwin A. Schmidl, "The Airlift That Never Was: Allied Plans to Supply Vienna by Air, 1948–1950," *Army History: The Professional Bulletin of Army History*, fall 1997/winter 1998, pp. 12–23. This article was also published as "'Rosinenbomber' über Wien? Alliierte Pläne zur Luftversorgung Wiens im Falle einer sowjetischen Blockade, 1948–1953," *Österreichische Militärische Zeitschrift*, fall, 1998, pp. 411–18.

90. COMDENUSFA-Vienna to COMGENUSAFE, EUCOM, July 23, 1948, no. P-2176, Box 177, RG 218; P&O File, "Air Supply from US Zone to Vienna [w/atchs.]," July 27, 1948, Box 177, RG 218.

91. COMDENUSFA-Vienna to COMGENUSAFE, EUCOM, July 23, 1948, Box 178, RG 218; P&O File, "Air Supply from U.S. Zone to Vienna," July 27, 1948, Box 178, RG 218; Note, Secretaries to Joint Chiefs of Staff, "U.S. Courses of Action in the Event of a Soviet Blockade of Vienna," Apr. 26, 1949, Box 178, RG 218; "U.S. Courses of Action in the Event of a Soviet Blockade of Vienna," Oct. 11, 1949, JCS 2000-2000/1, Box 178, RG 218.

92. Briefing sheet for chairman, J.C.S., "U.S. Courses of Action in the Event of a Soviet Blockade of Vienna," Oct. 11, 1949, Box 178, RG 218.

93. Memorandum for the president, July 16, 1948, President's Secretary's Files, Truman Papers.

94. McCullough, *Truman*, p. 647.

95. Millis, *Forrestal Diaries*, p. 498.

96. Memorandum for the president July 23, 1948, President's Secretary's Files, Truman Papers.

97. Ibid.

98. Ibid.

99. Ibid.

100. P&O File, "Military Implications Involved in Continuing Operation of the Berlin Airlift [w/atchs.]," Oct. 27, 1948, Box 103, RG 319.

101. Memorandum, James Forrestal to the National Security Council, "U.S. Military Courses of Action with Respect to the Situation in Berlin," July 26, 1948, Box 177, RG 218.
102. Ibid.
103. Mastny, *Cold War and Soviet Insecurity*, pp. 49–50.
104. Clay, *Decision in Germany*, p. 367.
105. Millis, *Forrestal Diaries*, pp. 469–70; Narinskii, "Soviet Union and the Berlin Crisis," pp. 68–70.
106. Narinskii, "Soviet Union and the Berlin Crisis," p. 70.
107. Ibid., pp. 70–71.
108. Memorandum, "Points on Berlin Situation for NSC," Sept. 7, 1948, Box 12, RG 335; Millis, *Forrestal Diaries*, pp. 480–81.
109. Clay, *Decision in Germany*, p. 375.
110. Telegram, [George C.] Marshall to [Philip C.] Jessup, Nov. 25, 1948, Box 14, RG 335.
111. [Kenneth] Royall to [Stuart] Symington, Sept. 26, 1948, Box 12, RG 335.
112. Mastny, *Cold War and Soviet Insecurity*, pp. 51–52.
113. Royall to Symington, Sept. 26, 1948, UnderSecArmy Project Decimal File.

Chapter 3. Tunner and the MATS Connection

1. Collier, *Bridge across the Sky*, pp. 97, 107, 112–23.
2. LeMay, *Mission with LeMay*, p. 416.
3. Owen, "Creating Global Airlift," pp. 21–22.
4. Tunner, *Over the Hump*, pp. 155–56, 159–60.
5. Owen, "Creating Global Airlift," pp. 74–83. The quote is on p. 81.
6. T. Ross Milton, "Inside the Berlin Airlift," *Air Force Magazine*, Oct., 1998, p. 49.
7. Ibid.; MFR, "Movement of Aircraft to Europe," June 29, 1948, Box 103, RG 319; Tunner, *Over the Hump*, pp. 162–65; Meilinger, *Hoyt S. Vandenberg*, pp. 98–99, 234–35, n. 235.
8. Quoted in Collier, *Bridge across the Sky*, p. 123.
9. Tunner, *Over the Hump*, p. 162.
10. Ibid.
11. Ibid., pp. 174–75.
12. Ibid., p. 174.
13. Daniel F. Harrington, "Against All Odds," *American History Illustrated*, Feb., 1982, p. 32.
14. Collier, *Bridge across the Sky*, pp. 122–23; Tunner, *Over the Hump*, pp. 175–78. The quotation is from Tunner, p. 177.
15. Tunner, *Over the Hump*, pp. 179–80.
16. Ibid., p. 221.
17. HQ MATS to Cmdrs., ATLD, PACD, "Movement Directives, Hqs. 518th Air Transport Group and Various MATS Air Transport Squadrons," July 25 1948, Berlin Airlift Files, History Office, Air Mobility Command; [Stuart] Symington to

Joseph J. O'Connell Jr. (chmn., Civil Aeronautics Board), Nov. 10, 1947, Secretary of the Air Force File 2 (Jan.–Feb., 1949), Box 59, Vandenberg Papers; "National Strategic Air Lift Capability (4-Eng Long Range)," Aug. 11, 1948, "Blitz Book," DCS/Ops, Box 38, Vandenberg Papers; CSAF to ICS, July 23, 1948, no. 50339, Box 118, RG 319; anonymous report, "Summary of Operation 'Vittles,'" Dec. 15, 1948, attachment to memorandum for Mr. Symington, "Status of Implementation of the NSC Recommendations for Augmenting the Berlin Airlift," Dec. 16, 1948, Box 808, RG 341, NA.

18. Hist, "USAFE and the Berlin Airlift, 1948," pp. 48–50.

19. Maj. Gen. William H. Tunner to Brig. Gen. Joseph Smith, "Operation Vittles," July 29, 1948, Berlin Airlift Files, History Office, Air Mobility Command.

20. Maj. Gen. William H. Tunner, Cmdr., Airlift Task Force (Prov.), to Maj. Gen. Laurence S. Kuter, Cmdr., MATS, Aug. 3, 1948, Berlin Airlift Files, History Office, Air Mobility Command; Tunner, *Over the Hump*, pp. 187–89.

21. The following paragraphs are based upon Tunner, *Over the Hump*, pp. 189–97.

22. Both quotations are from ibid, p. 197.

23. Memorandum to CSAF (Curtis LeMay to Hoyt Vandenberg), Aug. 23, 1948, File Memorandum (9), Box 45, LeMay Papers.

24. Ibid.; A.V. M. Spackman to General Tunner, Aug. 26, 1948, File Memorandum (9), LeMay Papers.

25. Quoted in Hist, "USAFE and the Berlin Airlift, 1948," p. 153.

26. Memorandum to CSAF, Aug. 23, 1948, File Memorandum (9), Box 45, LeMay Papers. See also Tunner's comments in Maj. Gen. William H. Tunner, Cmdr., Airlift Task Force (Prov.), to Maj. Gen. Laurence S. Kuter, Cmdr., MATS, Aug. 6, 1948, Berlin Airlift Files, History Office, Air Mobility Command.

27. Maj. Gen William H. Tunner to Lt. Gen. Curtis E. LeMay, Aug. 6, 1948, Berlin Airlift Files, Office of History, Air Mobility Command; Hist, "USAFE and the Berlin Airlift, 1948," pp. 56–61.

28. Hist, "USAFE and the Berlin Airlift, 1948," pp. 51, 61–62.

29. Memorandum to CSAF, Aug. 23, 1948, File Memorandum (9), Box 45, LeMay Papers; [Lt. Gen. Curtis] LeMay to [Gen. Hoyt] Vandenberg, Aug. 23, 1948, File Teletypes, Box 45, LeMay Papers; Maj. Gen. S. E. Anderson, dir., Plans & Operations, HQ USAF to Air Chief Marshal Sir Charles Medhurst, British Joint Services Mission, Aug. 30, 1948, Box 808, AF Plans–Project Decimal File.

30. Air Chief Marshal Sir Charles Medhurst, British Joint Services Mission, to Maj. Gen. S. E. Anderson, dir., Plans & Operations, HQ USAF, "Berlin Airlift-Integrated Control," Sept. 28, 1948, Box 808, RG 341.

31. Draft order, "R.A.F./U. S.A.F.. Directive to Berlin Airlift Transport Operations," n.d., Box 808, RG 341; Hist, "USAFE and the Berlin Airlift, 1948," pp. 155–57.

32. Hist, "USAFE and the Berlin Airlift, 1948," pp. 176–78.

33. Ibid., p. 159.

34. Ibid., pp. 163–64; Milton, "Inside the Berlin Airlift," p. 51; Combined Airlift Task Force, "Preliminary Analysis of Lessons Learned," June, 1949, 572.549-1, Air Force Historical Research Agency, p. 10.

35. Col. Gail S. Halvorsen, "Berlin, the Citadel of Freedom," *The Friends Journal*, summer, 1998, p. 6.

36. Collier, *Bridge across the Sky*, pp. 77, 86–87. Colonel Halvorsen later published a book-length account of his adventures, *The Berlin Candy Bomber*, (Bountiful, Utah: Horizon Publishers, Apr., 1990, rev. ed. Sept., 1997).

37. Quoted in Harold Nufer, "Uncle Wiggly Wings," *Air Power History*, spring, 1989, p. 27.

38. Collier, *Bridge across the Sky*, pp. 87–89.

39. Quoted in ibid., p. 105.

40. Tunner, *Over the Hump*, p. 207.

41. Collier, *Bridge across the Sky*, pp. 105–107; Nufer, "Uncle Wiggly Wings," pp. 28–29.

42. 1st Indorsement, Lt. Gen. Curtis E. LeMay, Cmdr., USAFE, to letter from Maj. Gen. William H. Tunner, Cmdr., Airlift Task Force (Prov.), to Cmdr., USAFE, "Maximum Tonnage to Berlin, September 28, 1948," Oct. 2, 1948, Box 808, RG 341; Hist, "USAFE and the Berlin Airlift, 1948," pp. 78–82, 218–19.

43. Hist, "USAFE and the Berlin Airlift, 1948," pp. 209–10.

44. Ibid., pp. 211–13; Col. Joseph Jansen, "An Army Engineer in Berlin during the Blockade and Airlift" (paper presented to the Conference of Army Historians, Bethesda, Md., June 9–11, 1998).

45. [Lt. Gen. Curtis] LeMay to [Gen. Lucius] Clay, June 17 and Aug. 20, 1948, Correspondence Files, Box 45, LeMay Papers; "USAFE and the Berlin Airlift, 1948," pp. 213, 218.

46. Memorandum, [Maj. Gen. William H.] Tunner to [Lt. Gen. Curtis M.] LeMay, "Construction Priorities at Tempelhof, Gatow, and Tegel," Aug. 26, 1948, File Memorandum (9), Box 45, LeMay Papers.

47. LeMay to Clay, June 17, 1948, LeMay Papers; Hist, "USAFE and the Berlin Airlift, 1948," pp. 211–13.

48. [Gen. Lucius] Clay to [Lt. Gen. Curtis] LeMay, Aug. 20, 1948, Correspondence Files, Box 45, LeMay Papers.

49. *Berlin Airlift: A USAFE Summary*, p. III; Hist, "USAFE and the Berlin Airlift, 1948," pp. 218–19; Hist, "Berlin Air Lift," 2:39–40; Clay, *Decision in Germany*, p. 384.

50. "Open for Business at Tegel Airport," *The Berlin Observer*, Nov. 19, 1948, p. 1. Copy thanks to Daniel Bunting, Santa Rosa, California.

51. Nicholas M. Williams, "Globemaster (The Douglas C-74)," *American Aviation Historical Society Journal*, summer, 1980: pp. 83–84, 88, 92–95; Swanborough and Bowers, *United States Military Aircraft since 1909*, pp. 297–98, 636; Hist, "USAFE and the Berlin Airlift, 1948," pp. 167–70.

52. Maj. Gen. William H. Tunner, Cmdr., Airlift Task Force (Prov.), to Maj. Gen. Laurence S. Kuter, Cmdr., MATS, Sept. 2, 1948 Berlin Airlift Files, History Office, Air Mobility Command; Owen, "Creating Global Airlift," p. 41; Kent A. Mitchell, "The Fairchild C-82 Packet," *American Aviation Historical Society Journal*, spring, 1999: pp. 2, 4–5, 7, 11, 14; Swanborough and Bowers, *United*

States Military Aircraft since 1909, pp. 310–16; Hist, "USAFE and the Berlin Airlift, 1948," pp. 169–72, 211–12.

53. Standard histories that describe this incident mention one radio tower. For example, see Collier, *Bridge across the Sky*, pp. 145–46. The earliest source found reporting the incident, however, specifically refers to two radio towers. CINCEUR to CSUSA (for General Bradley and Lieutenant General Wedemeyer), Dec. 17, 1948, Box 118, RG 319. More recently, a history of the French occupation in Berlin described the destruction of two towers based upon documents from the French Ministry of Foreign Affairs and an article published in the December 17, 1948, issue of *Der Tagesspiegal*. Cyril Buffet, *Mourir Pour Berlin: La France et l'Allemagne, 1945–1949*, p. 239.

54. *Berlin Airlift: A USAFE Summary*, p. 21.

55. Except where noted, the information on developments in flying the air corridors is from two letters to the author from Brig. Gen. Sterling P. Bettinger (USAF Ret.) dated June 2 and July 2, 1998, and subsequent telephone conversations with General Bettinger.

56. *Berlin Airlift: A USAFE Summary*, p. 24.

57. Ibid., p. 25.

58. Tunner, *Over the Hump*, pp. 152–53. Tunner's book misidentifies the pilot as Paul O. Lykins, but see "Texan Wins Award as Top Lift Pilot," *Stars and Stripes*, Aug. 14, 1948, p. 1.

59. Tunner, *Over the Hump*, pp. 153–54.

60. Ibid., p. 154.

61. *Berlin Airlift: A USAFE Summary*, p. 24; Combined Airlift Task Force, "Preliminary Analysis of Lessons Learned," pp. 20–21.

62. *Berlin Arilift: A USAFE Summary*, p. 45. The quotation is from Milton, "Inside the Berlin Airlift," p. 50.

63. *Berlin Airlift: A USAFE Summary*, p. 40.

64. Ibid., p. 45; Hist, "USAFE and the Berlin Airlift, 1948," pp. 198, 201, 203; "AACS: Building Highways in the Sky," *Intercom*, June, 1998, p. 16.

65. *Berlin Airlift: A USAFE Summary*, pp. 45–46.

66. Hist, "USAFE and the Berlin Airlift, 1948," pp. 199–200, 206.

67. Ibid., pp. 206–207; "Special Study of Operation 'Vittles,'" p. 66.

68. Hist, "USAFE and the Berlin Airlift, 1948," pp. 67–69.

69. Maj. Gen. William H. Tunner, Cmdr., Airlift Task Force (Prov.), to Maj. Gen. Laurence S. Kuter, Cmdr., MATS, Aug. 16, 1948; Maj. Gen. William H. Tunner, Cmdr., Airlift Task Force (Prov.), to Maj. Gen. Laurence S. Kuter, Cmdr., MATS, Aug. 21, 1948, Berlin Airlift Files, History Office, Air Mobility Command; Tunner, *Over the Hump*, pp. 189–90.

70. Maj. Gen. Laurence S. Kuter, Cmdr., MATS, to Maj. Gen. William H. Tunner, Cmdr., Airlift Task Force (Prov.), Aug. 3, 1948, and Maj. Gen. William H. Tunner, Cmdr., Airlift Task Force (Prov.), to Maj. Gen. Laurence S. Kuter, Cmdr., MATS, Sept. 10, 1948, Berlin Airlift Files, History Office, Air Mobility Command.

71. P&O File, "Possibility of Jamming Aircraft Landing Aides at Berlin Airfields [w/ atchs.]," Oct. 16, 1948, and P&O File, "Russian Capabilities to Interfere with U.S. Signal Communications with Berlin [w/atchs.]," Oct. 20, 1948, Box 103, RG 319.
72. *Berlin Airlift: A USAFE Summary*, pp. 51–53.
73. Hist, "USAFE and the Berlin Airlift, 1948," pp. 203, 204–205.
74. Ibid., pp. 66–67; *Berlin Airlift: A USAFE Summary*, p. 53.
75. Hist, "USAFE and the Berlin Airlift, 1948," p. 32; *Berlin Airlift: A USAFE Summary*, p. 55.
76. "Special Study of Operation 'Vittles,'" pp. 20–23, 38–41.

Chapter 4. The Airlift Meets "General Winter"

1. Hist, "USAFE and the Berlin Airlift, 1948," pp. 90–91.
2. Ibid., pp. 121–23.
3. Ibid., pp. 121–23.
4. Hist, "USAFE and the Berlin Airlift, 1948," attachment, "Supply and Maintenance Procedures for Air Lift Task Force (Prov.)," Aug. 19, 1948, USAFE letter 65–60.
5. Hist, "USAFE and the Berlin Airlift, 1948," pp. 111–12, 115.
6. "Special Study of Operation 'Vittles,'" pp. 75–76; *Berlin Airlift: A USAFE Study*, pp. 94–95.
7. Hist, "USAFE and the Berlin Airlift, 1948," pp. 93–95.
8. "Special Study of Operation 'Vittles,'" p. 78.
9. *Berlin Airlift: A USAFE Study*, p. 95.
10. Ibid., p. 95.
11. "Special Study of Operation 'Vittles,'" pp. 78–81.
12. Ibid.
13. Maj. Gen. William H. Tunner to Maj. Gen. Laurence S. Kuter, Aug. 3, 1948, Berlin Airlift Files, History Office, Air Mobility Command.
14. Hist, "USAFE and the Berlin Airlift, 1948," pp. 50–51, 63, 96–100; "Special Study of Operation 'Vittles,'" pp. 86–88.
15. Hist, "USAFE and the Berlin Airlift, 1948," pp. 96–100.
16. Ibid., pp. 100–102.
17. Memorandum, Maj. Gen. R. C. Lindsay, deputy director, Plans & Operations, "U.S. Military Courses of Action with Respect to the Situation in Berlin," Aug. [?], 1948, Box 177, RG 218; "200 Hour Maintenance—Burtonwood," *Task Force Times*, Dec. 8, 1948; "Special Study of Operation 'Vittles,'" p. 88.
18. *Berlin Airlift: A USAFE Summary*, p. 34.
19. Ibid., p. 94; Hist, "USAFE and the Berlin Airlift, 1948," pp. 100–102.
20. "Special Study of Operation 'Vittles,'" pp. 98–100.
21. Ibid., p. 101.
22. Maj. Gen. Laurence S. Kuter, Cmdr., MATS, to Maj. Gen. William H. Tunner, Aug. 13, 1948, Berlin Airlift Files, History Office, Air Mobility Command; anony-

mous report, "Summary of Operation 'Vittles,'" Dec. 15, 1948, attachment to memorandum for Mr. Symington, "Status of Implementation of the NSC Recommendations for Augmenting the Berlin Airlift," Dec. 16, 1948, Box 808, RG 341.

23. Anonymous report, "Summary of Operation 'Vittles,'" Dec. 15, 1948, attachment to memorandum for Mr. Symington, "Status of Implementation of the NSC Recommendations," Dec. 16, 1948, Box 808, RG 341; Hist, "USAFE and the Berlin Airlift, 1948," pp. 137–41.

24. Hist, "USAFE and the Berlin Airlift, 1949," pp. 88–90.

25. Maj James F. Rhodes, Asst. Adj. Gen., to Cmdr., Air Matériel Command, "Planning Factors for Replacement Training Unit at Great Falls Air Force Base, Montana," Oct. 12, 1948, Berlin Airlift Files, History Office, Air Mobility Command; D. M. Giangreco and Robert E. Griffin, *Airbridge to Berlin: The Berlin Crisis of 1948, Its Origin, and Aftermath*, p. 176.

26. Memorandum for the chief of staff, HQ USAF, "Increasing the Berlin Airlift [w/atchs.]," n.d., Box 808, RG 341; Memorandum for General Wedemeyer, "USAF Participation in the Berlin Airlift," n.d., Box 808, RG 341; "Special Study of Operation 'Vittles,'" pp. 116–17.

27. "The Fassberg Diary," copy in author's possession (typescript courtesy of Lt. Col. J. W. Bradbury [USAF Ret.], San Antonio, Tex.). John H. "Jake" Schuffert related the story of the diary to the author during conversations before his death in November, 1998. The author of the Fassberg Diary was the public information officer at Fassberg. Tunner immediately had the officer transferred to CALTF headquarters at Wiesbaden, according to Jake, "where he could keep an eye on him."

28. Hist, "USAFE and the Berlin Airlift, 1948," pp. 38–41; *Berlin Airlift: A USAFE Summary*, p. 5; Benjamin King, Richard C. Biggs, and Eric Conner, *Spearhead of Logistics: A History of the United States Army Transportation Corps*, pp. 290–94.

29. Hist, "USAFE and the Berlin Airlift, 1948," pp. 19–20.

30. Hist, "Berlin Air Lift," 2:44–47. A "railhead" was a transfer point where cargo carried by train was transferred from or to another form of conveyance, usually trucks. An "airhead" performed the same function for cargo consigned between air and ground transportation.

31. Ibid., 1:2; 2:44–47.

32. Ibid., 1:21–23.

33. Hist, "USAFE and the Berlin Airlift, 1948," p. 41.

34. Ibid.; Hist, "Berlin Air Lift," 2:34; Col. Lloyd D. Bunting, "TC Airhead Tempelhof Operations, 1 Apr.–12 Sept. 1948," n.d., pp. 1–2 (in possession of Daniel Bunting, Santa Rosa, Calif.).

35. Bunting, "TC Airhead Tempelhof Operations," pp. 2–3; Col. Lloyd D. Bunting, "Operation Vittles—Berlin End (T.C.)," n.d., p. 3 (copy of speech in possession of Daniel Bunting, Santa Rosa, Calif.).

36. Hist, "Berlin Air Lift," 2:47–49; *Berlin Airlift: A USAFE Summary*, p. 33.

37. Bunting, "Operation Vittles—Berlin End (T.C.)," p. 5.

38. Hist, "Berlin Air Lift," 1:24; Hist, "USAFE and the Berlin Airlift, 1948," p. 41; Bunting, "Operation Vittles—Berlin End (T.C.)," p. 3.

39. Bunting, "Operation Vittles—Berlin End (T.C.)," p. 6.

40. Memorandum, Brig. Gen. T. S. Timberman, chief, Operations Group, P&O, to General Wedemeyer, "Transportation Requirements to Maintain Berlin Tonnage," Oct. 19, 1948, attachment to P&O File, "Transportation Requirements to Maintain Berlin Tonnage [w/atchs.]," Oct. 19, 1948, Box 118, RG 319; Hist, "Berlin Air Lift," 2:34–36.

41. Bunting, "Operation Vittles—Berlin End (T.C.)," p. 7.

42. Hist, "Berlin Air Lift," 2:36, 38–39.

43. *Berlin Airlift: A USAFE Summary*, pp. 35.

44. Collier, *Bridge across the Sky*, p. 61. The story has been told many ways. According to LeMay: "I had only been on the job for six or seventh months when there came that all important telephone call from General Lucius B. Clay . . . could we haul some coal up to Berlin? Sure. We can haul anything. How much coal do you want us to haul? All you can haul." LeMay, *Mission with LeMay*, p. 415.

45. HQ USAFE Daily Diary, June 25, 1948, Box 47, LeMay Papers; Hist, "USAFE and the Berlin Airlift, 1948," p. 5, table G. Confusing the issue, the memoirs of Clay's political advisor, Robert Murphy, state that the conversation occurred after he and Clay returned from Washington, D.C., following the general's presentation at the NSC meeting on July 22, 1948, almost a month after the airlift began. Murphy, *Diplomat among Warriors*, p. 318.

46. Tunner, *Over the Hump*, pp. 204–205.

47. Quoted in Tina McCloud, "Berlin Airlift Vet: 403 Loads of Hope," *Gloucester* [Virginia] *Daily Press*, May 17, 1998.

48. *Task Force Times*, May 18, 1949, p. 2.

49. Memorandum, Maj. Gen. S. E. Anderson, Dir., Plans & Operations, to General Maddocks, "Use of B-29s in Berlin," June 30, 1948, Box 103, RG 319.

50. Hist, "Berlin Air Lift," 2:52–53.

51. Hist, "USAFE and the Berlin Airlift, 1948," pp. 77–78.

52. Ibid., 187; Tunner, *Over the Hump*, pp. 204–205; Swanborough and Bowers, *United States Military Aircraft since 1909*, p. 291.

53. Hist, "USAFE and the Berlin Airlift, 1948," pp. 192–94; Tunner, *Over the Hump*, p. 205; Stephens, "RAF Contribution to the Berlin Airlift," p. 11.

54. Collier, *Bridge across the Sky*, pp. 108–109.

55. Hist, "Berlin Air Lift," 2:50–51.

56. OMGUS to CSUSA (for Generals Bradley, Wedemeyer, and Maddocks), Oct. 28, 1949, Box 118, RG 319.

57. Howley, *Berlin Command*, pp. 230–31.

58. Anonymous report, "Summary of Operation 'Vittles,'" Dec. 15, 1948, attachment to memorandum for Mr. Symington, "Status of Implementation of the NSC Recommendations," Dec. 16, 1948, Box 808, RG 341.

59. Clay, *Decision in Germany*, p. 383.

60. Tunner to Kuter, Aug. 3, 1948, and Kuter to Tunner, Aug. 16, 1948, Berlin Airlift Archives, History Office, Air Mobility Command.

61. Hist, "USAFE and the Berlin Airlift, 1948," pp. 161–62.

62. MFR, "Berlin Airlift, October 20, 1948," attachment to P&O File, "Berlin Air Lift [w/atchs.]," Oct. 18, 1948, Box 103, RG 319; P&O File, "Increase of Berlin Air Lift [w/atchs.]," Sept. 23, 1948, P&O 381 TS, P&O Division Decimal File; Maj. Gen. Laurence S. Kuter, Cmdr., MATS, to COS USAF, "Further Reduction in Military Air Transport Service Lift to Augment VITTLES," Sept. 22, 1948, Box 808, RG 341.

63. Memorandum, Maj. Gen. F. R. Everest, Act. Dep. Chief of Staff, Operations, to Generals Anderson and Smith, "Policy Decisions by the Chief of Staff in Connection with 'OPERATION VITTLES,'" Sept. 24, 1948, Box 808, RG 341.

64. Ibid.

65. [Gen. Lucius] Clay to [Lt. Gen. Albert C.] Wedemeyer, Oct. 14, 1948, CC-6324, Box 17, RG 335.

66. Memorandum for the chief of staff, HQ USAF, "Increasing the Berlin Airlift [w/atchs.]," n.d., Box 808, RG 341.

67. Revised draft of enclosure to memorandum for the secretary of defense attached to memorandum, Maj Gen Alfred M. Gruenther, Dir., The Joint Staff, "Berlin Air Lift," Oct. 19, 1948, JCS 1907/9, P&O 381 TS, P&O Division Decimal File.

68. Memorandum, Brig. Gen. T. S. Timberman, Chief, Operations Group, to the director of Plans and Operations, "Impact on FLEETWOOD of Additional Allocation of C-54 Aircraft to Operation VITTLES" Oct. 27, 1948, Box 103, RG 319; P&O File, "'Vittles' (Duplications of Withdrawal of Eleven (11) C-54 Airplanes from Caribbean Command) [w/atchs.]", Oct. 26, 1948, Box 103, RG 319; "Military Implications Involving the Commander in Chief, Far East and Commander in Chief, Caribbean in Continuation of the Berlin Air Lift [w/atchs.]," Dec. 22, 1948, Box 103, RG 319.

69. MFR, "Berlin Airlift," Oct. 20, 1948, attached to P&O File, "Berlin Air Lift [w/atchs.]," Oct. 18, 1948, Box 103, RG 319; memorandum, Pres. Harry S. Truman to Exec. Sec., National Security Council, Oct. 22, 1948, attached to JCS-1907/18 (w/atchs.), Oct. 27, 1948, Box 103, RG 319; Clay, *Decision in Germany*, p. 384.

70. Hist, "USAFE and the Berlin Airlift, 1948," pp. 188–90.

71. [Secretary of the Army Kenneth] Royall to [Secretary of the Air Force Stuart] Symington, Sept. 26, 1948, Box 12, RG 335.

72. [Gen. Lucius] Clay to [Sir Brian] Robertson, Sept. 25, 1948, Correspondence File, Box 45, LeMay Papers; Williamson, *A Most Diplomatic General*, pp. 128–30, 132, 134–35. Robertson never accepted the airlift as an indefinite solution to the Berlin crisis. He remained uncertain about the airlift's capacity until January, 1949, when it was delivering an average of over 5,000 tons per day, but continued to worry about its prodigious cost.

73. [Gen. Lucius] Clay to [Gen. Omar] Bradley, Sept. 23, 1948, no. CC-6050, Box 177, RG 218.

74. Memorandum, Lt. Gen. A. C. Wedemeyer, DCS/Plans and Combat Operations, to Gen. Bradley, "Status of the Berlin Airlift," Nov. 15, 1948, Box 103, RG 319; [Lt. Gen. Albert] Wedemeyer to [Gen. Lucius] Clay, Oct. 18, 1948, no. WARX-91094, Box 17, RG 335; [Lt. Gen. Albert] Wedemeyer to Generals Clay, Huebner, and Cannon, Nov. 5, 1948, no. WARX-92253, Box 17, RG 335; memorandum Europe & Middle East Branch, P&O, HQ USAF, "Augmentation of the Berlin Airlift," Nov. 5, 1948, Box 17, RG 335; [Lt. Gen. John K.] Cannon to [Gen. Hoyt] Vandenberg, Nov. 10, 1948, no. UAX-1276, Box 17, RG 335.

75. Staff summary sheet for Maj. Gen. S. E. Anderson, Dir., Plans & Operations, HQ USAF, "Augmentation—Operation 'Vittles' by 54 USAF Aircraft [w/atch.]," Nov. 17, 1948, Box 808, RG 341; memorandum for Mr. Symington, "Status of Implementation for Augmenting the Berlin Airlift," Nov. 18, 1948, Box 808, RG 341; memorandum for General Wedemeyer, "USAF Participation in the Berlin Airlift," n.d., Box 808, RG 341; "Summary of Operation 'Vittles,'" Dec. 15, 1948, attachment to memorandum for Mr. Symington, "Status of Implementation of the NSC Recommendations," Dec. 16, 1948, Box 808, RG 341; "Factors and Implications affecting the Continuation of Operation Vittles at the Present or on an Expanded Scale," n.d., attachment to staff summary sheet for Maj. Gen. S. E. Anderson, Dir., Plans & Operations, HQ USAF, "Factors and Implications affecting Continuation of 'Vittles' [w/atchs.]," Apr. 13, 1949, Box 808, RG 341.

76. Lewis D. Whipple, Benton, Lousiana, to Dr. Roger G. Miller, Nov. 22, 1997, and Oct. 21, 1998, in the author's possession.

77. Staff summary sheet for Maj Gen S. E. Anderson, Dir., Plans & Operations, HQ USAF, "Augmentation of 'Vittles' Aircraft by 24 Navy R5Ds," Oct. 27, 1948, Box 808, RG 341; Maj. Gen. S. E. Anderson, Dir., Plans & Operations, HQ USAF, to MATS/Cmdr., "Movement of VR-6 and VR-8 Squadrons to Germany," Oct. 29, 1948, Box 808, RG 341; Anthony Atwood, "Operation Vittles: Mission with a Heart," *Naval Aviation News*, May–June, 1998, p. 37.

78. Hist, "USAFE and the Berlin Airlift, 1948," pp. 131–34.

79. Ibid., pp. 179–80; Tunner, *Over the Hump*, pp. 214–15; *Berlin Airlift: A USAFE Summary*, p. 5; Atwood, "Operation Vittles," p. 37.

80. Hist, "USAFE and the Berlin Airlift, 1948," pp. 135–37.

81. Atwood, "Operation Vittles," p. 38.

82. Memorandum, [General] Vandenberg to [Secretary of the Air Force] Symington, Apr. 22, 1949, Vandenberg Files (1949), Box 32, Vandenberg Papers; Hist, "USAFE and the Berlin Airlift, 1948," pp. 179–80.

83. *Berlin Airlift: A USAFE Summary*, p. 12; Hist, "USAFE and the Berlin Airlift, 1948," p. 213.

84. Howley, *Berlin Command*, pp. 230–31, 237.

85. *Berlin Airlift: A USAFE Summary*, p. 12.

86. Hist, "USAFE and the Berlin Airlift, 1948," pp. 207–208, 235.

87. Ibid., p. 234.

88. Memorandum, Lt. Gen. A. C. Wedemeyer, DCS/Plans and Combat Operations, to Gen. Bradley, "Status of the Berlin Airlift," Nov. 15, 1948, Box 103, RG 319.

89. Ibid.; Hist, "USAFE and the Berlin Airlift, 1948," pp. 164–65.

90. Memorandum, [General] Vandenberg to [Secretary of the Air Force] Symington, "Welfare of Dependents of 'Vittles Operation' Men," Dec. 10, 1948, Secretary of the Air Force File (2) 3, Box 59, Vandenberg Papers.

91. *Berlin Airlift: A USAFE Summary*, p. 12; Hist, "USAFE and the Berlin Airlift, 1948," p. 243.

92. Hist, "USAFE and the Berlin Airlift, 1948," pp. 241–42.

93. MFR, "Alleged Coal Crisis in Berlin," Jan. 4, 1949, attachment to P&O File, "Alleged Coal Crisis in Berlin [w/atchs.]," Dec. 23, 1948, Box 118, RG 319.

94. "Blockaded Berlin under the Airlift," *Intelligence Review*, Jan. 13, 1948, pp. 18–23.

95. Ibid.

96. Ibid., p. 23.

97. *Berlin Airlift: A USAFE Summary*, p. 12.

98. Ibid.

99. Commendation, Sect. of State Dean Acheson, Feb. 18, 1949, attachment to rec. control sheet, "Commendation from Dept. of Army to Dept. of Air Force re Berlin Airlift," Mar. 15, 1949, Box 808, RG 341.

100. CINCFE to CSGPO, Mar. 19, 1949, no. CX-68653, Box 178, RG 218, Central Decimal File; memorandum, Lt. Col. N. B. Edwards, P&O Division, "The Berlin Airlift," n.d., Box 14, RG 335.

101. Askold Lebedev, member of the Soviet Military Administration in Germany, quoted in Murphy, Kondrashev, and Bailey, *Battleground Berlin*, pp. 67–69.

102. OMGUS to CSUSA (for CSGPO), Dec. 9, 1948, Box 118, RG 319.

103. Except where noted, the following account was taken from Tunner, *Over the Hump*, pp. 218–22.

104. Memorandum, Col. Jack Roberts, Exec. to CSAF, to Col. Martin, OSAF, Apr. 28, 1949, File Secretary of the Air Force (1), Box 59, Vandenberg Papers.

105. P&O File, "Support of Berlin throughout an Indefinite Period of Blockade (Implementation of War Council Action) [w/atchs.]," Dec. 9, 1948, Box 103, RG 319; CSGPO to CINCEUR, Dec. 11, 1948, no. WARX-81069, Box 177, RG 218.

106. Air Commodore R. N. Waite, Hqts. "AIRLIFT," "The Supply of Berlin during the Winter Months," Sept. 15, 1948, Berlin Airlift Files, History Office, Air Mobility Command; Maj. Gen. William H. Tunner to USAFE Cmdr., "Maximum Tonnage to Berlin," Sept. 28, 1948, Box 808, RG 341.

107. Report to French, British, and United States Military Governors, "Berlin Airlift Requirements (1 Apr. 1949–30 June 1950)," Mar. 14, 1949, AG-3191, Box 618, RG 260, NA.

108. Col. Theodore R. Milton, chief of staff, CALTF, to Cmdr., USAFE, "Plans for Continuation of Airlift," Jan. 20, 1949, Berlin Airlift Files, History Office, Air Mobility Command; "Factors and Implications Affecting the Continuation of Operation Vittles," n.d., attachment to short staff report for Anderson, "Factors and Implications Affecting Continuation of 'Vittles,'" Apr. 13, 1949, Box 808, RG 341.

109. "Factors and Implications Affecting the Continuation of Operation Vittles,"

n.d., attachment to short staff report for Anderson, "Factors and Implications Affecting Continuation of 'Vittles,'" Apr. 13, 1949, Box 808, RG 341.

110. Maj. Gen. Robert W. Douglass Jr., chief of staff, USAFE, to chief of staff, USAF, "Assignment of Engineer Aviation Units," Jan. 20, 1949, Box 808, RG 341.

111. Maj. Gen. William H. Tunner, Cmdr., CALTF, to Cmdr., USAFE, "Future Organization and Deployment, CALTF [w/atch.]," Jan. 1, 1949, Berlin Airlift Files, History Office, Air Mobility Command.

112. Ibid.

Chapter 5. "Blockade Ends, Airlift Wins"

1. Mastny, *Cold War and Soviet Insecurity*, p. 61; Narinskii, "Soviet Union and the Berlin Crisis," p. 72.

2. Kohler to SecState, May 6, 1949, telegram #1154, Box 16, RG 335, NA.

3. Clay, *Decision in Germany*, pp. 388–89; Murphy, Kondrashev, and Bailey, *Battleground Berlin*, p. 72.

4. Mastny, *Cold War and Soviet Insecurity*, pp. 63–64.

5. Ibid., pp. 62, 64–65.

6. Smith, *Lucius D. Clay*, pp. 532–33.

7. Narinskii, "Soviet Union and the Berlin Crisis," pp. 72–73.

8. Representatives of France, the United Kingdom, and the United States of America to the Secretary-General, May 4, 1949, Box 178, RG 218.

9. Kohler to SecState, May 6, 1949, Box 16, RG 335.

10. Quoted in Smith, *Lucius D. Clay*, p. 532.

11. Jackson, *Berlin Airlift*, p. 140.

12. Memorandum for the National Security Council, "Phase-Out of the Berlin Airlift [w/atchs.]," July 28, 1949, Box 808, RG 341.

13. CSGPO to CINCEUR, COMGEN OMGUS, July 28, 1949, no. WARX-92098, Box 178, RG 218; COMGEN OMGUS to CSGPO, July 29, 1949, no. V-40678, Box 178, RG 218; Memo for the National Security Council, "Phase-Out of the Berlin Airlift," July 28, 1949, Box 808, RG 341.

14. Hist, "USAFE and the Berlin Airlift, 1949," pp. 334–39; *Berlin Airlift: A USAFE Summary*, p. 11.

15. Collier, *Bridge across the Sky*, p. 158.

16. "History of the 1st Airlift Task Force for September 1949," p. 8, quoted in Hist, "USAFE and the Berlin Airlift, 1949," pp. 347–48.

17. Jackson, *Berlin Airlift*, p. 9.

18. Ibid., pp. 124, 142; *Berlin Airlift: A USAFE Summary*, p. 12; Richards, "Whitfield's Circus," p. 17.

19. *Berlin Airlift: A USAFE Summary*, p. 12.

20. Ibid.; Richards, "Whitfield's Circus," p. 17.

21. *Berlin Airlift: A USAFE Summary*, p. 50.

22. Jackson, *Berlin Airlift*, pp. 151–52; Roger D. Launius, "Berlin Airlift, Constructive Air Power," *Air Power History*, spring, 1989, p. 19.

23. Zubok and Pleshakov, *Kremlin's Cold War*, pp. 51–52, 147; Gaddis, *Russia, the Soviet Union, and the United States*, p. 193.

24. Gaddis, *Russia, the Soviet Union, and the United States*, p. 197.

25. Wohlforth, *Elusive Balance*, p. 91.

26. Crockatt, *Fifty Years War*, pp. 81–82; Foster Rhea Dulles, *America's Rise to World Power, 1898–1954* (New York: Harper Torchbooks, 1963), p. 241.

27. Memorandum, Maj. Gen. S. E. Anderson, Dir., Plans & Operations, to General Norstad, "Preliminary Appreciation of the Defense of the Rhine River [w/ atch.]," Oct. 26, 1948, Box 807, RG 341; memorandum of conversation, British Ambassador, Secretary of State Marshall, and Mr. Lovett, July 14, 1946, Box 177, RG 218.

28. [Gen. Lucius] Clay to [Gen. Omar] Bradley, July 16, 1948, no. CC-5182, Box 7, RG 218, NA; [Gen. Omar] Bradley to [Gen. Lucius] Clay, July 16, 1948, no. WAR-85967, Box 7, RG 218; [Gen. Lucius] Clay to [Gen. Omar] Bradley, Sept. 6, 1948, no. CC-5839, Box 7, RG 218.

29. [Gen. Lucius] Clay to [Lt. Gen. Albert C.] Wedemeyer, "Transcript of a Meeting held by Field Marshal Montgomery at Melle on Nov. 8th," Nov. 10, 1948, no. CC-6692, Box 7, RG 218; [Gen. Lucius] Clay to [Gen. Omar] Bradley, Nov. 10, 1948, no. CC-6690, Box 7, RG 218.

30. Mastny, *Cold War and Soviet Insecurity*, p. 63; Dulles, *America's Rise to World Power*, pp. 242, 245; Doris M. Condit, *The Test of War, 1950–1953*, vol. 2 of *History of the Office of the Secretary of Defense*, pp. 309–11.

31. Clay, *Decision in Germany*, p. 388.

32. Murphy, *Diplomat among Warriors*, p. 318.

33. Mastny, *Cold War and Soviet Insecurity*, p. 50.

34. Ninkovich, *Germany and the United States*, pp. 66–71.

35. Ibid., pp. 71–73; Clay, *Decision in Germany*, p. 1; Mastny, *Cold War and Soviet Insecurity*, p. 65.

36. Roger D. Launius, "Lessons Learned, Berlin Airlift," *Air Power History*, spring, 1989, p. 23.

37. *Berlin Airlift: A USAFE Summary*, p. 37.

38. Hist, "USAFE and the Berlin Airlift, 1948," p. 236.

39. Maj. Gen. Laurence S. Kuter, Cmdr., MATS, to Maj. Gen. William H. Tunner, Cmdr., Airlift Task Force (Prov.), Sept. 2, 1948, Berlin Airlift Files, History Office, Air Mobility Command.

40. Maj. Gen. William H. Tunner, Cmdr., Airlift Task Force (Prov.), to Maj. Gen. Laurence S. Kuter, Cmdr., MATS, Sept. 3, 1948, Berlin Airlift Files, History Office, Air Mobility Command.

41. Maj. Gen. Laurence S. Kuter, Cmdr., MATS, to Maj. Gen. William H. Tunner, Cmdr., Airlift Task Force (Prov.), Aug. 23, 1948, Berlin Airlift Files, History Office, Air Mobility Command.

42. Maj. Gen. Laurence S. Kuter, Cmdr., MATS, to Maj. Gen. William H. Tunner, Cmdr., Airlift Task Force (Prov.), Sept. 16, 1948, Berlin Airlift Files, History Office, Air Mobility Command.

43. Maj. Gen. William H. Tunner, Cmdr., Airlift Task Force (Prov.), to Maj. Gen. Laurence S. Kuter, Cmdr., MATS, Sept. 10, 1948, Berlin Airlift Files, History Office, Air Mobility Command.

44. Ibid.; Lt. Gen. Elwood R. Quesada, Cmdr., TAC, to Lt. Gen. Curtis LeMay, Cmdr., USAFE, Sept. 22, 1948, Correspondence Files, Box 45, LeMay Papers.

45. Lt. Gen. Elwood R. Quesada, Cmdr.,TAC, to Lt. Gen. Curtis LeMay, Cmdr., USAFE, Sept. 22, 1948; [Lt. Gen. Curtis] LeMay to "Pete" Quesada, Oct. 9, 1948, Correspondence Files, Box 45, LeMay Papers.

46. Owen, "Creating Global Airlift," p. 84; Launius, "Lessons Learned, Berlin Airlift," p. 23; *Anything, Anywhere, Anytime: An Illustrated History of the Military Airlift Command, 1941–1991*, pp. 112, 115.

47. Owen, "Creating Global Airlift," p. 84.

48. Maj. Gen. Laurence S. Kuter, Cmdr., MATS, to Maj. Gen. William H. Tunner, Cmdr., Airlift Task Force (Prov.), Aug. 13, 1948, Berlin Airlift Files, History Office, Air Mobility Command; Tunner, *Over the Hump*, p. 198.

49. Kuter to Tunner, Aug. 13, 1948, Berlin Airlift Files, History Office, Air Mobility Command; Tunner to Kuter, Aug. 21, 1948, Berlin Airlift Files, History Office, Air Mobility Command; Tunner, *Over the Hump*, p. 198.

50. Tunner to Kuter, Sept. 10, 1948, Berlin Airlift Files, History Office, Air Mobility Command.

51. Rear Adm. John P. Whitney, Vice Cmdr., MATS, to Maj. Gen. William H. Tunner, Cmdr., CALTF, Apr. 28, 1949, Berlin Airlift Files, History Office, Air Mobility Command; Maj. Gen. William H. Tunner, Cmdr., CALTF, to Rear Adm. John P. Whitney, Vice Cmdr., MATS, May 8, 1949, Berlin Airlift Files, History Office, Air Mobility Command; memorandum, "Meeting Held in Office of Chief of Staff Combined Airlift Task Force," May 2, 1949; Col. Richard W. DaVania, Cmdr., 61st Troop Carrier Wing, to Cmdr., 1st Airlift Task Force, "Summary of First Weekly Operation of Service Test of YC-97A on the Airlift," May 10, 1949, Berlin Airlift Files, History Office, Air Mobility Command; *USAFE and the Berlin Airlift, 1949*, pp. 155–56; Swanborough and Bowers, *United States Military Aircraft since 1909*, pp. 125–29.

52. Tunner, *Over the Hump*, pp. 198–99.

53. Ibid., p. 199.

54. Kuter to Tunner, Aug. 23, 1948, Berlin Airlift Files, History Office, Air Mobility Command.

55. Memorandum, [General] Vandenberg to [Secretary of the Air Force] Symington, "Development of Heavy Cargo Aircraft," Dec. 10, 1948, Box 32, Vandenberg Files (1948), Vandenberg Papers; Tunner, *Over the Hump*, p. 200.

56. Owen, "Creating Global Airlift," p. 84.

Bibliography

Archival and Manuscript Sources

Air Force Historical Research Agency, Maxwell AFB, Alabama.
   Combined Airlift Task Force, "Preliminary Analysis of Lessons Learned," June,
      1949, 572.549–1.
   "USAFE and the Berlin Airlift, 1948: Supply and Operational Aspects." HQ USAFE
      History Office, April 1, 1949.
History Office, Air Mobility Command, Scott AFB, Illinois.
   Berlin Airlift Files.
History Office, United States Air Forces in Europe, Ramstein AFB, Germany.
   "USAFE and the Berlin Airlift, 1949: Supply and Operational Aspects," HQ USAFE,
      April 1, 1950.
   Lt. Col. Lester H. Gallogly, et al., "Report of Department of the Army Observer
      Group Concerning Study of Operation VITTLES," February 16, 1949, HQ USAFE
      History Office, microfilm #Z-0038, frame 1701ff.
   Task Force Times.
Library of Congress, Washington, D.C.
   Muir S. Fairchild Papers.
   Curtis E. LeMay Papers.
   Hoyt S. Vandenberg Papers.
National Archives, Washington D.C.
   Record Group 218, Records of the U.S. Joint Chiefs of Staff, 1941–78.
   Record Group 260, Records of U.S. Occupation Headquarters, World War II,
      1923–72.
   Record Group 319, Records of the Army Staff, 1903–92.
   Record Group 335, Records of the Office of the Secretary of the Army, 1903–80.
   Record Group 341, Records of Headquarters, United States Air Force (Air Staff),
      1934–89.
United States Army Military History Institute, Carlisle Barracks, Pennsylvania.
   "The Berlin Air Lift." 2 parts. Karlsruhe, Federal Republic of Germany, U.S.
      European Command, Historical Division, 1952.

Books

Alsop, Joseph, and Stewart Alsop. *The Reporters Trade.* New York: Reynal & Company, 1958.

Anything, Anywhere, Anytime: An Illustrated History of the Military Airlift Command, 1941–1991. Scott AFB, Ill.: Military Airlift Command History Office, 1991.

Aviation Operations Magazine. *A Special Study of Operation Vittles.* New York: Conover-Mast Publications, 1949.

Barker, Dudley. *Berlin Air Lift: An Account of the British Contribution.* London: His Majesty's Stationery Office, 1949.

Bates, Charles C., and John F. Fuller. *America's Weather Warriors, 1914–1985.* College Station: Texas A&M University Press, 1986.

Berlin Airlift: A USAFE Summary, 26 June 1948–30 September 1949. Ramstein AB, Ger.: HQ USAFE, n.d.

Bohlen, Charles E. *Witness to History, 1929–1969.* London: Weidenfeld and Nicolson, 1973.

Bowyer, Chaz. *History of the RAF.* New York: Crescent Books, 1977.

Buffet, Cyril. *Mourir Pour Berlin: La France et l'Allemagne, 1945–1949.* Paris: Armand Colin, 1991.

Charles, Max. *Berlin Blockade.* London: Allan Wingate, 1959.

Christienne, Charles, and Pierre Lissarrague. *A History of French Military Aviation.* Translated by Francis Kianka. Washington, D.C.: Smithsonian Institution Press, 1986.

Churchill, Winston S. *Triumph and Tragedy.* Vol. 6 of *The Second World War.* Boston: Houghton Mifflin, 1953.

Clay, Lucius D. *Decision in Germany.* New York: Doubleday, 1950.

Collier, Richard. *Bridge across the Sky: The Berlin Blockade and Airlift, 1948–1949.* New York: McGraw-Hill, 1978.

Condit, Doris M. *The Test of War, 1950–1953.* Vol. 2 of *History of the Office of the Secretary of Defense.* Washington, D.C.: Historical Office, Office of the Secretary of Defense, 1988.

Condit, Kenneth W. *The History of the Joint Chiefs of Staff 1947–1949.* 2 vols. Washington D.C.: Historical Division, Joint Chiefs of Staff, 1976.

Crockatt, Richard. *The Fifty Years War: The United States and the Soviet Union in World Politics, 1941–1991.* London: Routledge, 1995.

Davis, Franklin M., Jr. *Come as a Conquerer: The United States Army's Occupation of Germany, 1945–1949.* New York: Macmillan, 1967.

Davison, W. Phillips. *The Berlin Blockade: A Study in Cold War Politics.* Princeton, N.J.: Princeton University Press, 1958.

Djilas, Milovan. *Conversations with Stalin.* Translated by Michael B. Petrovich. New York: Harcourt, Brace, & World, 1962.

Donovan, Frank. *Bridge in the Sky.* New York: David McKay, 1968.

Eisenberg, Carolyn Woods. *Drawing the Line: The American Decision to Divide Germany.* Cambridge: Cambridge University Press, 1996.

Ferrell, Robert H. *George C. Marshall.* Vol. 15 of *The American Secretaries of State and Their Diplomacy.* New York: Cooper Square Publishers, 1966.

Fredericksen, Oliver J. *The American Military Occupation of Germany, 1945–53.* Karlsruhe, FRG: Historical Division, USAREUR, 1963.

Futrell, Robert Frank. *Ideas, Concepts, Doctrine: Basic Thinking in the United States Air Force, 1907–1960.* 2 vols. Maxwell AFB, Ala.: Air University Press, 1989.

———. *The United States Air Force in Korea, 1950–1953.* Rev. ed. Washington, D.C.: Office of Air Force History, 1983.

Gaddis, John Lewis. *Russia, the Soviet Union, and the United States.* 2nd ed. New York: McGraw Hill, 1990.

———. *The United States and the Origins of the Cold War, 1941–1947.* New York: Columbia University Press, 1972.

———. *We Now Know: Rethinking Cold War History.* Oxford: Clarendon Press, 1997.

George, Alexander L., and Richard Smoke. *Deterrence in American Foreign Policy: Theory and Practice.* New York: Columbia University Press, 1974.

Giangreco, D. M., and Robert E. Griffin. *Airbridge to Berlin: The Berlin Crisis of 1948, Its Origin, and Aftermath.* Novato, Calif.: Presidio Press, 1988.

Goldberg, Alfred, ed. *A History of the United States Air Force, 1907–1957.* Princeton, N.J.: Norstrand, 1957.

Halvorsen, Gail S. *The Berlin Candy Bomber.* Bountiful, Utah: Horizon Publishers, April 1990, rev. ed. September 1997.

Harrington, Daniel F. *"The Air Force Can Deliver Anything!": A History of the Berlin Airlift.* Ramstein AB, Ger.: USAFE History Office, 1998.

Haydock, Michael D. *City under Siege: The Berlin Blockade and Airlift, 1948–1949.* Washington, D.C., & London: Brassey's, 1999.

Heller, Deane, and David Heller. *The Berlin Crisis.* Derby, Conn.: Monarch, 1961.

Heukin, Louis. *The Berlin Crisis and the United Nations.* New York: Carnegie Endowment for International Peace, 1959.

Howley, Frank. *Berlin Command.* New York: Putnam, 1950.

Huschke, Wolfgang J. *The Candy Bombers: The Berlin Airlift 1948–49: A History of the People and Planes.* Berlin: Metropol Verlag, 1999.

Jackson, Robert. *The Berlin Airlift.* Wellingborough, Eng.: Patrick Stephens, 1988.

King, Benjamin, Richard C. Biggs, and Eric Criner. *Spearhead of Logistics: A History of the United States Army Transportation Corps.* Fort Eustis, Va.: U.S. Army Transportation Center, 1994.

Knight, Clayton. *Lifeline in the Sky: The Story of the U.S. Military Air Transport Service.* New York: Morrow, 1957.

Korb, Lawrence J. *The Joint Chiefs of Staff: The First Twenty-Five Years.* Bloomington: Indiana University Press, 1976.

LeMay, Curtis E. (with MacKinley Kantor). *Mission with LeMay: My Story.* Garden City, N.Y.: Doubleday, 1965.

McCullough, David. *Truman.* New York: Simon & Schuster, 1992.

Mastny, Vojtech. *The Cold War and Soviet Insecurity: The Stalin Years.* New York: Oxford University Press, 1996.

Meilinger, Phillip S. *Hoyt S. Vandenberg: The Life of a General.* Bloomington: Indiana University Press, 1989.

Miller, Roger G., ed. *Seeing Off the Bear: Anglo-American Air Power Cooperation during the Cold War.* Washington, D.C.: Air Force History and Museums Program, 1995.

Millis, Walter, ed. *The Forrestal Diaries.* New York: Viking Press, 1951.

Moody, Walton S. *Building a Strategic Air Force.* Washington, D.C.: Air Force History and Museums Program, 1996.

Morris, Eric. *Blockade: Berlin and the Cold War.* London: Hamish Hamilton, 1973.

Murphy, David E., Sergei A. Kondrashev, and George Bailey. *Battleground Berlin: CIA vs. KGB in the Cold War.* New Haven, Conn.: Yale University Press, 1997.

Murphy, Robert. *Diplomat among Warriors.* Garden City, N.Y.: Doubleday, 1964.

Naimark, Norman N. *The Russians in Germany: A History of the Soviet Zone of Occupation, 1945–1949.* Cambridge: Harvard University Press, 1995.

Naimark, Norman N., and Leonid Gibianski, eds. *The Establishment of Communist Regimes in Eastern Europe, 1944–1949.* Boulder, Colo.: Westview Press, 1997.

Narinskii, Mikhail M. "The Soviet Union and the Berlin Crisis 1948–9." In *The Soviet Union and Europe in the Cold War, 1943–1953,* edited by Francesca Gori and Silvio Pons, 57–75. Fondazione, Italy: Giangiacomo Feltrinelli, 1997.

Ninkovich, Frank. *Germany and the United States: The Transformation of the German Question Since 1945.* Boston: Twayne Publishers, 1988.

Parrish, Patricia. *Forty-Five Years of Vigilance for Freedom: United States Air Forces in Europe, 1942–1987.* Ramstein AB, Ger.: USAFE Office of History, n.d.

Parrish, Thomas. *Berlin in the Balance, 1945–1949.* Reading, Mass.: Addison-Wesley, 1998.

Pearcy, Arthur, Jr. *Berlin Airlift.* Shrewsbury, Eng.: Airlife Publishing, 1997.

Provan, John, and R. E. G. Davies. *Berlin Airlift: The Effort and the Aircraft, the Greatest Humanitarian Airlift in History.* Illustrated by Mike Machet. McClean, Va.: Paladwr Press, 1998.

Rearden, Steven L. *The Formative Years, 1947–1950.* Vol. 1 of *History of the Office of the Secretary of Defense.* Washington, D.C.: Historical Office, Office of the Secretary of Defense, 1984.

Reynolds, David, ed. *The Origins of the Cold War in Europe: International Perspectives.* New Haven, Conn.: Yale University Press, 1994.

Rodrigo, Robert. *Berlin Airlift.* London: Cassell, 1960.

Shlaim, Avi. *The United States and the Berlin Blockade, 1948–1949: A Study in Crisis Decision Making.* Berkeley and Los Angeles: University of California Press, 1983.

Smith, Jean Edward. *Lucius D. Clay: An American Life.* New York: Henry Holt, 1990.

Smith, Jean Edward, ed. *The Papers of General Lucius D. Clay: Germany, 1945–1949.* 2 vols. Bloomington: Indiana University Press, 1974.

Swanborough, Gordon, and Peter M. Bowers. *United States Military Aircraft Since 1909.* Washington, D.C.: Smithsonian Institution Press, 1989.

Truman, Harry S. *Memoirs: Years of Trial and Hope, 1946–1953.* London: Hodder and Stoughton, 1956.

Tunner, William H. *Over the Hump.* New York: Duell, Sloan, and Pearce, 1964.

Tusa, Ann, and John Tusa. *The Berlin Airlift*. New York: Atheneum, 1988.

Ulanoff, Stanley M. *MATS: The Story of the Military Air Transport Service*. New York: Franklin Watts, 1964.

U.S. Department of State. *Germany, 1947–1949: The Story in Documents*. Washington, D.C.: U.S. Government Printing Office, 1950.

Weinberg, Gerhard L. *A World at Arms: A Global History of World War II*. Cambridge: Cambridge University Press.

Williamson, David. *A Most Diplomatic General: The Life of General Lord Robertson of Oakridge*. London: Brassey's, 1996.

Wohlforth, William C. *The Elusive Balance: Power and Perceptions during the Cold War*. Ithaca, N.Y.: Cornell University Press, 1993.

Ziemke, Earl F. *The U. S. Army and the Occupation of Germany, 1944–1946*. Washington, D.C.: Center of Military History, U.S. Army, 1971.

Zubok, Vladislav, and Constantine Pleshakov. *Inside the Kremlin's Cold War: From Stalin to Khrushchev*. Cambridge: Harvard University Press, 1996.

Articles

"AACS: Building Highways in the Sky." *Intercom*, June, 1998, pp. 16–17.

"Airlift to Berlin." *The National Geographic Magazine*, May, 1949, pp. 595–616.

Atwood, Anthony. "Operation Vittles: Mission with a Heart." *Naval Aviation News*, May–June, 1998, pp. 36–39.

"Blockaded Berlin under the Airlift." *Intelligence Review*, January 13, 1948, pp. 18–23.

Borowski, Harry R. "A Narrow Victory: The Berlin Blockade and the American Military Response." *Air University Review*, July–August, 1981, pp. 18–30.

Davis, Shelley. "The Human Side of the Berlin Airlift." *The Retired Officer Magazine*, December, 1998, pp. 68–75.

Fisher, Paul. "The Berlin Airlift." *The Bee-Hive*, fall, 1948, pp. 3–31.

Halvorsen, Col. Gail S. "Berlin, the Citadel of Freedom." *The Friends Journal*, summer, 1998, pp. 2–9

Harrington, Daniel F. "The Berlin Blockade Revisited." *International History Review*, February, 1984, pp. 88–112.

———. "Against All Odds." *American History Illustrated*, February, 1982, pp. 53–59.

Haydock, Michael D. "Out of Thin Air." *Invention & Technology*, fall, 1998, pp. 42–51.

Judt, Tony. "Why the Cold War Worked." *New York Times Book Reviews*, October 9, 1997, pp. 39–44.

Launius, Roger D. "Berlin Airlift: Constructive Air Power." *Air Power History*, spring, 1989, pp. 9–22.

———. "Lessons Learned, Berlin Airlift." *Air Power History*, spring, 1989, p. 23.

McCloud, Tina. "Berlin Airlift Vet: 403 Loads of Hope." *Gloucester [Virginia] Daily Press*, May 17, 1998.

McLaughlin, J. B. "Berlin Airlift: Plus Fifty." *IFR: The Magazine for the Accomplished Pilot*, June, 1998, pp. 6–9, 21.

Milton, Gen. T. Ross. "The Berlin Airlift." *Air Force Magazine*, June, 1978, pp. 57–65.

———. "Inside the Berlin Airlift." *Air Force Magazine*, October, 1998, pp. 48–51.

Mitchell, Kent A. "The Fairchild C-82 Packet." *American Aviation Historical Society Journal*, spring, 1999, pp. 2–14.

Morrissey, Bill. "Over Berlin Thirty Years Ago: The Tree Grows." *Phi Delta Kappa Magazine*, August, 1978, pp. 6–9.

Moseley, Lt. Col. Harry G. "Medical History of the Berlin Airlift." *U.S. Armed Forces Medical Journal*, November, 1950, pp. 1249–63.

Nauman, Lt. R. D. (USN). "Medical Aspects of 'Operation Vittles.'" *Journal of Aviation Medicine*, February, 1951, pp. 4–12.

Nufer, Harold. "Uncle Wiggly Wings." *Air Power History*, spring, 1989, pp. 26–29.

Orion. "The Berlin Airlift." *Journal of the Royal United Service Institute*, February, 1949, pp. 82–86.

Powell, Stewart M. "The Berlin Airlift." *Air Force Magazine*, June, 1998, pp. 50–63.

Schmidl, Erwin A. "The Airlift That Never Was: Allied Plans to Supply Vienna by Air, 1948–1950." *Army History: The Professional Bulletin of Army History*, fall, 1997/winter, 1998, pp. 12–23.

———. "'Rosinenbomber' über Wien? Allierte Pläne zur Luftversorgung Wiens im Falle einer sowjetischen Blockade, 1948–1953." *Österreichische Militärische Zeitschrift*, fall, 1998, pp. 411–18.

"Soviets Harass Western Allies in Berlin." *Intelligence Review*, April 11, 1948, pp. 53–59.

Stevenson, Irene. "A Berliner's Memories of Berlin." *The Friends Journal*, summer, 1998, pp. 16–17.

Stivers, William. "The Incomplete Blockade: Soviet Zone Supply of West Berlin, 1948–1949." *Diplomatic History*, fall, 1997, pp. 569–602.

West, Col. Marcus C. "'Operation Vittles': A 50th Anniversary Salute to the Berlin Airlift." Parts 1 and 2. *The Friends Journal*, summer, 1998, pp. 10–13; winter, 1998, pp. 30–34.

Williams, Nicholas M. "Globemaster (The Douglas C-74)." *American Aviation Historical Society*, summer, 1980, pp. 82–106.

Unpublished Material

Gobarev, Victor M. "Soviet Military Plans and Activities during the Berlin Crisis, 1948–1949." Paper presented at the Conference on the Soviet Union, Germany, and the Cold War, 1945–62: New Evidence from the Eastern Archives, Essen and Potsdam, Germany, June 28–July 3, 1994.

Narinskii, Mikhail M. "Soviet Policy and the Berlin Blockade, 1948." Unpublished paper in author's files.

———. "The USSR and the Berlin Crisis, 1948–1949." Paper presented at a conference on the Soviet Union and Europe in the Cold War, 1943–53, Cortona, Italy, September 23–24, 1994.

Pennacchio, Chuck. "Origins of the Berlin Blockade Crisis: New Evidence from the

East German Communist Party Archive." Paper presented at the Conference on
the Soviet Union, Germany, and the Cold War, 1945–62: New Evidence from the
Eastern Archives, Essen and Potsdam, Germany, June 28–July 3, 1994.

Owen, Robert Charles. "Creating Global Airlift in the United States Air Force, 1945–
1977: The Relationship of Power, Doctrine, and Policy." Ph.D. diss., Duke
University, 1992.

Richards, Clive. "Whitfield's Circus: The British Civil Contribution to the Berlin
Airlift, August 1948–August 1949." Paper presented at Freedom through Air
Power: A Historical Symposium Commemorating the Berlin Airlift, 1948–49,
Berlin, Germany, July 7–8, 1998.

Stephens, A. B. "The RAF Contribution to the Berlin Airlift, 1948–1949." Paper
presented at Freedom through Air Power: A Historical Symposium Commemorating the Berlin Airlift, 1948–49, Berlin, Germany, July 7–8, 1998.

Index

LaVergne, TN USA
13 January 2010
169923LV00003B/5/P